THE THORNY ROSE OF TEXAS

THE THORNY ROSE OF TEXAS

AN INTIMATE PORTRAIT OF GOVERNOR
ANN RICHARDS

Mike Shropshire and Frank Schaefer

A BIRCH LANE PRESS BOOK
Published by Carol Publishing Group

A Birch Lane Press Book
Published by Carol Publishing Group
Birch Lane Press is a registered trademark of Carol Communications,
Inc.
Editorial Offices: 600 Madison Avenue, New York, N.Y. 10022
Sales & Distribution Offices: 120 Enterprise Avenue, Secaucus,
N.J. 07094
In Canada: Canadian Manda Group, P.O. Box 920, Station U, Toronto,
Ontario M8Z 5P9
Queries regarding rights and permissions should be addressed to
Carol Publishing Group, 600 Madison Avenue, New York, N.Y. 10022

Carol Publishing Group books are available at special discounts for
bulk purchases, sales promotion, fund-raising, or educational
purposes. Special editions can be created to specifications. For
details, contact: Special Sales Department, Carol Publishing
Group, 120 Enterprise Avenue, Secaucus, N.J. 07094

Manufactured in the United States of America
10 9 8 7 6 5 4 3 2 1

Library of Congress Cataloging-in-Publication Data

Shropshire, Mike.
   The thorny rose of Texas : an intimate portrait of governor
Ann Richards / by Mike Shropshire and Frank Schaefer.
       p.   cm.
   "A Birch Lane Press book."
   ISBN 1-55972-232-0
   1. Richards, Ann, 1933-   . 2. Governors—Texas—Biography.
I. Schaefer, Frank, 1936-   . II. Title.
F391.4.R53S57   1994
976.4'063'092—dc20
   [B]   93-42170
                                                     CIP

CONTENTS

PROLOGUE

It was party time in Austin, and Ann Richards, birthday girl and governor of the great and sovereign state of Texas, was having one more time of her life. Who wouldn't, with a brand-new parrot named Amazing Grace, a new 250 cc specially built Harley-Davidson motorcycle (actually, donated to the state in her name), and some two million dollars raised for her 1994 reelection coffers. It was quite a show, and if turning sixty isn't at the top of most people's wish list, there are worse ways of passing that milestone.

The party that had simmered for a week culminated on the night of nights with a Texas-sized bash at the Austin Coliseum down by Town Lake, which is really a fancy name for part of the Colorado River. A tent had been erected for the Names, the High Rollers, and Big Givers who live on perks and a sense of their own importance, and whom a politician can't afford to offend or ignore in a day when dollars are more than ever of the essence. But far outnumbering the insiders were the more than two thousand Ann Richards fans, friends, and campaign workers who had gathered to drink Lone Star Beer out of paper cups and sweat it out again on the searing macadam parking lot and to honor one of the most colorful and best-loved politicians of our day. People who had only read about her or seen her on television and wanted to see her in real life as well as those who remembered her—as she remembered them—from long before she had political aspirations.

People who had gone to grade school, high school, and college with her and people who, later, were her students when she ttaught at Fulmore Junior High in Austin.

People who had fought the liberal fight with her in the overwhelmingly conservative Dallas of the sixties.

Women, especially, with and for whom she had worked in the early days of the women's movement in Austin, when to be a woman was automatically to be an outsider, without clout or power.

People with and for whom she had stuffed envelopes, worked the phone banks, and trudged from door to door hustling votes during the years she was busy learning the nitty-gritty of politics from the grass roots up.

People who couldn't believe it when she said she was going to run for county commissioner, and then by golly won: the first female county commissioner in Travis County.

People who came from next door, from Tyler and Amarillo and El Paso and Houston and points between, from as far away as New York and Chicago and Los Angeles.

People who were black and brown as well as white, male and female, gay and straight, all in all as democratic and inclusive a constituency as can be found anywhere in America.

Governor Ann Richards is proud of that constituency, of those people from all walks of life, up and down and across the Lone Star State, and more and more, the whole country. She speaks their language, laughs with them, works with them, feeds their hopes, encourages their aspirations, and rewards their loyalty with a fierce loyalty of her own. They are her people, as she is theirs.

This is her story.

CHAPTER 1

A WOMAN'S PLACE IS IN THE DOME

November 6, AWR arises.

So begins the calendar of Democrat Ann Willis Richards's day, November 6, 1990, the final day of what has been called by some "the last great American political campaign." It was also one of the dirtiest.

The race for the governorship of Texas had begun in the spring of 1988 when Ann Richards retained pollster Harrison Hickman to research Texans' feelings about the possibility of a woman in the governor's office. The campaign that followed had stretched through two and a half grueling years, during which Republicans *and* Democrats attacked her with every weapon at their disposal.

She was a woman; worse, a proven feminist who surrounded herself with women, which raised the specter of a flock of pushy, bitchy females running the state into the ground. She was divorced and enjoyed the support of lesbians and gays, which led opponents to question her sexual preferences. She was a liberal running from the most liberal city and county in the state, and was charged with being soft on the death penalty. She was an admitted recovering alcoholic, and was accused of having used illegal drugs.

9:00 A.M.–10:00 A.M. Hair appointment.

The polls opened at 6:00 A.M. across the state, from Uncertain in the East Texas cypress swamps to high, dry El Paso in the Hueco Mountains in the far west, a span of some eight hundred miles. From Texline, far north in the Panhandle, to the lighthouse at Port Isabel at the southern tip of the state, nearly a thousand miles. Seven point seven million of the 12.1 million Texans old enough to vote were

1

registered, the highest registration ever for a nonpresidential election.

When the day dawned bright and clear, with no forecast of rain, Ann Richards said, "Somebody upstairs must be looking out for me. It's an absolutely gorgeous day and that translates into a greater voter turnout. And that's good news for us."

10:00 A.M., return to her house [on Shoal Creek Boulevard] with her son.

Dan, Ann's second child, and the elder of her two sons, had spent the last nine months campaigning with her. As he had during the campaign for her first state-wide office, state treasurer, in 1982, he had been of inestimable value, possibly irreplaceable as her caretaker and confidant, especially on the road.

Dan had picked her up in the morning and driven her to the airport. He had escorted her into and out of crowds and press conferences. He had hurried her along when she was late and slowed her down to make sure she spoke to key supporters. He had found food for her and eaten on the run with her. He had accompanied her to parties, fund-raising dinners, and private interviews with newspaper editors, local political leaders, and big donors. He had calmed her when she was angry and cheered her when she was depressed. As well as being her son, he had been her friend.

10:30 A.M. To Town Lake Hike and Bike Trail.

For months, weather and schedule permitting, Virginia Whitten had taken her to Town Lake to walk in the morning. Virginia was one of Ann's closest friends. They had met in Dallas shortly after Ann and her husband, David, moved there in 1957 and had remained close friends over the years.

With them that morning were Cecile and Ellen, Ann's daughters, and Lily Adams, her three-year-old granddaughter, on whom she dotes and lavishes attention.

Some fifty reporters were present. Ann Richards, when she was elected state treasurer in 1982, also became the first woman in fifty years to win a state-wide election. Having been reelected in 1986, having achieved instant national attention for her keynote address at the 1988 Democratic convention, having won a no-holds-barred primary contest, and now having at least an even chance of becoming Texas's next governor, the Town Lake "media hit," or photo opportunity, was an unqualified success.

Rarely has anyone gone for a brisk walk so immaculately coiffed. "Lily, it's like I'm always telling you, girl. If you're going to make it in this world, you've got to run hard," Ann said, and then picked up the pace leaving the reporters behind.

11:30 A.M., went for lunch.

"This is a joke," Gordon Hensley, Republican candidate Clayton Williams's press secretary, had crowed to reporters. "Richards is going down in this election.... Ann Richards is a pathetic candidate. She can do whatever she wants to and we're going to ignore her."

Ann did not think so. "I'm going to become a really good governor. I think the toughness of this campaign tempered me to do that."

If she won, she would not be the first female governor of Texas. That honor went to Miriam "Ma" Ferguson, who took over the reins of state from her husband, Jim, when he was impeached in 1917, and then, as his surrogate, was elected to that office in 1932, the year before Ann—Dorothy Ann Willis—was born. Since then, Frances "Sissy" Farenthold had been the only other woman to make a creditable run for the governorship, in 1972. Her second race, in 1974, had been a disaster of such magnitude that the very idea of another woman running was out of the question until Hickman's poll suggested that Ann could win.

2:30 P.M., invited Claire Korioth to play bridge. Present were AWR, Claire, Dan R., Paula Smith, Carol Fowler, Pat Cole, Robert Spellings, Ray Carrington.

This is the last entry for the day, because who, then, had time to write down trivia of this nature?

Claire Korioth, later named chair of the Insurance Board, was an old Dallas friend from the early sixties. Pat Cole and Ann had worked together in the early seventies on women's issues in Austin at the Austin Women's Center. Robert Spellings and Ann went back to 1976, when he supported her in her campaign for county commissioner. All were old friends with whom she felt comfortable, with whom she could laugh and joke. Spellings describes her as a better-than-average bridge player and says that she was relaxed that afternoon. The campaign was over, the election won or lost. The phone rang every half hour or so, Ann took the call, "Mm-hmm. Mm-hmm," hung up, and then it was "Two hearts." Her supporters had worked hard; her organization had done everything as well as anyone could have asked. Living in the moment, as she had learned the hard way, was the only way. She could wait. They would all know soon enough.

They played until a little after 5:30 P.M.. Ann caught supper, then disappeared, which disappearance was to be explained later that night at the Texas Ballroom in the Hyatt Regency.

The tension mounting, Ann, Dan, Mary Beth Rogers, and Jane Hickie, the latter two friends and close political allies since the early seventies, went to election headquarters to be briefed by Jack Martin. The numbers he gave them, however, were secondhand, having been compiled by Nancy Clack at campaign headquarters on West Avenue. The party moved there.

The numbers were terribly close. The exit polls, surprisingly, showed Ann losing ground. Williams was up one minute, Ann the next. The networks vacillated and refused to name a winner. When, around 9:30 P.M., the Hyatt Regency called to say the crowd waiting for her was turning unruly, Ann almost demanded that Clack call it. Clack took a deep breath and told her, "I'll stick with my numbers: 50.03 percent. You've won."

It was a bold statement, but one to be taken on faith. Her decision made, Ann and her party left headquarters. Ann and her mother and father, Iona and Cecil Willis, piled into one car with her old friend, Bud Shrake. Dan, her daughters Cecile and Ellen, and granddaughter Lily rode in a second car with Mary Beth Rogers and Jane Hickie. A mini-caravan of two vehicles, they crossed the Colorado River and turned left toward I-35 and the Hyatt Regency, where, nearly eight months earlier, they had celebrated her primary victory over Jim Mattox, the "mad dog" of Texas politics.

They went into the Hyatt through a back entrance, up the stairs to a holding area in a hallway behind the Texas Ballroom. There they waited, the waves of sound from the ballroom almost palpable, even through the heavy door.

The crowd was clamoring for Ann Richards. "Ann Richards! Ann Richards!" they chanted. But Ann waited and refused to go out to them. Waited until Jane Hickie handed her the portable phone she was carrying to take a call from Clayton Williams.

The sound was deafening. Ann crouched, one finger in her ear, as she listened. "Thank you very much, Clayton. I appreciate your kind thoughts," she said, and then hung up and, turning to Bill Cryer, her press secretary, said, "Well, that's it."

The rumor that Ann had won had spread, and the sound swelled to a roar as the door opened and Ann pushed into the ballroom. To the strains of the theme song from *Chariots of Fire*, her unofficial campaign song, she made her way to the dais. There, flanked by Dan and Cecile, holding Lily, and by Mary Beth Rogers, Jane Hickie, and Barbara Jordan, she raised her arms as the tidal wave of shouting beat against her, echoed off the walls, enveloped her. It went on and on, and was nearly fifteen minutes before she could calm them enough to be heard, and then, instead of speaking, she held up a T-shirt on which was emblazoned, "A Woman's Place Is In The Dome."

The Dome was the capitol: The news of her victory was verified! The crowd erupted again and stilled only after another wild five minutes. When she finally spoke, she promised, as she had throughout her campaign, that she would make room for women and minorities. "It means," she said, "the doors are open to everyone and they're not going to be closed again!"

"We're going to join hands and march up Congress Avenue and we're going to take back the capitol for the people of Texas!" she said, in a voice thick with fatigue and emotion.

"There are going to be a lot of little girls who are going to open their history texts and see my picture, hopefully along with Barbara Jordan, and say, 'If she can do it, so can I.'"

That she was there, that she—and they—had won, was the message that mattered.

Bill Cryer described the next three quarters of an hour as absolute mayhem. There were perhaps twenty cameras set up around the room. The governor-elect, preceded by a pair of Department of Safety officers who forced a path through the crowd, went from camera to camera giving short statements. "It was horrendous," Cryer said. "The crowd was going berserk. They were pushing her, shoving her, everybody trying to touch her and so forth, so we decided we'd better stop that and get her out of there because it was getting out of hand."

Out of there was upstairs to a suite filled to overflowing with over a hundred big donors, personal friends, and political people. The air almost literally throbbed with emotion as she made a few remarks, then circulated from room to room, from group to group.

It was a mixture of euphoria, exhilaration, and exhaustion. Ann Richards was a professional and had hired professionals to run her campaign, but she and her campaign had brought more to the process than mere professionalism. They had brought the passion of empowerment to women and to minorities. They had spoken for "the ignored and the injured." They had set out to take "the capitol back for the people of Texas," and had done so.

Giddy, hysterical laughter turned into tears, and seconds later, tears back into laughter. Her mother and father. All her children. Old friends. This woman they had known as daughter and mother. This West Austin housewife with whom they had raised children and played bridge, who they had watched compost kitchen scraps. This companion with whom they had fought for women's and minorities' rights. And they and the people of Texas had just elected her governor!

Suddenly, around midnight, the days and weeks and months, all the miles and endless hours, caught up with her. "She was absolutely exhausted," Bill Cryer said, and offered no resistance as they "whisked her out of there," loaded her into her friend Bud Shrake's car, and sent her packing home for a night's sleep. Tomorrow would come soon enough. A different kind of tomorrow, for Texas, when a woman's place would, indeed, be in the Dome.

CHAPTER 2

ROOTS

A trip to the Dome, unlike the proverbial thousand-mile journey that starts with a single step, begins with time, place, and people. In Ann Richards's case, the last quarter of the last century, on the central plains of Texas, and with sturdy second-generation pioneer stock. No one starved, but the land did not yield a living easily. Summers were hot, and when the rainfall fell too far below the annual average of thirty-one inches and the hundred-degree days stretched into weeks on end, crops could be devastated. Winters were on the whole mild, but punctuated, too, by bitter cold in the form of stock-killing northers that swept down from Canada with little warning, no more between Texas and the North Pole, they said, than a barbed wire fence, and it was down.

If there was no air-conditioning, people didn't miss it. If long hours of manual labor were the norm, there was time for church and chatter, for quilting and quiet hours with books and family. Nostalgia exists today for the cyclic nature and rich texture of daily ritual that filled people's lives a century ago, but that nostalgia is perhaps misplaced: Despite stability and consistency, the times cried out for variety, entertainment, and spectacle.

The unusual was prized, even if it meant only the toll bridge that spanned the Brazos River on the northern edge of Waco with the longest—475 feet, with cables designed by John A. Roebling of Brooklyn Bridge fame—freestanding suspension bridge in the world when it was built in 1870, in the heartland of nowhere. People came from miles around to gawk and wonder at the sight. More to the liking of the spectacle-starved blackland farmers and their wives was the action-packed adventure of Buffalo Bill Cody's Wild West Show, which included a reenactment of Custer's Last Stand. For pure showmanship, though, nothing before or since matched the great train wreck.

George Crush, a splendidly apt name as it turned out, was general passenger agent for the Missouri-Kansas-Texas railroad when he conceived the idea of the stunt to end all advertising stunts. Visions of nation-wide publicity spinning in their heads, the M-K-T signed on quickly. Newspaper ads were taken out and fliers pasted on walls across the country. Crush, Texas, complete with saloons, restaurants, lawmen, and a jail, was hastily incorporated, said incorporation to terminate the day after the crash. The idea caught on and some fifty thousand spectators streamed toward Crush from nearby Golinda and Honey Grove and China Spring, and on thirty-two special trains from around the state and across the whole country.

September 15, 1896, was the big day. Admission was free, the price of the train tickets more than paying for all expenses. The crowd perched in mesquite trees, sat on wagons and improvised platforms, and jostled for position on the rolling hills, many of them perilously close to the tracks. Suddenly, with a distant blast of steam whistles, two huge red and green locomotives, each trailed by a string of dilapidated box and flat cars, appeared over slight knolls to the north and south. And as the awed crowd roared and then stilled, the massive machines, their throttles tied wide open and their brakes off, accelerated in a monstrous chicken game toward their doom.

The concussive effect of the collision and explosion of two locomotives hitting head-on at over ninety miles an hour proved so great that a farmer's wife riding along a road a half mile away was knocked out by a piece of timber thrown from the wreckage. Two nearby spectators were killed instantly and scores of others wounded, either scalded by the expanding wave of superheated steam or lacerated by flying chunks of shrapnel. The railroad settled the claims of the injured as quickly as they were presented. Just as quickly, the M-K-T decided that once was enough and, in spite of the brief popularity of Scott Joplin's "The Crash at Crush," canceled all plans for an annual train disaster festival.

In the very nearly one hundred years to follow, Wacoans would see only two other events to match that of Crush's train wreck spectacle. Both of them, the great tornado of 1953 and the David Koresh/Branch Davidian tragedy, in 1993, would take many more lives and be heard much farther away than a pair of exploding trains. And in both of them, too, Ann Richards would be a more than interested spectator. In the meantime, though, folks headed back toward their homes and the humdrum of daily existence.

Home, for Nat and Alta Willis, a few years down the road in 1908, was the tiny community of Bugtussle, Texas, just three miles south of Lorena, Texas, in the middle of the rolling Central Texas prairie. Nat had come to Texas from Tennessee, and Alta, née Fryer, from Kentucky. How they met and married is not recorded, nor how they found the farm in Bugtussle, where Nat worked part-time at a cotton gin when he wasn't raising a cotton crop of his own, pressing cane for molasses, or cooking up modest batches of corn whiskey, not for sale, but for private consumption.

Not found on any maps, Bugtussle was more a state of mind than a town, according to Jimmy Willis. Jimmy was the third of six Willis children, two boys and four girls. Now eighty, shorter and stockier than he appears in the photographs of him stunt riding his Harley-Davidson back during the thirties in Waco, he is still feisty and salty of tongue, a Willis trait. He recalls his big brother, Cecil, Ann Richards's father, with fondness.

Born early in 1909, Robert Cecil Willis—he later dropped the Robert—fit the description of millions of other American farm youths of the early years of the century. He lived in a world in which the day-by-day hummed by like the steady drone of summer cicadas. Home with Mama, feed the chickens, pick up the yard. The increasingly harder and more important chores came as he grew into responsibility. Too, there were the visits to the creek with a cane pole and a tin of night crawlers and, early on, initiation into the time-honored rituals of rabbit and squirrel, dove and deer hunting, as much for the sheer fun of it as to put badly needed meat on the table. Not to be mistaken for a choirboy, he could be counted on for his share of high jinks.

Whether it was due to hard times or a question of taste and inclination, Ann's grandfather, Nat Willis, wasn't one to sink roots too deep. He left the farm and moved the family into Lorena, where

Jimmy was born in 1913, shortly thereafter returned to the farm and then moved back into Lorena, where he acquired a livery stable that was doomed to failure by the increasing popularity of automobiles. In the early 1920s he moved everyone again, this time fifteen miles north to Waco, where he had found a job driving a truck for the Humble Oil Company.

Waco, a city that has played an enormous role in Ann Richards's life, took its name from the Waco Indians, a Wichita tribe closely related to the Tawakoni, who were supposedly established there long before they were "discovered" in 1541 by a Spanish expedition led by Hernando de Soto. Legend says that an early shaman had suggested the location because the soil was rich and the buffalo plentiful along that stretch of what later became known as the Brazos River, and because the area was supposed to be blessedly free of the tornadoes. It wasn't, however, free of Cherokees, who conquered the Wacoans in the 1820s, killing and enslaving much of the tribe. Their remnants were later rounded up with other Indians and imprisoned on an Oklahoma reservation. The Wacoans passed from the scene, and left only the name of a white man's city to memorialize them.

Formally laid out in 1849 and incorporated in 1856, Waco had become, by the early twenties, a Central Texas farming and cotton trading center of some forty thousand inhabitants. It lay in the heart of the Bible Belt, whose Baptist buckle could be said to be Baylor University. It was also a severely segregated town, extending even to laundries that advertised that they washed for white people only. Laundries, however, were only the broken tooth in the smiling white face that so fervently maintained that the Negroes (a relatively benign and rarely used word) were not only accustomed to but actually enjoyed their way of life.

Just to be on the safe side, however, should anyone have dared to challenge that notion, the Ku Klux Klan was ready to enforce it during its heyday in the early twenties. Indeed, the Saxet Klan Number 33, in January of 1923, had little trouble recruiting some two thousand robed and hooded men to march through the downtown streets of Waco. This terrifying event took place well before Ann Richards's time, but segregation and its effects would linger to touch and sicken her, and she would later choose to fight discrimination in all its forms.

Jimmy doesn't remember his mother and father as particularly outgoing, but his big brother Cecil was, and "hit the ground running" when they landed in Waco. Already quick with a quip and endowed with the ability to make people laugh, he was immensely popular both in South Junior High School and then Waco High, where he dropped out, sometime during the tenth grade, to find full-time work to help support his brother and sisters. Already over six feet tall, he was a lanky, clean-cut, good-looking teenager. Smart, personable, and used to the idea of putting in a full day's work for a day's pay, he was quickly hired by Jim Penland at Southwestern Drug Company.

There were worse places for a young person to start, for Southwestern was one of the premier drug companies in Texas. The four-story brick headquarters and grounds occupied nearly a full city block on Fifth Street, hard by the railroad tracks and kitty-corner from what is now the Dr Pepper Museum. There, one could find name-brand elixirs and tonics, salves and unguents, braces and appliances—virtually all, from Carter's Little Liver Pills to Lydia Pinkham's Skin Oil, now either in disrepute or relegated to medical museums. They were off-loaded from boxcars, stored, and trans-shipped to Southwestern Drug stores in Waco, Corpus Christi, Amarillo, San Antonio, and a half dozen other cities around the state. There, too, Southwestern Drug mixed and manufactured its own brand of popular nostrums from headache powders to a dizzying array of preparations for "male" or "female" problems.

Cecil started as a buy-out boy, an employee dispatched to buy from a competitor when a customer needed a product that the warehouse could not supply. That task did not prove challenging enough to suit him. He was soon picking up on very nearly everything else. No buys to make, and he would run a delivery. A quiet day, and he would help with a customer's inventory, and could soon write down stock faster than anyone else. A rapid and willing student, he quickly learned all the medicines Southwestern stocked, and took to filling orders as well. Sadly, Jim Penland died, but Boots, who took over, liked Cecil and looked after him. By the time he had turned twenty, he was well known for his hustle and had been promoted to a buyer for five drugstores. He was moving up rapidly, and in the process learning the salesman's techniques of tact and timing, and the soft and hard sell. As well, he learned how to organize, plan ahead, maintain and expand his contacts, and, perhaps most important of all, build the trust upon which all else is based.

And he was having a good time. The Volstead Act was in force and Prohibition in full swing, but even in Waco, bastion of the Baptists, beer could be found to slake dry throats when the day's work was done. There were parties and dances, and girls to chase and date—he was considered a good catch, according to his brother, Jimmy—but all of that slowed measurably during the months after a friend introduced him to Iona Warren at the Cotton Palace one night.

Jimmy remembers Iona as a "nice-looking, streamlined brunette with a dark eyes and a real good smile," a memory that is reinforced by early photographs. Iona—nicknamed Ona, which most people called her, and which she herself used—was born near Hico, Texas, a town south of Fort Worth, in a small community called Hogjaw, which, when combined with Bugtussle, makes a colorful background for a politician. At any rate, Iona had no intention of being stuck in a country town called Hogjaw. In her own way as ambitious as Cecil—certainly more adventurous, given that she was a girl—she struck out for the big city, Waco, where her uncle, I.V., worked, and found a job at the Rosenberg Dry Goods Company on the square. Not too long afterward came the night she went to the Cotton Palace with a girlfriend and her boyfriend, who introduced her to Cecil, a tall young man, six foot four by then, with a shock of light brown hair, blue eyes, an infectious smile, and a gift of gab. One thing slowly leading to another, they were married two years later in the home of a friend.

Marriages that last for more than sixty years weren't always as rare as they are these days, and the tendency now is to marvel and ask, why? Love, is the easy answer, but the outsider is tempted to analyze. That Cecil and Iona were as different as night and day, and so complemented each other perfectly, seems as good a second easy answer as any.

Iona was nineteen going on thirty. Exceptionally mature, serious, pragmatic, and frugal, she may not have known exactly what she wanted from husband and marriage, but she did know that she had not come that far to allow herself to become the urban equivalent of a poor farmer's wife. Marriage was more than fun, games, and jokes, and there was serious business at hand.

Cecil, on the other hand, was a splendid raconteur and hail-fellow-well-met who was well supplied with off-color jokes. He was also driven to success and determined to be more than just another drummer selling one product after another, little different from floating from farm to livery stable to behind the wheel of an oil truck. Giving up beer with the boys of an afternoon was worth the price of stability, and one he would happily pay.

One way or another, love and pragmatism, fun and goals, merged and matched. Not only would this formula produce a successful marriage, but it would play an overwhelmingly important role in the life of the newlyweds' only child, who was as yet only a gleam in their eyes.

The times, though, in the wake of the great stock market crash of that October, 1929, were rapidly becoming perilous. Cecil earned about one hundred dollars a month, Iona somewhat less. It was not a princely sum, even then, but enough for newlyweds with stars in their eyes, not to speak of Iona's practicality and the brash optimism of a born salesman that Cecil wore as prominently as his hat. Depression or no, though, Cecil and Iona were country people at heart and, with both of them getting enough city during the day, they looked outside of town for a house in which to begin not only their marriage but a family. And they found one on Walnut Street in Lakeview, an unincorporated community in the country but inside the Waco city limits, eight miles north of the square and the Southwestern Drug Company's headquarters.

The house that was to become their home was by no means a palace, but it was their own. A typical country house of its day, the one-bedroom, wood-frame structure was painted white, and boasted a walk-up front porch and a surrounding white picket fence. The cost, seven hundred dollars, was on the steep side, but that covered an acre of land as well, which in time would pay for itself with the money they would save by growing virtually all of their own food and raising chickens for meat and eggs.

Hunger, unemployment, and homelessness had become a feature of existence for too many families throughout America, draining individual dignity and self-respect and, worst of all, hope. As devastating as the Depression was for many, Cecil and Iona, while not escaping entirely unscathed, were relatively well off. True, Cecil's salary was reduced to $81.50 a month when times were at their toughest, but there was that garden and those chickens, and Iona, who made most of their clothes by hand, saw that they made do. She managed so well that, on those meager rations, she and Cecil paid off the $700 mortgage in two years, a prodigious feat.

Nothing was easy in a time when frugality was a necessary virtue and dollars were as scarce as snowflakes in August. Cecil, honing skills he would later pass on, drove the roads and met and became friends with the owners and operators of every drugstore and general store in his eight-county territory. He paid the poorest of his customers respect by dressing immaculately, even snappily. He memorized names and preferences and patiently listened to the woes of men and women who were barely managing to exist.

Trust, Cecil learned, was not freely given, but had to be earned over days and months of honest endeavor, value given for value received. He believed in the merchandise he sold. He was extensively self-educated about over-the-counter drugs and was capable of acting as stand-in for a country doctor when it came to dispensing common-sense advice on everyday health problems. Storekeepers perked up when Cecil arrived, unwound from his car and ducked on his way in the door so he wouldn't crumple his hat. The contagious smile he brought with him was genuine, because he genuinely liked his customers, who generally grinned in response.

He often led off with a story before he tried to pitch them on a sale. "Say, now," he'd begin, "did you boys hear about that yellow hound ol' Tom Higgins up in Lorena bought from the lightning rod salesman who was working his way through that part of the country last week?" And the grins would widen in anticipation of a new story they hadn't heard before, usually on the raunchy side but funny enough to make a tree stump laugh. No doubt about it. Cecil Willis was better liked than Willy Loman ever dreamed of being.

"Cecil Willis? Oh, yeah, I knew him," said one old-timer who years ago owned a little corner grocery a half dozen miles west of Lorena. "A salesman's salesman. Knew his customers and *their* customers, and took care of 'em. Why, one time, I recall, back in oh, thirty-eight, thirty-nine, maybe, he spent two hours helpin' me do an inventory, and I didn't buy a damn thing from him that day!"

At $81.50 a month, Cecil Willis was cheap at double the price, which Boots Penland knew even if he couldn't afford to pay it. Cecil had learned, though, that if a man worked hard and was honest, gave cheerfully of himself and truly cared about others, he profited, and not merely with a fat paycheck, but with respect returned, with friendship, affection, loyalty, and a sense of accomplishment, of leaving the world a better place than he found it.

It was a lesson he would pass on to his only offspring, who would insist that women and minorities be included in that formula for success, and adopt it as her own.

CHAPTER 3

A PLACE IN FRONT

"Little girls, like butterflies," a Robert Heinlein character, Lazarus Long, wrote, "need no excuses." Iona and Cecil no doubt shared that sentiment on September 1, 1933, as they gazed down at their newborn daughter.

The weather had been hot the day before, and Iona, alone and in the initial throes of labor, had walked the dusty road in front of their house to hurry the process. It was a long day, with Cecil on the road, unable to be summoned unless and until he called in to the office, but Iona was not unduly worried. As was her way, with the practicality of a farm girl who had some experience in matters maternal, she had planned ahead and was prepared. That afternoon, when the labor pangs began in earnest, she called Waco to tell Dr. Beidlespach her time had come and summoned a neighbor who had promised to help.

Iona, though, for all her planning and arranging, for once had little to say about nature's timing, and Dr. Beidlespach, fearful of sleeping through the birth if he lay down on a regular bed, camped out on the front porch of the tiny prairie-style wood-frame house that was the mid-twentieth-century equivalent, for a politician, of the nineteenth-century log cabin. At last, mistress of her own fate, a characteristic she would cultivate down through the years, Dorothy Ann Willis made her appearance at six in the morning. It was some way to start the day.

On that day, far around the world, Mahatma Gandhi, with his usual sense of laconic humor, announced that he would fast for three weeks unless someone could convince him that the devil had told him he should, and Adolf Hitler finally wrested dictatorial powers from a reluctant Reichstag, just months before he became the Führer.

In the United States, the NRA was the National Recovery Act—not the National Rifle Association—and Greta Garbo had titillated the nation by speaking to the press for the first time, which, for most people, was vastly more interesting and important than the stranglehold that Huey P. Long, the Kingfish, had on the politics of Louisiana.

In Texas, Clyde Barrow and Bonnie Parker were still paying the occasional visit to Central Texas to knock over a bank, and Ma Ferguson, who had been elected Texas's first female governor in 1924, was back in office again, once more issuing pardons by the dozen, fighting the Klan and the Depression, and advocating that women should be allowed to enter the business world and dress as they pleased.

Closer yet to home, as reported in the *Waco News-Tribune* on the day Ann Richards was born, there were exactly five Male Help Wanted ads in the classified section, and nobody thought it was out of the ordinary that a headline should read "Girl Murdered by Negroes."

And five miles north of Waco, life in Lakeview, where there was neither lake nor view to speak of, was about as exciting as an afternoon nap. The affairs of dictators, governors, Hindu religious leaders, and glamorous movie stars were as far removed from that little rural community as the moon. Even a murder was unthinkable, which made it the perfect place to rear a child.

"Lakeview was a wonderful place to raise children," Bessie Smith, the mother of Ann's childhood friend Regina Garrett, said, repeating an often-heard theme. "People knew each other, cared about and watched out for each other." Today once-quiet Lakeview has been invaded by small industry housed in low-cost galvanized-tin buildings that squat amid the usual suburban homes, stores, gas stations, and even a minimall. All well manicured, lit, and boostered by a chamber of commerce, it is difficult to picture as it was sixty years ago.

Lacy Lane, the only paved street in town, connected to the Dallas Highway, which led south to the suspension bridge over the Brazos River and downtown Waco. The Interurban train tracks were good for the high drama of the hourly trains that ran north and south between Waco and Dallas. Bolfing Grocery was down at the corner of Lacy Lane and the highway, a block or so up the road from the filling station, and the Montgomery Store sat on the far side of the highway and tracks, which the children were not allowed to cross without an adult accompanying them.

The school consisted of a two-story wood-frame building that came with large oak trees. Legend had it that under one were buried two children who had died when their family passed through the area in a covered wagon. Not to be forgotten were the Baptist and Methodist churches, neither of them impressive or imposing but, in the days before malls enticed people to Waco or television isolated them in their homes, the focal points of social life. No one complained: The citizens of Lakeview had never been accused of being worldly-wise sophisticates, but they did know what suited them, and that did not include the infernal commotion of the big city.

Dorothy Ann, as she was called until she dropped the Dorothy when she enrolled in high school, may not have needed any more excuse than a butterfly, but some of the neighbors thought she could have done with a bit more flesh on her bones. "Birdlegs," she was called on at least one occasion in her teens, but "grasshopper" evidently fitted her as a better description. When she was younger, Iona thought her daughter was dangerously pale and thin, which is an assessment that probably needs to be put in historical context.

Regina Hoffman, née Garrett and now called by her high school nickname, Rusty, is some six months older than Ann. Rusty recalls hearing her own grandmother openly speculate about how long Cecil and Iona would have a child to raise. That sounds dire, but understandable, for that was a time when typhoid, diphtheria, scarlet fever, and whooping cough were grave threats to children. Penicillin did not exist and sulpha drugs were the best medicine, and they were not always readily available. It made sense, then, for grandparents, most of whom could count brothers and sisters who hadn't made it through childhood, to worry.

Actually, thin wasn't at all that uncommon then. Pick any class or group photograph today, and there will always be at least three or four chubby kids, but look at some from the thirties, especially from rural schools, and the chubby youngster will be a rarity. According to a photo of the Lakeview Central School rhythm band taken when Dorothy Ann was about eight, not a one of those twenty-six girls and boys had an ounce of fat to spare.

Whether other mothers worried, it seems clear that Iona did, and perhaps excessively. Reading Ann Richards's autobiography and talking to friends who knew the family then, it becomes clear that Iona had an incredibly powerful emotional investment in her daughter. Perhaps the fact that Dorothy Ann was an only child, with no more planned, had something to do with it, but Iona was constantly after her to eat and hounded her with frequent doses of cod liver oil and other tonics Cecil brought home from Southwestern.

If Iona perhaps worried too much, Ann seems hardly to have worried at all. She remembers herself as a skinny slip of a thing, but not at all sickly. Quite the opposite. Quoting from her autobiography: "My daddy said I was a perpetual motion machine, always squirming around like a worm in hot ashes." "I can't remember ever walking; I ran everywhere." "I climbed trees. When *Superwoman* comics came out,...I got on the roof of the garage with a rope...and jumped off." Bearing similar witness, Rusty Garrett recalls them always running, climbing, and, using their secret names for each other—Dorothy Ann was Sybil and Rusty was Trellis—playing make-believe. In truth, her grasshopper build and pale skin notwithstanding, Dorothy Ann was hardly a child at risk. And as the years passed, she proved to have the constitution of an ox.

As she has been with rare exceptions, Ann was too busy to be sickly. Lakeview may have been off the beaten path, but it was a great place to rear children. It is difficult today to visualize life for children before the great baby-sitter and time filler, television, but they did survive, playing with cutout paper dolls and eating homemade ice cream. The long summer afternoons with no adult-directed entertainment could be lazy and boring, but there were cardboard boxes to be turned into palaces, chinaberry wars, and, going nowhere in particular, riding bikes along the dusty streets. And always, there were books—Nancy Drew and the Bobbsey Twins, for example—to be read and dreamed about.

There were, too, for Dorothy Ann, piano and "expression" lessons—"Thank God nobody was giving ballet lessons in Lakeview, or I'd've had those, too," she later said—which meant some hours of practice. Cecil and Iona had added to and rebuilt their house to include two bedrooms, a formal living room with finished pecan floors, a dining room, a small kitchen, and a screened-in back porch. Ann was assigned chores, cleaning and polishing that pecan floor, for one, and on her hands and knees, which to this day Iona says is the only way to do a floor correctly. The floor finished, there were ivy leaves to polish—every leaf, and start from scratch if she missed one—and pots and pans to wash. There were chickens to care for, a garden to weed, beans to snap both for supper and canning. There were jams, jellies, and pickles to be put up for winter, clothes to be made, repaired, and ironed, all of which a girl was expected to know how to do, even if fond parents might wish the day would come when she did not have to.

There was more for Dorothy Ann, though, than friends, Mama, and housework. Just as important, and certainly having an enormous influence on her life, was Cecil. Fathers of only children who happen to be girls have often been accused of trying to make them into boys, and there are those who feel Cecil did so with Dorothy Ann. He certainly included her in activities that were thought of as boyish. An avid hunter, he taught her how to shoot and took her deer and bird hunting with him. A fisherman from childhood, he initiated her in the mysteries of trotlines and blood bait. "It wasn't as spectacular as deep sea fishing in the Gulf of Mexico," Ann later remembered in a sports feature in *The Dallas Morning News*, "but when we'd set a trotline in the Bosque River, I felt like I was first mate to the captain." Introduced her, too, to the quiet whisper of river water and the call of night birds, to the spooky ways of cottonmouths, copperheads, and rattlesnakes that lay in wait for careless little girls. To this day, she is a good shot and enjoys hunting, and is an above average fisher.

From Cecil, too, she learned the art of storytelling, of the punch line timed for maximum effect. Iona's living room, and no doubt the living rooms of the other neighborhood women, was off-limits for virtually everything except the Home Demonstration Club, and certainly for a bunch of men given to smoking, drinking beer, and wearing shoes that would mark that satin-sheened pecan floor. For the men to have a place to call their own, Cecil built a gazebolike affair they called the pavilion. There, in the backyard, friends and neighbors would gather on summer evenings, and while the women sat and chatted in the house or on lawn chairs outside, the men congregated inside the low-walled and screened pavilion to play dominoes and tell stories.

There was no shortage of material in the current events section of the story department, and it was there, perhaps, that the events of the wide world first piqued the interest of a little girl who seemed to be curious about everything. Governor Pappy O'Daniel, he of the Light Crust Doughboys, was a colorful character good for a half hour on any given night. An up-and-coming young fellow named Lyndon Baines Johnson had started to make a name for himself. Talk still turned, now and again, to Miriam "Ma" Ferguson, who had been elected for a full term in office the year before Ann was born, and she and Jim were still stirring the pot of Texas politics.

Cecil, a font of Texas sayings and colloquialisms, was the champion storyteller of the pavilion crew. Not just because he was a natural and loved to tell stories, but because, like salesmen everywhere, he heard more stories than the other men. And of all of Ann Richards' memories related in her autobiography, none comes across with more warmth than those of the hours she spent listening to her daddy tell stories. It doesn't take much imagination to see her, a little girl up past her bedtime, sneaking down to the back porch to curl up in a corner and listen to those wonderful stories, and the men laughing.

Some fifty years later, during her keynote address at the 1988 Democratic National Convention in Atlanta, she recalled some of those times. "I can remember summer nights," she said, "when we'd put down what we called a Baptist pallet, and we listened to the grown-ups talk. I can still hear the sound of the dominoes clicking on the marble slab my daddy had found for a tabletop.

"I can still hear the laughter of the men telling jokes you weren't supposed to hear, talking about how big that old buck deer was, laughing about Mama putting Clorox in the well when a frog fell in." Few images out of Ann Richards's past are more endearing, and it's difficult to imagine her where she is today without those clandestine lessons that she soaked up, a bright-eyed, inquisitive sponge, those many years ago.

There was more, of course, as there always is. Playing with her other best friend, Virginia Lynn Douglas, who lived across the road with her mama, Gladys, and her daddy, Boots (a popular nickname), who carved wooden shoes for the girls. (Old ties last. In the middle of December, 1993, Ann traveled to Lakeview to announce her candidacy for a second term as governor. After her remarks, delivered on the front porch of the house in which she'd grown up, she hired Boots, then well into his eighties, to make a dollhouse for her granddaughter, Lily.) The Douglases were readers, and introduced Dorothy Ann to the printed page and a love of books that would last a lifetime. There was learning to ride a bicycle, and going on neighborhood excursions with Regina and Virginia. Discovering that Cecil, her daddy, had defended a married teacher the school board was about to fire because she was pregnant and beginning to show, and either forced or shamed the board into letting her keep her job. More fondly remembered, summer trips to Hico to visit her aunts, Elta and Oleta, and to Grandmother and Grandfather's farm in the country, where the electricity had yet to come.

Her granddaddy Warren was a storyteller, too, and she loved to listen to his tales, but the lesson that sank in deepest was the reality of the women, who had done all the cooking, getting whatever was left over after the men finished eating. It didn't occur to the women to question that arrangement, but the memory of men ruling the roost as a matter of course, just because they were men, was an image that would remain with Dorothy Ann and, reinforced in later years, would be instrumental in shaping the political course she charted.

It was a rich life for a small-town girl who, today, society would be tempted to call socially disadvantaged. Playing with Trellis and Virginia Lynn. Chores under her mama's tutelage, and lessons. The occasional sales trip or visit to her daddy's office at Southwestern Drug headquarters. The late-night talk and laughter of men, the soft and ageless talk of the women. All wove a rich tapestry of experience and tradition upon which a child could stitch her future. But we've left out, still, two more factors that contributed in no small amount. Church and Mama.

Church, as in most small communities of the time, was very much a part of a youngster's life and education. Both the Baptist and Methodist churches in Lakeview were small and intimate, with a lot of attention paid to individuals. Dr. Bruce Weaver was pastor of Lakeview Methodist Church from 1943 through part of 1946. Today he runs a full-time Russian program for the Global Ministry of the United Methodist Church.

The American Methodist movement was founded largely on the inspiration of John Wesley, who traveled the frontier on horseback, preaching the gospel from town to town and encampment to encampment. According to John Wesley's roving legacy, Methodist ministers are periodically assigned by a bishop to a church, then replaced after two or three years. The revolving-door policy is fundamental to the denomination, and it is rare that a Methodist minister is attached to one congregation on a permanent basis. It was, then, a fortunate event for the community when the bishop selected young Bruce Weaver—Brother Weaver, as he was called—to take his turn in Lakeview.

Lakeview Methodist Church was small, with some two hundred and fifty members, of whom perhaps seventy or eighty consistently attended Sunday services. Dr. Weaver remembers Dorothy Ann and her parents well. He and his wife, Doris, he told us, "were almost children of the parents more than we were pastor, but we went in there and took care of the church for them." Soon highly regarded by the whole community, he was asked, in the fall of 1943, to teach sixth grade in the Lakeview School, and so became Dorothy Ann's teacher as well as pastor. Too young and energetic to know he couldn't possibly simultaneously teach school full-time, minister to a congregation, and finish his own degree work, he did, and was loved by congregants and students alike.

Fifty years is a long time to remember, and memories vary. Ann Richards, in her autobiography, says she "remembers many more times than once hearing, 'Dorothy Ann, if you don't quit talk-ing…'"

Dr. Weaver, when asked about that, remembers differently. "Oh, no," he said without hesitation. "She was very well behaved. A big reader. Always working. She didn't idle away her time." He went on to describe her as petite, smiling, open faced, friendly and quiet, not really shy but not pushy, either, like some of the girls.

Whatever the case, Brother Weaver was a natural with the children, who, according to Rusty Hoffman, adored him. He and

Doris, who was also a student at Baylor, spent much of their time in Lakeview and tailored most church activities with their young charges in mind. There were outings, with picnics and trips to the Waco Zoo and Cameron Park high on the list. Music played an important role, to the point that the church choir was a children's choir. Special, too, were the covered-dish suppers on the church grounds, when the weather was nice.

The church itself was simple and poor. The most valuable item there for many years was a blue and white Shirley Temple cup, which Ann has said she was baptized with. White clapboard covered the wood frame and small steeple. The wood floors creaked and squeaked, and some of the window sashes hung off plumb. The walls were bare with low wainscoting, and a polished hardwood railing separated the nave from the altar area, where there was a plain podium for the preacher and rows of straight-backed chairs for the choir. The fanciest thing in sight was the choir, twenty or so little girls on any given Sunday, dressed in white surplices with large dark bows at the neck and, judging by an old and faded photograph taken when Dorothy Ann was in the third or fourth grade, looking very nearly like angels. And the leader was Dorothy Ann, as poised and confident as if by some inherent right she belonged there.

Leaders may be born, but they must also be taught. Which is another way of saying that while nature undoubtedly favored Dorothy Ann Willis's position in front, she wouldn't have been there without the nurture provided by doting parents. That said, and recognizing Cecil's contribution to shaping and honing Dorothy Ann's social skills, the real push more likely came from Iona, who was not only determined that her daughter should have the very best she could possibly give her, but was also ambitious for her and appears to have been somewhat of a stage mother. "Mainly because she never thought she was going to get anything herself, and somehow, through me, she would bask in some kind of glory," Ann recalled in a 1979 tape made for a Travis County oral history project.

Iona could well be proud of her daughter when, very nearly a Shirley Temple look-alike, she was the leader of the grade school rhythm band. Her hair in ringlets, dressed in the white and gold costume Iona made and the fancy boots that she scrimped and saved to buy, Dorothy Ann stood relaxed and poised, at home in the only place Iona could imagine her on that stage, which was down center, in front.

Tough times, they say, make for tough people, and the Willises are as good an example as any. They came from poor families and found themselves with few resources and little formal education in the middle of a depression. Neither wept bitter tears or lost much sleep over their fate, but neither was about to let their daughter suffer that same fate.

And so, while Cecil could indulge his happy-go-lucky streak when the day's or week's work was done, Iona rarely let up. The rules—home in an hour, chores done, practice the piano, finish the homework—were enforced. From piano and expression to dusting and sewing, everything was a lesson to be learned and mastered, no detail left undone. Always, whatever limelight was to be found in Lakeview was to be sought. Always, in choir, band, school plays, down center stage was to be taken, in order, perhaps, that the daughter should vindicate the mother by achieving or attaining that which the mother could not.

Luckily, that young ego wasn't brittle and breakable but proved to be as resilient as it was strong. Luckily, too, unlike so many other children driven by stage mothers, Dorothy Ann came to relish her place in front and flourished.

CHAPTER 4

CLASS FAVORITE

Dorothy Ann was going to be as prepared as a Boy Scout, as far as Iona was concerned. What she couldn't be prepared for, however, was the dimming of the lights across Europe and the shock of Pearl Harbor. The ripple effects were felt all the way to tiny Lakeview.

Nothing changed for the kids. The Rhythm Band practiced, donned white and gold costumes, and clicked, clacked, jingled, and drummed for proud parents. The living room still had to be dusted, those ivy leaves polished. Paper dolls still held parties, and chinaberries still ripened. Sybil and Trellis rode their bikes two miles down the road to Mrs. Glenn's for their piano lessons. Homework had to be finished—neatly—and there was the occasional day trip to Southwestern with Cecil. And, with the advent of sugar rationing, there were fudge-making parties with, each week, a different designated sugar supplier so no one family would have to spend too many coupons.

And yet, a dark and frightening undercurrent ran under the calm surface of daily life. True, Cecil and the men still gathered at night to sip a brew or two and spin tall tales, but new and mysteriously troubling words, for Dorothy Ann, crept into the conversation. Words like Nazis and Japs, who were evil people, and did unspeakable things to women and children. Words that were names of faraway places where bombs fell, fires raged, and men died. Names of men, like Hitler and Tōjó, who the men swore they would shoot as soon as they would a mad dog if they ever got them in their sights. More talk of war and killing and how we would teach the sons-a-guns, and this time a lesson they would learn for good.

Confusing, too, was the mixture of pride and pain, of hope and despair. Some days a figurative band played patriotic marches as, one after another, friends' fathers and older brothers caught the Interurban or the bus for boot camp or basic training. Other days, a gold star appeared in someone's window, people spoke in hushed whispers, and mothers baked extra casseroles or pies that they carried to the gold-star house, where the answer to the age-old question "Why?" was still "For God and country."

People meant it, too. Waco was 100 percent behind the war, and the sentiment spilled out into Lakeview. Ernie Pyle, John Steinbeck, Ernest Hemingway, and other war correspondents were devoured as the *Waco Herald-Tribune* was bought, passed around, and read. People listened to Walter Winchell or Edward R. Murrow on the radio. Children gathered milkweed, which the government bought for ten cents a pound and turned into life preservers, and spent spare dimes on savings bond stamps that were pasted in books that were exchanged for the bonds themselves, proof that the youngest could participate in the war effort. Tin cans and cooking grease were collected and recycled, modern term though that is, to be transformed into armor and explosives. New cars were simply out of the question for the duration—hardly any were made for the civilian market—and copper plumbing and wiring, when they could be bought, were worth a small fortune. Tires, gasoline, and sugar, to name only three, were rationed, as was even daylight with the advent of National Daylight Savings Time, in the name of the war effort which, Americans were sure, would end in victory.

War, however fascinating, and fear go hand in hand, and those who are old enough will remember the gory posters that generated both resolve and, at least in children, terror. Waco Army Air Field, today Texas State Technical College, was only a mile and a half to the northeast, just across the M-K-T tracks. A training base, it filled the air with planes on good flying days. Because people were understandably proud of "their" base and imbued it with so much importance, Dorothy Ann, barely eight years old when Pearl Harbor was attacked, was terrified the Japanese would bomb it and get her house, too. More frightening was the Navy's drafting her daddy, at age thirty-four, in the spring of 1944.

The government stopped drafting men with children a couple of weeks after Cecil was inducted, but that was no help to a ten-year-old girl, even if she was one of many so deprived. No help, either, to Cecil who, not at all a man to cry, did so when he reached for and hugged her the night before he left. Since a Seaman Fourth Class's pay wasn't nearly enough for a wife and daughter to live on, he arranged for Iona to be taken on part-time at Southwestern Drug during his absence.

With Cecil gone, the Willis household joined the ranks of fatherless families. Iona took the new bus that ran between the air field and downtown to work, and back home early enough to be there after school when Dorothy Ann arrived. On Saturdays and occasionally during the week, when school was out, Dorothy Ann was treated to a day with her mother in the sample room at Southwestern, or wandered the halls to be entertained by the rest of the employees, and to entertain whoever would listen, carrying on in Cecil's stead with stories and jokes.

Ann Richards reports that she doesn't remember much about the months when Cecil was gone and she and Iona lived alone. Perhaps so, but even as Cecil had been her great teacher when he was home, also, in a way, his absence itself provided a lesson: However unformulated the notion, she experienced the fact that women alone could make it. Women were perfectly able to keep the car running, pay the bills, and make decisions. Women had the power and the ability to manage their lives and affairs as effectively as men. Loving Daddy was one thing, but being absolutely dependent on him was another: Love and independence were not mutually exclusive. It was a lesson that strong women had learned and relearned, and that would in the coming decades in America be transformed into an explosive movement of women's rights and empowerment.

In any case, Dorothy Ann and Iona were not alone for long, because Iona, in her own determined way, quickly decided that she and Dorothy Ann would move to San Diego to be with Cecil for the duration. It was to be quite an adventure for an eleven-year-old sixth-grader who had never been farther away than Hico.

Iona enlisted her cousin, Fannabee Fryer, whose husband was also in California, to accompany her and Dorothy Ann. Arrangements were made to rent out the house in Lakeview. The two women pooled their gas rationing stamps and set the date for their departure in late May, as soon as school recessed for the year. As the time to leave neared, Iona and Fannabee killed the chickens and canned them and whatever was ready to be picked in the spring garden. Finally, school out and the old Chrysler loaded down with clothes, utensils, and baskets packed with boiled eggs, fried chicken, cookies, and whatever else would keep—Iona was not one to waste money on restaurant fare—they headed west.

It was not a trip for the faint of heart in those days of narrow roads and sparse accommodations, but then, Iona had never been accused of being any less than stout of heart. As it turned out, there was no need to worry. The trip went well, with no problems. They spent the first and only night on the road in El Paso and arrived in San Diego the next night.

Housing was a big problem right away. It was next to impossible to find an apartment that did not ban children. Finally they rented a basement apartment as a stopgap. Dorothy Ann slept on a cot that they folded up and put in a closet early each day. "It was horrible," Iona says of the circumstances, "but we had just endured a depression and had lived on a farm under tough circumstances. We knew what we had to do to survive."

After a few months, through connections of friends from Texas, they located an apartment that was more liveable. Iona cannot remember the names of the friends but recalls the address: 2078 First Avenue. Dorothy Ann attended school on the other side of town. She rose at dawn to catch a bus that took her downtown, where she transferred to a streetcar that took her the rest of the way. Ann "didn't seem to mind at all," and, of the whole experience, "seemed to make out just fine."

Cecil was a Hospitalman Fourth Class (lowest grade in the Navy). He "just hardly got enough money to be worth standing in line for," Iona said, so she took in sewing to help make ends meet. She and Cecil were "kind of homesick," but she doesn't recall Ann "fretting over it." California was "nice in many aspects," and the people "were friendly, curious about Texas and asked a lot of questions about Texas." One of the worst parts of the experience was the constant fear that Cecil would be sent overseas. "He always dreaded it," Iona said, but it was a possibility faced by everyone. "We never knew what the next day would bring."

Whatever her parents' feelings, Dorothy Ann felt she might have landed in Oz. In Lakeview, she and Regina could walk the three or four blocks to school. In contrast, San Diego sprawled over miles of countryside. The view in Lakeview was limited to low, rolling hills that were not, once she had seen the real thing, proper hills. Of course, there were flowers in Lakeview, but they paled in comparison to the naturally growing hedges of magenta bougainvillea, the banks of delicate pink and white geraniums or, almost beyond belief, poinsettia shrubs the size of small trees. And as for trees! The live oak, mesquite, white oak, and chinaberry that shaded Lakeview were not as beautiful and romantic as the towering palms that lined so many of San Diego's streets.

The wonders went on. Balboa Park and the zoo were filled with trees and animals never seen before. The naval base, with the huge hospital in which Cecil worked, seemed larger than Waco, and the warships, bristling with weaponry and riding at anchor in the bay, boggled the mind. The Spanish architecture, with its tile roofs and barely glimpsed courtyards, seemed more like movie sets than mere houses. Most amazing of all, though, were doughnuts. Biscuits and bread, cookies, pies and cakes, were all standard fare in Lakeview, but real doughnuts, deep-fat fried, were until then only myth.

But more than Dorothy in Oz, Dorothy Ann was a Miranda in a brave new world peopled by men and women, boys and girls, with exotic names unlike any she had heard before. Czechs, mostly, lived in the bustling town of West, twenty miles north of Lakeview, and Fredricksburg was German, but few Czechs or Germans were seen in Lakeview, and they were regular white people anyway. Some Mexicans, as most Hispanics were called then, lived in Lakeview and Waco, but most in the 1940s lived in San Antonio, and along the Mexican border in the Rio Grande valley. As for blacks, Texas was still rigidly segregated, and most people were not yet enlightened enough to call them Negroes, even. Ann speaks of knowing only one black, a man named Smoke Munson, who worked with Cecil at Southwestern Drug.

The white world she grew up in and knew would never be quite the same for Dorothy Ann after San Diego. In the seventh grade at Theodore Roosevelt Junior High School, she met and got to know classmates who were Greek and Italian, French and British, black and brown, too, and discovered they were all remarkably like her. More than anything else that had happened in her young life, the revelation opened her eyes to the way blacks and, later, other minorities, were discriminated against. Dorothy Ann Willis the child, and Ann Richards the housewife, mother, and politician she became, would never be a party to racial intolerance or prejudice in any form.

The end of the war began in Europe on May 8, 1945, when Germany finally surrendered. Men and provisions, weapons and munitions streamed toward the West Coast in preparation for the final drive against Japan. Within months after Japan surrendered, Cecil was discharged in San Diego on, ironically, December 7, 1945. "We were very elated," Iona said, and wasted no time heading back to Texas in the same old Chrysler. "We drove all night and made the trip nonstop." And despite the dislocation and stress, Cecil, when it was over, "was glad that he had a part in the war."

Cecil stepped back into his job with Southwestern Drug as if he hadn't missed a day, and Iona was happy enough to be back in her own home. As for Dorothy Ann, the adventure was over and, she and Regina agreed after a jubilant reunion, there really was no place like home. Armed with hundreds of new stories about exotic places and experiences, she took up where she had left off.

Dorothy Ann's eighth- and ninth-grade years passed quickly. School and church, Cecil once again holding forth with stories in the pavilion, covered-dish suppers, lazy afternoons riding bikes with Trellis, Virginia Lynn, and her other girlfriends. The ageless chores, for a twelve- or thirteen-year-old, of wiping the ivy leaves, of hemming a skirt, of weeding the garden. If, as an eight- and nine-year-old, the possibility of the Japanese bombing Waco Army Air Field had frightened her, Dorothy Ann and her generation had in the intervening years grown accustomed to images of death and destruction. The atomic bomb seemed to be just another bomb. Algebra seemed more important than Albania. Geography and English took precedence over geopolitics. The history of the Lone Star State—the Alamo, James Bowie, Sam Houston—was emphasized by Texas educators. Choir, basketball, school plays, and most of all football were immediate and infinitely more exciting than the changes taking place on the world stage.

The war had spawned a technological revolution that started a massive population shift from country to city. Cecil, perhaps better than Iona, saw the changes taking place as he drove around the countryside, but Iona, too, after having been exposed to San Diego, was as fully aware that the future lay in the education the cities offered. Consequently, both wanting—Iona perhaps driven—to give Dorothy Ann the best, the decision was made in the spring of 1947 to move into Waco so she could go to a "real" high school where she would have all the advantages. Luckily for Dorothy Ann, Regina's mother had made a similar decision, so the girls would enter high school with at least one old friend.

Census figures show Waco growing from 58,000 to 86,000 between 1940 and 1950, a direct result of the war boom. The General Tire Company operated a huge plant, and Bluebonnet Ordnance was retooled for a transition from gunpowder and ordnance to fertilizers and rocket propellants. The Waco Army Air Field, newly commissioned as Connally Air Force Base, was still in operation, and returning G.I.'s swelled Baylor's enrollment, which meant, too, an expanded faculty. This new, sophisticated, and relatively highly educated constituency demanded a modern education for its children. As a result, Waco High School was said to be one of the better schools in the state, and gave its students "more education than most of us thought we needed," Norman Hay, a banker and one of Dorothy Ann's classmates, told us. More education in more than one sense, especially as compared to the dearth of extracurricular opportunities in Lakeview. The Waco Tigers, in their gold and white uniforms, consistently posted winning seasons. Waco High's band, an award-winning marching ensemble, led loud, proud parades along Austin Avenue, Waco's main street, on the frequent occasions of Tiger victories. Mattie Bess Coffield ran a debate program that quietly but consistently placed as high in state-wide competition as the football team.

The move was a defining one for Dorothy Ann Willis. For whatever the reason, she had never liked the name Dorothy, so failed to mention it when she registered. Both her parents had taken freedom with their given names, but Ann had just turned fourteen, and how many barely-fourteen-year-olds have the temerity to change their names and make the change stick? Whatever the reason—rebellion or a true sense of what better suited her personality—she had taken charge of her own destiny. The message that she sent might not have been clear to her at the time, but it is crystal clear in retrospect: Ann Willis would be who and what Ann Willis, not someone else, wanted her to be.

Waco High School consisted of an imposing cream-colored brick four-story building on the southeast edge of downtown, a couple of blocks south of the McClennan County Courthouse. There were three grades, ten through twelve. The student population was all white, with the exception of eight students with Hispanic surnames in the class of 1950, and with the black children segregated in Moore High, in East Waco.

Ann Willis neither understood nor agreed with segregation, but she was a child of a conformist era and probably did not then imagine challenging it. In those simpler times, girls wore loafers or saddle oxfords, plaid skirts and plain blouses, and perhaps the occasional string of artificial pearls. Boys sported dress slacks and loafers, dress shirts with sweaters when the weather turned chilly, and slicked their hair back Tyrone Power–style with Brylcreem. Boys held all the class offices, with the exception of secretary, which was generally reserved for a girl. Teachers were respected, and while a student was free to argue a point, no one thought of talking back, using bad language, or striking someone.

Conformity was not taken lightly in the Willis household, because conformity was the stuff and essence of society. One was accepted or rejected, and rose, fell, or, worse, remained ensnared in mediocrity according to how well and to whose standards one conformed. The house, then, that Iona set about having built soon after they moved to Waco, became an important part of her program to give her daughter nothing but the best. Built on the west side of town within a few blocks of the country club and Lake Waco, on a large corner lot at North Twenty-ninth and Sturgiss streets, it connected the have-not Willises with more affluent and better-established families, among whom were the Coffelts.

Mary Kay Coffelt, now Trautschold, was a tall, dark-haired girl with a no-nonsense approach to daily affairs that later served her well during a thirty-three-year career as a junior high school English teacher. Kay's house sat behind a brick fence fitted with wrought iron gates, well back from the road and shaded by large live oak trees. Her father was a cardiologist and clearly well-to-do, but by no means beyond treating people who had no money and could pay their bills only in kind—with a pound or two of butter or a sack of blackeyed peas.

Mary Kay and Ann became best friends. Their mothers took turns driving them downtown to school, often stopping to pick up Rusty—Regina's new nickname—on the way. Weekends, they either went to or hosted "Coke parties,"—no party was considered a success unless Ann was there—where they played records and danced, ate potato chips and drank sodas. The parties were closely chaperoned, with a doused light in the party room the signal for the quick arrival of a parent. Dances, too, were subjected to the same intense scrutiny, but there, at least, the wilder kids could sneak out into the Texas night for an illicit beer or a smoke.

As for dates, there were not many places for fifteen- and sixteen-year-old boys and girls to go in Waco. If someone had access to a car, they could drive down to the circle for a hamburger and fries at the Elite Cafe. More often they went to a movie at the Waco Theater, the Orpheum, or the Rivoli, which showed B movies, followed by a stop at Otis Stahl's Pharmacy or the Palace of Sweets for a soda or sundae. Summertime was more of the same, with hours spent reading or playing bridge in the shade under the oak trees at home or at the Fish Pond Country Club where, Ann says in her autobiography, the sons and daughters of the "haves" congregated.

"That was the only thing about her book that kind of irritated me," Kay told us as we chatted about the old days. "I never...we never...thought of ourselves as haves, or her as a have-not." It was difficult, though, for a girl who grew up poor to think of herself as anything but poor. Poor people grew and canned their own food. Poor people wore homemade clothes, not the ready-mades their friends bought. But ironically, according to Shirley Frank, now Eller, one of Ann's college debating partners, "As I recall, she dressed better than the rest of us. Her mother made exquisite clothes for her."

We talked to Bill Dosher, a heavy-set man with a Texas drawl, now in real estate in Waco. Bill met Ann in the fall of 1947, shortly after she enrolled in Waco High and became best friends with his buddy, J.B. Little. He describes her then as "not the prettiest girl in school, but she was pretty, and maybe not the smartest, but she was darn smart." He adds, "There were girls who had a lot of boy friends and some who had a lot of girl friends, but damn few who were popular with both, and Ann was universally popular...with all groups and cliques."

From very nearly the first day of school, she took center stage and told the funniest, and raunchiest, stories in the joke telling sessions outside the schoolhouse at lunch and other free times. Acceptance came easily for a pretty and personable girl who was bold enough to walk up to strangers, stick out her hand, and introduce herself. People naturally liked a girl who was funny—her laconic, often self-defacing humor laid everyone out—but smart enough never to be thought of as the class clown. They enjoyed being around a girl who did not play the snob and who got along with everyone, including the teachers. They looked up to a classmate who, quickly enough, brought honor to her school as a debater.

Ann was introduced to debate early in her first year in Mattie Bess Coffield's speech class. Bill Dosher, who took the same course, describes their teacher as a large—she weighed over two hundred pounds—cheerful woman with an infectious smile. She had "immaculate enunciation," Bill recalls, and "was as good a teacher as I had in high school."

Mattie Bess, debate teacher and coach, had the ability to energize her students, and as proof could point to a shelf of victory cups among the more usual gilded footballs and crossed baseball bats that filled Waco High's trophy case. She was also tough, and if a student failed to meet her standards, she would quietly and kindly suggest, at the end of the year, that he or she should move on to something else. There was no such suggestion for Ann, who quickly turned into one of her stars.

The Interscholastic League—the debate club—rated only one page as compared to ten for football in the 1950 *Daisy Chain,* the Waco High School yearbook. Nonetheless, debate was one of the unsung American high school and college passions. For Ann, discovering debate was like learning that she could be paid—in this case, get good grades—for doing what she loved best, which was to talk. Mattie Bess set up the class so each student worked alone and with a partner of the same and opposite sex.

Alone or with a partner, Ann was glib, facile, and had, it turned out, a logical mind. She was calm under fire and intensely competitive. Serious when it counted, she was given to losing patience and her temper with a partner who in her consideration fouled up. She and her usual partner, Joanne Sheehy, delighted in destroying the opposition, especially on the rare occasions when, during interscholastic competition, the opposition turned out to be boys. She was good enough, by her second, or junior, year, to be paired with Bob Schmidt—girls and boys usually debated separately in tournaments—to participate in a demonstration debate at the University of Texas against a mixed boy-girl team from Austin High. The old Texas Quality radio network broadcast the debate and recorded the program when it was aired.

Guy Bizzell was Mattie Bess Coffield's counterpart at Austin High. In his eighties now, his voice is still mellifluous and commanding. He had forgotten all about that debate, he told us, until the original electric transcription of it was discovered and sent to him.

The proposition to be debated was, Resolved: that the President of the United States should be elected by a direct vote of the people. With a toss of a coin, Austin High won the affirmative, and Waco High, the negative. The quality of the transcription is excellent, and one can hear how hard Ann was working, how well she had mastered the basics.

"First of all," she declares, "the members of the opposition say that unit rule is unfair, and yet we find that were it not for unit rule, we would not have our two-party system in the United States, that has made one of the strongest governments in the world."

She speaks in complete sentences, with barely an "um" or "ah." She selects her points and emphasizes them. She is well prepared in her opening response, which required little adjustment since she herself had argued the affirmative on other occasions, and strongly attacks her opponents' arguments in her final rebuttal.

"First of all, it will encourage fraud....Since one vote will equal one vote...ballot boxes will be stuffed." (Not as naive as it sounds, recalling Lyndon Johnson's mysteriously packed Duval County boxes in his senatorial race in 1948.)

"Second, it will destroy one of our two theories of fundamental representation...(for) it will destroy all states' rights...." (And this from a one-day liberal Democrat!)

"Third, we find that a candidate will appeal to a thickly populated section. Did you know that New York could outvote twenty-five states west of the Mississippi under this plan?"

To Guy, now as then, the impression was that the substance was shaky and sometimes naive, but that was easily forgiven in a high school junior. The important point is that she was the most polished of the four contestants, and a listener today, as did the judges then, has to agree that the negative prevailed.

There was more to debate than shredding a competitor's arguments. Preparation demanded wide reading in current affairs and history, a logical examination of issues, and the development of strategy and timing. It taught the fine art of listening and *hearing*, and then exploiting an opponent's weak spots or, when taken off guard, quickly contriving a defense. By no means, though, was it all practice and work. Debate, using ideas and words, proved to be *fun*, as did meeting and contending with the sharpest minds from schools in her district and across the state as she and her partner, Joanne Sheehy, rose in the rankings. It was fun traveling, more fun being on the radio, and the most fun of all, winning the Texas Interscholastic League Double-A category championship in her senior year.

It's a little-known fact that Ann Willis, at the age of fifteen and a junior in high school, was the attorney general of the state of Texas. Sort of. For a few hours.

The occasion was Bluebonnet (Texas) Girls State, which met at the Texas School for the Blind in Austin. Politics for girls in the late

1940s was a man's world in which women were allowed to help with the chores and little more. Nonetheless, girls were supposed to learn about and understand politics. To this end the Girls State program, sponsored and run by the American Legion Auxiliary, was founded in 1937 and was expanded to include Girls Nation in 1948. The program gave most of the girls who attended their first view into the workings of politics and their first chance to be elected for anything other than secretary or treasurer of a club or class.

Ann was one of 185 girls who attended Bluebonnet Girls State in 1949. It was heady stuff for her. With parents along as chaperones, she had been to Dallas with Kay, Rusty, and other friends to visit the Texas State Fair and watch the Ice Capades. She had accompanied the rest of the school on chartered trains to Texarkana and Port Arthur for the quarter- and semi-final football games the previous fall, and to Fort Worth for the state 6-A level championship game at Texas Christian University Stadium against Amarillo, which the Tigers won on Christmas Day. She had debated at other schools in Central Texas, but Girls State was special because, even more than winning debates, she loved to meet new people.

And what people! Bright girls, they came from El Paso, the Rio Grande Valley, and the Panhandle. They came from small towns like Spur, in West Texas, and the biggest and most sophisticated cities, like Houston and Dallas. They were smart and personable, and she worked her way through them, introducing herself and shaking hands, telling stories and making friends. The real politicians called that working a room, as she would later learn, but already she was a natural.

Running for office at Bluebonnet State was part of the exercise, and Ann Willis ran with a vengeance, first for mayor of her town, next for county judge of her county, and finally for state attorney general. Which last is where the trouble started, because she won, and having won, was sworn in and attended a reception at the governor's mansion, where she shook Lieutenant Governor Allan Shivers's hand. Only to learn, hours later, that she had *not* won, that someone had miscounted the votes, and that her opponent was the victor.

"When Ann came back, she was full of stories about what a great experience that had been," Kay Coffelt Trautschold said, and added, about her belatedly discovered loss, "If she had been disappointed, she didn't show it. She was gracious about the whole thing, which was characteristic of her. If that had happened to me, I'd hadda fit." In fact, evidently feeling quite miserable, she hurriedly found the real winner and apologized, though the error hadn't been hers.

The gesture and her obvious sincerity so impressed the staff that it chose Ann as one of Texas's two representatives to Girls Nation, in Washington, D.C. There, as they have been for almost fifty years, the girls were introduced to the inner workings of the federal government and Washington politics. They toured the city and met with representatives or heads of departments and agencies in the three branches of government. Notable for Ann was a meeting with Georgia Neese Clark, the Treasurer of the United States, a woman who had aspired and achieved. Most impressive of all was the traditional highlight of the session, a tour of the White House and the Rose Garden, where she shook hands with President Harry Truman.

Ann has remained active in the Girls State program, Frances Goff, the legislative coordinator from 1947 to 1951, and Bluebonnet Girls State director since 1952, told us. She was invited the next year, 1950, to be a counselor, and served in that capacity for six years. Later, when she became a county commissioner of Travis County, Frances invited her to visit with and address the girls, as she has every year since.

"At Girls State," Ann has written in the American Legion Auxiliary *National News*, "I developed a lifelong interest in politics and government. I was electrified when the elected officials stood up and talked about their jobs and serving people. It seemed their work must be the finest thing anyone could possibly do."

—

Back in the real world of a teenager, Ann's senior year of high school awaited her. High school, football games, debate, the senior play, fishing with Cecil, and boys, of course. She had dated J.B. (J.B. Little later became the editor in chief of *Architectural Digest,* and was murdered during a holdup in Los Angeles), but her first really serious boyfriend was David Richards.

David, like Ann, was an only child. Tall, with dark eyes and a prematurely receding hairline, he was well-read for his age, and self-assured. The girls at Waco High thought he was handsome, and he was considered a "good catch." His parents, Dick and Eleanor Richards, had moved to Waco after Eleanor made Dick give up coaching football because he had become so excited during one game that he had had a heart attack and almost died. They had worked their way into affluence with the Richards Equipment Company, which sold equipment and supplies for general and road construction, and explosives.

Ann Willis and David Richards had known each other in passing in their first year at Waco High, but then he had been sent to Phillips Academy in Andover, Massachusetts, for his junior year. Back in Waco, they met again when Kay Coffelt introduced them at the A&W root beer stand. Soon, David carrying Ann's books, they were holding hands in the halls at school. They were bright, funny, and the life of the parties they attended, and friends who knew them thought they were made for each other.

The match that seemed made in heaven was endorsed on earth by Iona and Eleanor. For Iona, David Richards was a dream come true. He dressed well, was polite, didn't track dirt into the house, and, above all, was one of the "haves," one more plank in her ongoing campaign for the best for her daughter. For Eleanor, Ann Willis was not only bright, personable, and funny, but she had a mind of her own, as attested to by the photograph of her sitting next to a black girl at Girls Nation that had raised eyebrows in Waco.

Dick and Eleanor Richards were somewhat of an anomaly in Waco. Eleanor, or Mom El, as the kids called her, had been educated at Grinnell and Radcliffe and served on the board of trustees at Coe College in Iowa. Suspected of being Yankee carpetbaggers, she and Dick compounded the sin by being two of the tiny minority of liberals that was frequently at odds with the ultraconservative Citizens Council that ran Waco.

Their house on Bernard Avenue, near the Fish Pond and thus within a mile or so of the Willises, was more conventional. Large and lavishly appointed, it also had the Mom El personalized touch, with the downstairs powder room papered with old *New Yorker* covers. On Sunday afternoons, guests gathered there to discuss and argue politics. While she and David dated, Ann spent most Sunday afternoons there. Sometimes she found the talk confusing, as she admits in her autobiography. In contrast to her own family discussions, the conversations and views expressed at the Richardses seemed more sophisticated, as they ranged from the internecine skullduggery of party battles to the world-wide implications of Washington policies she barely knew and little understood. And feeling very much the naïf—Ann—she who twenty and thirty years later would understand as well as anyone the convoluted, Byzantine structure and mechanisms of modern politics—would retreat to the safety of the kitchen, where she still believed a woman belonged, to wash dishes.

The image of Ann Willis as a naïf, though, is probably one of her own invention. Her fellow students obviously didn't think of her that way. Neither, forty-five years later, does the observer who spends a moment looking at the photograph of her as one of six class favorites in the 1950 edition of the Waco High School yearbook, the *Daisy Chain*. There, very much a girl of her times in a strapless gown with a lace throw, in three-quarter profile, she was more than just pretty. One perceives a sureness and quiet elegance that isn't matched by the conventionally toothy smiles on the faces of the other five girls. More than most sixteen-year-olds, Ann Willis had a sense of who she was, and where she might be going.

CHAPTER 5

GREEN AND GOLD

We'll fling our green and gold afar, to light the ways of time...so guide us as we onward go...that good old Baylor line.
—BAYLOR ALMA MATER

Ann Willis would rather have gone away to college, an idea that seemed so much more romantic than enrolling in Baylor in Waco, but Iona, with her Depression mentality counting the dollars, said no. Money was not an issue. Cecil was doing well at Southwestern Drug, and they were not deeply in debt. Tuition, fees, and books cost about three hundred and fifty dollars a semester. On the strength of her debating talent, Ann had been offered tuition scholarships to Southern Methodist University and the University of Texas. Actually, Baylor would have been acceptable had she and David been able to go there together, but David's mother had decided that their romance had gone too far too fast and had sent her son back east to Andover for another year. So, no David and no Dallas and no Austin, it was Baylor or nowhere.

Baylor had dominated East Waco since it had been moved there and absorbed tiny Waco University in 1886. It appeared to be a typical American liberal arts college. Ivy grew on classroom buildings and dormitories tastefully and symmetrically arranged around Waco Hall, the Austin-chalk, pseudo-Greek, domed four-story administration building and campus centerpiece. Sidewalks crisscrossed well-kept green lawns and slipped past park benches placed under gracious live oak trees.

The oldest continuously operating university in Texas, Baylor was founded in 1845 by a most unconventional man. Robert Emmett Bledsoe Baylor served as a soldier in the War of 1812, and later became a Kentucky and Alabama state legislator. Having moved to Texas, he was a judge in the Republic of Texas and helped write the Texas Constitution when Texas became a state. A judge under the new constitution, he was also a Baptist preacher and is best known as the predominant member of a trio of staunch Baptists intent on creating a school where higher learning was reinforced by an expanded exposure to matters of the spirit, where Shakespeare was dispensed with equal dosages of Ecclesiastes and Jeremiah. That was a common enough notion in the mid to late nineteenth century—most colleges and universities when founded were denominationally affiliated—but the trend, by mid twentieth century, was toward secularization. Baylor itself was subject to secular pressure, but had the three founding fathers been able to visit Baylor in 1950, their vision, to an astonishing degree, would have been that of a dream fulfilled.

The jewel in the crown of theological orthodoxy was the hour-long chapel service, daily attendance at which was mandatory on weekdays for freshman, sophomores, and faculty. Chapel consisted of panel discussions and lectures of an inspirational or philosophical nature, with an occasional hellfire-and-damnation Baptist sermon, replete with amens and glory hallelujahs, to remind the students on which side their theological bread was buttered.

The conservative bent did not stop with chapel, and life for most students was highly structured by today's standards. Wednesday night was religious hour, and everyone was urged to take religion courses. On weeknights, female students were required to sign in at their dormitories by 8:30 P.M. Slacks and shorts, for coeds, and shorts for men, were forbidden on campus. The use of cigarettes or alcohol could result in expulsion. As for dancing, those who wished to could, but if so, they would probably be happier elsewhere.

The restrictions did not seem that extreme for most students. Many came from strongly religious backgrounds, and some, taking the rules one step further, were known on occasion to include prayers in their nightly meetings for those students licentious enough to chew gum. Others who were married and had children, worried about losing their GI Bill benefits, and had little time for playing around.

But college is college, and there was no dearth of students who sought more sophisticated and worldly adventures than those to be found hanging around their hometown root beer stands. Baylor allowed no formal affiliations with national Greek letter fraternities or sororities, but equivalent social clubs existed, and to be rushed and pledged was highly desirable. Boys and girls courted, as was required of college kids, and those who had their hearts set on drink and dance could sneak off unseen to one of a multitude of roadhouses and honky-tonks, none of which are reported to have gone out of business for lack of Baylor students.

Still, a good share of the single men made classroom, homework, and grades their highest priority to protect student exemptions that kept them out of the military. They had good reason to do so. In Europe, tension remained high. The United States had recently joined the North Atlantic Treaty Organization, and American troops faced the Communist bloc armies across the Iron Curtain. More dangerous by far was the war that raged up and down the Korean peninsula where, ultimately, over 54,000 Americans died and some 103,000 were wounded.

Avoidance of the draft wasn't the only reason. Girls, clubs, and parties generally were kept in perspective, because "most of us were intense and really kind of fervent about excelling academically," recalls David McHam, who became a journalism professor at both Baylor and Southern Methodist University. "That was because so many of the kids came from small towns and a time when hardly anybody had any money. And many were there only because their folks had scrimped and saved to give something that they, the parents, never had. So if you didn't do well at Baylor, there wasn't really a home to return to, nothing to fall back on."

The "Baylor Line"—the title of Baylor University's alma mater—referred to the cord of faith that bound the spirits of generations of students and alumni. The cord, too, that pulled some fifteen hundred green freshman from town and country to the golden opportunity of education in Waco, Texas, where, in the fall of 1950, secularization, permissiveness, and modern technology were nipping at the heels of that old-time religion.

There was good news for the girls and bad for the boys. In that year, there was a ratio of about three thousand boys to two thousand girls in the overall student population of some five thousand. Good news for all, with air-conditioning finally installed in the library, and bad news, especially for the boys, as President Truman committed more American troops to the Korean conflict. Worst news of all, as reported in the *Daily Lariat*, the Baylor student paper, Waco stood on the alert for a possible atomic bomb attack. A few months later, in January 1951, the *Lariat* reported that eighty-six students had withdrawn from classes to enter the service and, "academically, professors report a decided drop in interest....Men and women alike give evidence of being preoccupied—much more interested in the possibility of WW III...or in the conflict between democracy and communism."

News for the Baylor community at large was grist for the grinds in the debate club when Professor Glenn Capp formally greeted the new and returning members at the opening of the forensic, or debating, season. Professor Capp, known to the students and members of his debate teams as Prof, was regarded as a giant of a man on the Baylor campus. He has been described by former students as "a driving force," and "the epitome of a gentleman." Prof, now Professor Emeritus, taught at Baylor from 1934 to 1981. He served as the director of forensics for thirty-six years, the chairman of the Speech Department for thirty years, and wrote or coauthored some twenty educational books. Now eighty-two, he is in frail health and visits his campus office infrequently, but his memory is sure and his voice is still a deep, resonant baritone.

Prof was a teacher and coach who knew exactly what he wanted of his students, and ran one of the most successful debate programs in the state, if not the nation. He was so well respected that a few freshmen every year chose Baylor solely because of him. Like any other coach, he recruited aggressively. Throughout the year, he attended the local high school debates, and never missed the regional and state tournaments, where he heard, was impressed by, and offered a tuition scholarship to Ann, which Iona could not reject. And if Ann was initially disappointed, she did not stay so for long. Her prior reservations to the contrary, she would soon credit Baylor and Professor Capp as being two of the most important influences in her life.

In Glenn Capp's view, a team could never overprepare. Freshmen on scholarship were required to enroll in his advanced course,

Debate 401, which stressed mechanics and technique, and for which the textbook was *Excellence in Forensics*, by himself. Students attended the three-hour-long Union discussion program held each Tuesday evening in the South Lounge of the Union building and broadcast over KIYS, the student radio station. There, they listened to guest speakers or themselves debating topics like the place of intercollegiate athletics or organized religion on campus. Students were expected to keep up with *Time*, *Life*, the *New York Times*, the *Christian Science Monitor*, and other periodicals, none of which except *Life* were widely read in Central Texas at the time. Students studied tactics, both for affirmative and negative positions, and were tested in drills and practice debates. And when it came time to take the podium, Prof was there to nudge, to assure, and to motivate, but only rarely, because "we were already highly motivated. All of us," remembers Shirley Frank Eller, Ann's partner during her two years as a debater at Baylor.

Shirley Frank came from Temple, some thirty-five miles south of Waco. A year ahead of Ann, she had been awarded her scholarship by winning first prize in Interscholastic League Extemporaneous Speaking competition finals after speaking without the usual forty-five minute preparation period. She was flustered only because she had lost her belt and felt half dressed. "Everybody in the program had already been very successful in debate and competitive public speaking in high school. We were propelled by a strong desire to win," Shirley recalled as we leafed through a scrapbook filled with memorabilia of her Baylor years.

Shirley is a kind, sweet, matronly grandmother now. But when she began talking about her debating years, the killer instinct that all good ex-debaters have hidden away appeared. "We were a loud and competitive group who expected to win," she said, relishing the memory. "Because of our winning reputation, we had a bit of an edge in competition. Our reputation preceded us, and yes, we might have been a little bit cocky. It was unnerving to face Baylor.

"'No mercy!' was our battle cry, and we took it seriously. Our strategy was to present ourselves as innocent and kind of sweet. We wore tailored suits with high lace collars. That was the come-on. In truth, we were treacherous. We were tough skinned, dead set on discrediting the opposition.

"Ann's style was very forceful, very direct. But as soon as the thing was over, she'd snap back into her true self, joke and tease. That outgoing personality that you see as her political style isn't something that emerged later. She was just like that as a freshman in college. Years later I wasn't particularly surprised that she would become governor of Texas, although I wouldn't have been surprised if *anybody* from that group would have done the same."

Glenn Capp emphasized a logical, no-nonsense, businesslike approach to tournaments, and expected his teams to win, as they usually did. Weekend after weekend, they piled into cars and traveled to meets in Fort Worth and Dallas, Baton Rouge, Houston, College Station (Texas A&M), and elsewhere in the region, and usually left the tournament with a superior rating. On the rare, embarrassing occasions when they did lose, Capp, who was never lavish with praise when they won, was never harsh or critical. In truth, he didn't have to rant, rave, or assign blame, because however loudly his students complained about the incompetence of the judges, they knew that they had come up short.

It usually takes freshmen a while to work their way into the system. Ann shows up as early as February 2, 1951, in a story in the *Lariat* about a big debate meet in which thirty colleges participated. The story mentions senior men and women, junior men and women, and one mixed team—Ann Willis and Jim Brubaker, the latter being one of the Baylor team's big guns. Soon thereafter, she and Jim Slatton are mentioned as participating in a match in Natchitoches, Louisiana, from which she returned "with honors."

By the time another year had passed, Ann and Shirley were "big guns," too. In March 1952, the Baylor debate teams traveled to College Station and Texas A&M for a major meet, at which they whipped a prominent men's team. The men were blasé and maddeningly patronizing. The women had ambushed them, taken them unawares, because the men had not really taken them seriously. The problem was, the men's team did well enough to be invited to what amounted to the world series of intercollegiate debate at West Point later that year. Ann did not think that the laurel wreath should go to losers. Wronged, she confronted Prof Capp, who "was not a man to be questioned," according to Shirley, and bluntly told him that she and Shirley had won and deserved to go to West Point. Glenn Capp could not go that far, in 1952. He did agree, however, that they deserved some reward and recognition, and sent them to the Southern Speech Communication Association tournament in Jackson, Mississippi. There, Ann and Shirley received another superior rating. And, a distinct honor, Ann's "After Dinner" category offering was the only one chosen to be showcased at the closing banquet.

—

Over and over, in every stage of her life, people remark on the prodigious amounts of energy Ann Richards brought and brings to everything she sets her hand to. College, in all its aspects, was no different, so, in spite of the demands placed on her at home and by Prof and her other professors, she found time for boys.

Distance may make the heart grow fonder, but proximity exerts its own influence, too, especially given seventeen-year-olds caught up in an intense and charged atmosphere like that found in the debate club. Ann met James Slatton in Prof's Debate 401 class. James, who came from Dallas, was tall and "nice looking, with brown eyes and hair." He and his partner had been national debate champions in his senior year in high school. He had wanted to enlist in the Marine Corps and serve in Korea with some of his high school pals but was under age and couldn't convince his father to sign the release form.

"You have to remember," Kay Coffelt reminded us, "that sexual intimacy wasn't indulged in, in those days. At least by good girls." Nor by good boys like Jim Slatton, who was a ministerial student.

"It was all pretty tame," Dr. Slatton recalled, on the phone from Richmond, Virginia, where he is the pastor of River Oak Baptist Church. Neither of them had cars, so "dates," even after Iona relented and Ann moved into a dormitory for the spring semester, were limited going to to the Student Union, the debate club, or a football game, or sitting and holding hands on one of the benches scattered around the campus.

You would think that Jim, coming from Big D, would be more sophisticated than Ann, but he thought of her as "more worldly-wise than the average student." Outspoken, too, as she encouraged him to call himself Jim instead of James, which she considered a name for a country boy. He now looks on himself as uncivilized enough at the time for her to "take me to school on table manners."

Jim didn't care. He was in love. "Puppy love," he admits, "but remember, puppy love is very real to the puppy." Real enough that he was not unduly bothered that Ann did not share his profound devotion to the Scriptures and the Baptist faith, which too was real enough that he was glad when she was "saved" by the still young but already charismatic Billy Graham when he came to Baylor to wave his Bible, prowl the stage, and preach the word.

What more could a nice boy from Dallas want? Ann was pretty, well known and well liked on campus, and it must have felt good to be seen with her and to be known as her boyfriend. She was a crackerjack debater who could hold her own with anyone. She wasn't completely within the Baptist fold, but her head, if not her heart, was in the gate. Moreover, she liked him, and everybody *knew* that girls went to college to find a husband. Surely, God was in His heaven. The only trouble was, Iona was right there across town in Waco, and proximity again, won out.

Table manners aside, Iona didn't hold much with Jim Slatton. One day, she envisioned, Jim would become a Baptist minister, stuck forever in Discouraging Word, Oklahoma, while his wife, Ann, wrote hymns with titles like "His Bed of Roses Is My Crown of Thorns" and raised a brood of baby Baptists on a salary envied only by a night watchman. Iona hadn't worked like a Trojan to give Ann every advantage possible only to watch her marry into poverty, so when Ann wouldn't stop seeing Jim, she played a variant on Eleanor Richards's gambit by cutting off the dorm money and forcing Ann to move back home.

Actually, it wasn't the end of the world for Jim, however smitten he had been. Armed, no doubt, with the same droll sense of humor that comes across the telephone today, he must have known he faced trouble long before Ann moved home. Had, in fact, faced it since David Richards returned to Waco from Andover and, refusing to go back east, was shipped by Mom El to the University of Texas in Austin, which was close enough to drive home on the occasional weekend to see Ann.

There were no hard feelings, for puppies do grow up. And if details fade, vague shapes and impressions remain, of a pretty, vivacious, smart girl, the life of the party who bubbled with energy and made other people feel good just by being in the same room with them. A girl not mean or critical, but frank and outspoken. A girl who went prepared and gave no quarter during the heat of battle, but was quick to quip and laugh when the battle was over and, winner or loser, walk away with new friends. And a girl who, however short the time, had chosen him from among the many boys available. There were worse ways to lose.

There were worse places to be in love, too, than Baylor in the 1950s. Male/female roles were still pretty well engraved in stone, but the upheaval caused by two wars and shifting technology left room for interpretation, room to maneuver through the rules. Changes, also, in the theological walls that had long protected Baylor brought intellectual and social ferment to students and faculty alike.

In some ways, it was a strange time for an intellectual awakening. The Communist witch-hunters had raised the hue and cry against "pinkos" and "red sympathizers." In Washington, Senator Joseph McCarthy had declared the government riddled with Communists, and was ruining reputations. The House Un-American Activities Committee found more "reds" and "pinkos" in unions, the entertainment world, and elsewhere.

Reflecting this atmosphere, the Intercollegiate Scholastic League debate topic in the 1950–51 college year was, Resolved: that the non-Communist nations should form a new international organization. In late November, 1950, Resolved: That the communist party should be outlawed in the United States, was debated at a meet at the University of Texas. If these topics make it sound as if the anti-Communists were setting the agenda, it must also be noted that the Baylor team, arguing the negative, won, with the contest being decided by the audience.

While the Southern Baptists fought against the "erosion of morals," male and female mixed swimming was announced for Saturday morning at the university pool. The Waco School Board and Waco businessmen fought hard to maintain segregation, but the Baylor student council voted unanimously for the admission of Negro colleges to the Texas Intercollegiate Student Association. On a wider front, the House Un-American Activities Committee subjected college debaters to scrutiny for debating the affirmative on Resolved: that China should be admitted to the United Nations, but at least one Baylor professor, Dr. Ralph Lynn, lectured to his Twentieth-Century Western History students on "the stupidity of United States diplomacy."

Ralph Lynn and his colleague, Bob Reid, are still remembered by former Baylor students when they talk about the flowering of liberal views on the Baylor campus and among the faculty in the early fifties. That story starts when Pat Neff, a former governor of Texas and a fundamentalist autocrat, retired in 1948 from the presidency of the university and was replaced by W. R. White, more a proponent of intellectual freedom.

W. R. White was revered by Ralph Lynn as a man of "great integrity and warmth," a feeling that was fortified by the pastor-educator's willingness to allow professors to teach courses in which they expressed personal convictions that did not necessarily conform to Southern Baptist dogma. The atmosphere of intellectual freedom, individuality, and honesty allowed by White was unprecedented at Baylor and coincided with the influx of students who, for all their surface conformity, would pave the way for the explosion of student unrest and activism in the sixties.

"They should never be confused with flag-burning, long-hair, bomb-throwing radicals," Baylor alumnus David McHam said. "But there was certainly a trend toward a more low-key fervency based around attitudes of a prointegration, anti-McCarthyism kind of mind set." A progressivism that eventually led to the candidacy of men like Adlai Stevenson, the inclusion of more women and minorities at all levels of government, and the presidencies of John Kennedy, Jimmy Carter, and Bill Clinton.

This overview may seem on the surface to have little bearing on the teenage Ann Willis and the politician she became. It is, however, of key importance because Ralph Lynn and Bob Reid are the two professors who made history come alive for Ann.

Dr. Ralph Lynn was unconventional. Lynn served in the army during World War II, then ran a dry-cleaning establishment. He taught high school for three years while studying for his doctorate in history at age forty, then taught history at Baylor for thirty years before retiring. Lynn is a tall, powerfully built man who looks younger than his eighty-two years. He is still a recognized figure on the Baylor campus.

"I endear myself to all my students," Bob Reid told us, but "Ralph isn't as popular with some of the kids because he forces them to think. Let's face it, for many college students, that's a torturous thing."

The year was 1952, the course Modern Asian History. One day, several of Lynn's students who were well versed in anti-Communist rhetoric challenged his unflattering description of Chiang Kai-shek and his politics and policies. Now, dissent in class was welcome, but not uninformed dissent, and when the students persisted, Lynn finally told them to get out of his class and not return until they had read at least six articles in scholarly—i.e., not red-baiting—periodicals on the subject. They did, he readmitted them, and the discussion continued, presumably on a more informed level.

Bob Reid is in his latter sixties and recently retired, though he still teaches one class a semester. Ann Richards herself, in a speech on the occasion of his retirement, best described him as a lanky and highly appealing bachelor who left "undergraduates and unmarried faculty members of the female persuasion absolutely aquiver.

"It's hard to imagine how Bob Reid could look out over a classroom full of moonstruck and dewy-eyed coeds—of which I was one—and keep a straight face, much less teach history, but he did. And despite ourselves and our distractions, we learned a great deal because with Bob Reid it was show time. It wasn't dull stuff from a book. It was real and alive."

There is an old saying that the teacher will appear when the student is ready, and that seems to be the case with Ann. Naturally inquisitive, her curiosity regarding the past was due at least in part, according to Lynn, to Iona's obsession with history. Add to that her wide reading in current affairs, which also required extensive historical research, and Prof Capp's insistence on preparation and logic, and she was not only ready, but fired with enthusiasm and a thirst, for "ideas, concepts, insight, and understanding."

Bob Reid agreed. "This was a bright breed," he recalled, "but nobody, and I mean this, was any brighter than Ann Willis Richards, and during my years at Baylor, I taught over twenty thousand students." And more, "Ann was a standout who was quick to grasp the entire scene, the overview. She listened, her hand was up all the time. And she realized what was important and what was not, which current events might someday qualify as history and which ones would not."

Ann took only three courses from Lynn and Reid: Twentieth Century Western History from Lynn; Middle Eastern History and Eighteenth-Century European History from Reid. The courses, though, were not in the long run nearly as important as the teachers, which holds equally true for her debate courses under Prof Capp.

It is a measure of Ann Richards that, unbidden, she attended the dinner given for Bob Reid on the occasion of his retirement. And while Bob Reid is the name used in the remarks that follow, they could have been directed as well to Ralph Lynn and Prof Capp. She begins with jokes, typically Ann Richards, that slow, droll-sounding Texas speech that makes you wait for the zinger and leaves you holding your sides with laughter. But then, subtly sneaking up on you, she is suddenly serious, and the room stills, and laughter turns into a lump in the throat.

Forty years down the road, looking back at where we've been, people like Bob Reid we remember with real awe. He taught us to think for ourselves, to see the big picture, and to believe in the power of our own small brains to see this old world as it really is.

Harry Truman said the only thing new in the world is the history we don't know. Bob Reid opened thousands of new worlds for the students and we're profoundly grateful for his work and for steadily hitting our brains with knowledge, understanding, and encouragement.

While we were with 'ya, Bob, you made it fun. You gave us perspective. You made us understand the importance of the past and how it impacted the present, and the future.

What a joy you were to all of us.

CHAPTER 6

A Fingertip Veil

Ann Willis's junior year was a year of giving up as well as getting. In March of her freshman year she had been rushed by and pledged Pi Alpha Lambda, *the* women's social club of distinction at Baylor. Iona, no doubt, had been pleased by Ann's acceptance into the social elite. What else could a mother ask, after all? For Ann, though, the distinction was poisoned during pledge week of her sophomore year when she was privy to the selection of suitable pledges. A natural egalitarian who accepted people on their merits and personalities, she listened to her "sisters" blackball prospective pledges who seemed perfectly fine to her but whose parents were socially unacceptable. Though she liked the girls individually, she decided after some soul-searching to distance herself, and stopped participating in the daily activities of the club. One can almost see the matrons-to-be rolling their eyes in wonder. Almost see, too, Iona expressing her displeasure at some length—and Cecil, slightly off to the rear, winking his approval.

The big change, though, stemmed from David's decision not to return to the University of Texas but to enroll in Baylor. On the surface, given the conventional wisdom of the day, not to speak of gossip in a small town like Waco, David had reached down a rung on the social ladder. The Richardses were "haves," well educated, well-to-do, and well connected. David had been sent back east to a prestigious school for part of his high school education—a rarity for a Waco youngster—and then breezed not only into the University of Texas, but the Kappa Sigma fraternity, which latter conferred on him the status of a bona fide member of the elite and nicknamed him "Dirty Dave."

At the University of Texas in Austin, there were independent students, members of other fraternities, and atop the heap, Kappa Sigmas. Kappa Sigma was the domain of young Texas patricians, but money and family alone were not the only criteria for acceptance. "These were guys who might be extremely rich or extremely bright or extremely crazy, but everybody was extremely something," one ex-fraternity member explained. They were also extremely successful later in life, too, he might have added, citing Kappa Sigma alumni like Beauford Jester, governor of Texas when David was at the University of Texas, or, later, Bill Wittliff, who wrote the CBS teleplay of *Lonesome Dove*, pioneer heart transplant surgeon Denton Cooley, or American Airlines founder Cyrus Rowlett Smith. The Kappa Sigs saw in David Richards an extremely smart and self-assured pledge who was willing to be subjected to the torturous hazing inflicted on initiates. He could also survive the heavy-duty drinking—they were known as the "Kappa Swigs"—either at home in the red brick fraternity house on Nineteenth Street or on the far side of the bridges of the Rio Grande in festive little communities like Ciudad Acuña, Piedras Negras, and Nuevo Laredo.

The sybaritic life, however, had palled. "My two years at UT were pretty crazy," David recalled, adding, only somewhat face-tiously, "I had to go to Waco to dry out after two years of being a Kappa Sig." A more satisfying reason was Ann. "I went back for the romance," he said. "Ann and I were in love."

The romance flourished, with David back in town. Once again, well enough read by now to parry and riposte with the best, Ann joined the Richardses' Sunday afternoon discussions and shouting matches. She held not only her own, but her beer and bourbon, too, on the nights when she and David and a handful of friends hit the honky-tonks and dance halls so beloved by Baylor students. She was, in short, seen from a purely objective and sociological point of view, not in the least a step down anyone's ladder, and David knew it.

When school began again, Ann quit the debate club. Reading and filing articles, attending practice sessions, and spending weekends on the road and at tournaments took up too much time and left little for romance. Resigning from the debate team meant losing her scholarship, of course, but David was worth the sacrifice, even to Iona, who most likely saw him in the long run as much more valuable than the cost of two years' tuition.

Universities are traditionally hotbeds of student unrest, but not in Texas. The University of Texas in Austin, to the consternation of a politically conservative Board of Regents, was one of a few glaring exceptions in the 1950s. If David was not a full-fledged radical, he was certainly, his own term, "politicized."

"I had read a lot," he said. "I had been to school [at Andover, ex-President George Bush's alma mater] with black students, and had black friends, [and had] different ideas from prevailing Texas mores." Most of all, he said, "I hated [Governor] Allan Shivers," who in the spring of 1952 whipped liberal Ralph Yarborough, and in November ran for governor on both the Republican and Democratic tickets.

David carried his outrage back to Waco and Baylor. There, "drying out," working part-time for his father, going to school, and spending every spare moment available with Ann, he railed against the Republicans and the conservative Democrats. Ann, in love with him and similarly, if not as radically, inclined by nature, was an easy convert. Were they of another generation, they might well have become flower children and run off to San Francisco or a commune, burned draft card and bra, or fallen in with militant Marxists, but they were too solidly middle-class, too much the product of their times. The seeds were sown, though, and the gulf between them and Texas's conservative Democrats widened and became permanent. In a yellow-dog Democratic state in which progressive Democrats were more conservative than liberal Republicans in most other places, they would be identified by most Texans as extreme liberals if not pinkos or worse.

Not campus leaders in any accepted sense—many old acquaintances were confused and appalled by the new David—Ann and David were barely mentioned in the 1953 and 1954 editions of *The Roundup,* the Baylor yearbook. Attending classes, doing homework, enjoying the usual weekend parties—a radical philosophy did not preclude drinking beer and dancing—and simply being together

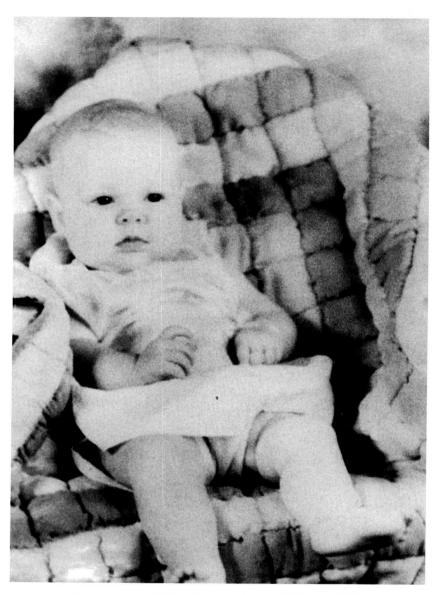

Dorothy Ann Willis baby portrait, late 1933/early 1934.
(Courtesy Ann Richards Committee)

Dorothy Ann, at front and center of the Lakeview Methodist Church children's choir, circa 1938. *(Courtesy Rusty Hoffman)*

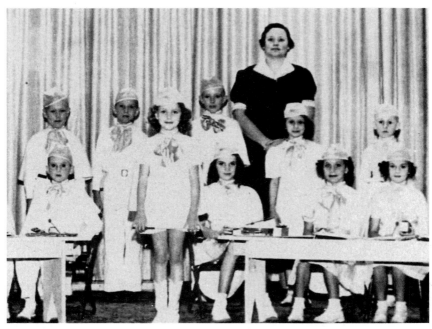

Dorothy Ann, at front and center, leader of the Lakeview Central School Rhythm Band, circa 1940. *(Courtesy Rusty Hoffman)*

"Sybil and Trellis."
Dorothy Ann Willis, left,
and Regina Garret, right,
at the State Fair of Texas,
circa 1946.
(Courtesy Rusty Hoffman)

Ann Willis, left, Iona Willis,
right. Photo taken on front
porch of the house at 29th
and Sturgiss in Waco, upon
her graduation from Waco
High School, May 1950.
*(Courtesy Ann Richards
Committee)*

Ann Willis, senior high school portrait, 1950.
(Photo by Jimmy Willis, her uncle,
who was a photographer for the Waco Tribune Herald)

Scene of the destruction wrought by the Waco Tornado,
May 11, 1953, that killed 116. *(Photo by Jimmy Willis)*

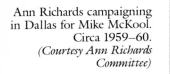

Ann Richards campaigning in Dallas for Mike McKool. Circa 1959–60. *(Courtesy Ann Richards Committee)*

The 1963 Christmas card sent by Betty McKool, left, and Ann Richards, right. This was a 12″ x 18″ flyer folded for mailings, as the crease marks indicate. Neither Ann nor Betty ever signed the cards, which they sent for eight years to a list of friends that grew to over five hundred.
(Courtesy Marlene Sparks)

Ann Richards portrays Lyndon B. Johnson in the 1968 Political Paranoia
show mounted by the North Dallas Democratic Women.
(Photo by Tad Hershorn)

Ann Richards, left, an unidentified union bus driver, center, and David Richards, right at a 1973 fundraiser. *(Photo by Alan Pogue)*

·filled most of the time. As the year went on they became almost inseparable. Finally they decided they no longer wanted to live apart and announced that they planned to marry at the end of the school year. What they did not, could not, have planned on was a disaster that came close to stilling those wedding bells.

The old shaman who predicted that the Wacos' territory along the Brazos River would be tornado-free was right for every known day since the day he made that prediction, with the exception of Monday, May 11, 1953.

May is tornado time in Texas and across the Midwest. Tornadoes had killed ten in Wisconsin and Minnesota on the tenth. On the tenth, too, the small town of Hebron, Nebraska, was blown off the map, and folks said it was a miracle that the twister that clipped Russellville, Arkansas, did not kill anyone.

Wacoans read the headlines that morning, clucked and shook their heads, and glanced at the weather forecast. Morning cloudiness, clearing skies in the afternoon, with a high temperature of eighty, gave no cause for concern. Of more concern, to many, was the news that the local minor league baseball team had officially integrated the day before and that, in the Big State League game at Katy Field, the Waco Pirates' Negro catcher had hit a home run during a 9–8 win over Wichita Falls.

Elsewhere, those who had television sets looked forward to *I Love Lucy, Studio One,* and Arthur Godfrey's *Talent Scouts* that night, and those who didn't wondered if "good credit" meant theirs, with which they could buy a set for next to nothing down and thirty-two cents a day.

For anyone who cared, as the day went on, the weatherman was dead on when, around noon, the clouds began to break up and move out. Those who listened to the three o'clock news on the radio heard sketchy reports that a tornado had hit San Angelo, two hundred miles to the west, at 2:30 P.M., and there were fatalities. With no reason for concern, the faculty at a Waco elementary school told the honor students that a party in their honor at Sun Pool would be held as planned. Elsewhere around town, appointments were made to meet at Luby's Cafeteria for the Monday Money Saver Special of barbecued meat patties, mashed potatoes, rolls, and iced tea for thirty-five cents.

Weather radar technology was a thing of the distant future, so no one in a position to make a difference realized that the same system that had spawned the tornado that hit San Angelo was slanting across the open prairie between San Angelo and Waco. As the afternoon wore on, most Wacoans went about their business as usual.

By 3:30 P.M., as divinity student Raymond Vickery studied in the Baylor library, the clouds began to return. With the sky blackening, retired Texas Ranger Elijah Coffelt, Kay Coffelt's grandfather, traded stories with other old-timers at the Feed Store Cafe downtown. Jimmy Willis, Ann's uncle, the photographer, did not see the ominous weather sign because he was inside the News-Tribune building processing film. And Ann was at work downtown at Morris Jewelers, with but one hour to go before David arrived to drive her home. By the time he picked her up, the sky had turned dark black. Moments after he left her at her home, and as he drove to his own, the sky became "as green as an emerald."

Red sky at night, sailors delight, red sky in morning, sailors take warning. Whether there is truth to that old adage, Texans and others who live in tornado country know they are in for heavy weather when the sky turns what others describe more as a deep, dark jade green. When Raymond Vickery finished at the library, at 4:30, the sky overhead was an odd mixture of green and black, it was nearly dark out, and the wind had picked up ominously. Suddenly a nearby utility pole began to whip back and forth, and wires snapped and lashed out as if to snare a pair of telephone booths tumbling down the sidewalk and across the green. As Vickery, who was attending Baylor on a track scholarship, sprinted for the athletic dorm where he lived, a sheet of almost horizontal rain drenched him.

Downtown, at 4:40 P.M. precisely, the downpour ended as quickly as it had begun. Seconds later people felt a sudden pain in their ears, and later remembered "feeling funny" as their heads filled with "an odd buzzing noise." Then, suddenly, the tornado, which had hooked around town from the west, crossed the Brazos and bore down on the central business district, a direct hit.

The tornado was "a motheroo," David recalled. The clock was

stopped at 4:41 P.M. on the outside wall of the First National Bank downtown, where the devastation was nearly complete. The Joy Theater, Sammy's Cafe, and Luby's Cafeteria were destroyed. The Dennis Furniture building, six brick stories and a fixture for a half a century, had imploded and was reduced to a pile of rubble. The four-story Tom Padgitt building that occupied half a block across the street had been torn to pieces. Destroyed, too, were the Feed Store Cafe and the bathhouse at the Sun Pool, where many of the elementary school honor-student party lay dead and buried in the rubble. Spared—structural engineers still wonder how and why—was the Alico skyscraper, although some half of the windows from the ground floor to the twenty-third and top story were sucked out.

"Oh, yes, I remember it well," Iona told us on the phone. "Ann was on her way home from Baylor and just got home in time. Cecil had been on the road that day in Waco, calling on drugstores, and got home just after it hit." Which made them some of the lucky few who knew the whereabouts of friends and relatives. Later Cecil and Iona "got in the car and drove down there and waded around in that mess." And mess it was, with water, mud, buildings blown apart, and live wires down all over the place.

Downtown the dead seemed to some to outnumber the living. Bodies were stacked, as someone said, like cordwood. Everywhere, it seemed, the trapped and wounded screamed for help from beneath caved-in walls and jumbles of beams. "There was rubble six feet deep in the streets," David said. The flood of debris covered crushed and flattened cars. Fading slowly as batteries weakened and died, unseen car horns blared eerily.

Everyone helped, that night. Dr. Coffelt, Kay told us, dug for hours through the rubble that had been the Feed Store Cafe until he found the lifeless body of his father, ex-Ranger Elijah Coffelt. Raymond Vickery, the rest of the jocks, and other students hurried downtown to search through the debris for the living and the dead. Airmen from Connally Air Force Base were trucked to the scene to administer first aid to the wounded, to help search for the living and dead, and to supply transportation. Pastors of all faiths tried to console the bereaved. Hospitals, doctors, and nurses worked around the clock for no charge.

The week that followed saw little rest. Ann, Rusty, and dozens of other young women worked the neighborhoods collecting food and supplies for those hardest hit. Kay Coffelt, who was attending Southern Methodist University in Dallas, returned to attend her grandfather's hastily arranged funeral. Funeral parlors were hard pressed, and forced to import help from surrounding communities. The next day, May 12, workers began tearing down walls and buildings that tilted dangerously during a deluge that dumped another seven inches on Waco and raised the Brazos River to near flood stage. By the time the workers were finished, a good share of downtown had been razed. Much of the land, to this day, remains empty parks and parking lots, and there is a general consensus that Waco never completely recovered, has never been the same.

Worst of all and more devastating by far, 116 souls were finally accounted for, and stories persist, even now, of others buried in filled-in basements or swept away down the Brazos. In an ironic postscript, after filling pages with stories of death, injury, and destruction, the *Tribune-Herald* noted that no "white people" had died of natural causes in the five days following the storm.

Curiously, to a nineties mentality that tends to linger on and explore or exploit the anguish of the survivors of a disaster of the magnitude of the Waco tornado, Ann does not even mention the tornado in her autobiography. A few others recall one overriding memory, like ministerial student Raymond Vickery, who said at one point they were no longer looking for the living, but for the dead, or Phil Hardberger, a longtime friend of David Richards's, who remembers lifting a wall panel at the pool hall to discover five bodies, one a young man killed as he handed money to an attendant. Most of those we talked to had little or nothing to say. The limited recollection may be because the tornado was a long time ago, and memory fades. But a greater reason, perhaps, may be attributed to a certain toughness of character of people whose lives were shaped to a great extent by the Depression and World War II. They understood and were willing to accept that life was sometimes unfair, and could pick up and move on, because as surely as ill winds blew, so did fair.

Everyone, Ann Willis included, studied Texas and U.S. history as either a freshman or sophomore, so she was certainly familiar with the concept of manifest destiny. She probably didn't, however, connect the term with another kind of destiny as manifest as one could find in the United States at the time, which was an early marriage with children not far behind.

Marriage and family, then, was virtually a definition of the meaning of life. As a rule, high school graduates who went no further than high school married high school sweethearts. Girls went on to college often with marriage in mind, and at least could choose from a wider pool of eligible men. In either case, as Betty Friedan points out in *The Feminine Mystique,* the conventional wisdom of the age for women was found in the women's magazines (edited by men), which assiduously and determinedly avoided the Cold War, nuclear confrontation, and politics at any level. Women, assigned the role of homemakers, mothers, and nurturers, were not supposed to be interested in issues. Granted that more and more of them were going to college, but they did so in order to talk intelligently to the bread-winning mates they found there and to better prepare to become nutritionists, secretaries, nurses, purchasing agents, hostesses, administrators, all the varied and multitudinous roles that keeping house and raising children required.

Ann Richards herself, in an oral history tape recorded in 1979, admitted that it never occurred to her that she should be anything other than a housewife and mother. It had seemed natural, therefore, after she and David had spent a few months together at Baylor, that the future be considered. The wedding was set for the end of the school year—almost but not quite the traditional June wedding—on May 30, 1953.

If there is one thing in Middle America that has not changed since the fifties, it is that first wedding. The men had it easy. Buy or rent a tux—in Cecil's case, write the checks, of course—appear when and where they were told, and otherwise stay out of the way. For the women, it was an endless round of showers, and oohing and aahing over china, flatware, and toasters. The interminable discussions about who would wear what. Arrangements for service and reception, for church, yard, flowers, decorations, guests, and a seemingly endless list of details to be agonized over. No small addition to the confusion was caused by Ann's and David's final exams and the disruption caused by the tornado.

On Thursday, two days before the wedding on Saturday, David and his buddies caroused the better part of the night at a traditional stag party, and set the stage for a mini-disaster when, according to Ann in her autobiography, he scratched himself on a rusty nail and had to get a tetanus shot. Reacting violently, he blew up "like a frog," and barely made it through not only the rehearsal dinner the next night but the wedding itself.

Meanwhile, the traditional pandemonium reigned at the Willises', and Ann was so tense and nervous after the rehearsal dinner—the house was packed with friends and relatives, last-minute details kept cropping up, and everything seemed to go wrong—that Kay and her mother informed Iona they would take Ann home with them, and did. There, away from the hullabaloo, Mrs. Coffelt led the girls out to the sun porch, served them strawberry shortcake on her best blue Wedgewood, and, when the tension eased, packed them off to bed for a few hours' sleep.

The next day promised to be perfect for a wedding. Sadly, Rusty would not be there. As children, she and Ann—the childhood Sybil and Trellis—had promised to be each other's maids of honor, but Rusty had married that April in California and was unable to make the trip back to Texas. No matter, for a Baylor friend, Miss Scottie Gayle Stevenson of Austin, would do the honors, with bridesmaids Kay Coffelt and Mary Holt.

"Baylor Couple Repeats Vows Here Saturday," the *Waco Tribune-Herald* headlined the next day. "An heirloom gold bar pin was worn for sentiment by Miss Ann Willis when she became the bride of David Read Richards Saturday evening in Austin Avenue Methodist Church," which had escaped the wrath of the tornado.

What a contrast to Iona's and Cecil's wedding at a friend's house! The bride wore a wedding dress "of imported white silk tissue taffeta in bridal white over bleached beige net, with a draped strapless bodice and brief bolero. The bouffant skirt of inverted pleats extended into a chapel length train.

"Her fingertip veil of imported French illusion in candlelight shade was caught to a halo of pearls with tapered ends to which small pearl droplets were attached. Her bouquet was of white orchids and stephanotis."

Dr. A. Norman Evans performed the ceremony, the altar was

decorated with emerald green ferns, baskets of white majestic daisies, and candelabra with white candles. Mrs. Fred Smith played the organ; Mrs. Merle Alexander, the harp. Cecil—one imagines the pomp and formality rendering him for once speechless—gave away the bride. Iona, stage mother supreme in a "waltz length dress of gold silk organza [and] a hat of matching shades of gold flowers," basked in the glow as the ritual unfolded.

Ann was elegant, David still befuddled by the reaction to the tetanus shot, and the guests appropriately moved and impressed by the solemnity of the occasion, but there was more to come. Back at 3500 North Twenty-ninth, a garden reception waited. There, under the live oak trees, the guests found a bride's table covered with white organdy and a three-tiered wedding cake encircled with ivy leaves. There, too, the champagne flowed, Cecil once again found his tongue, and Iona glowed as the bride and groom held court.

Finally Ann disappeared into the house, to emerge in "a beige shantung suit piped in white, a white straw hat with burnt orange velvet trim, and white accessories." It was 1953. It was perfect. It was as life was meant to be. And to ribald catcalls, leering winks, and tears, Ann and David—Mr. and Mrs. David Read Richards—drove off for a honeymoon in New Orleans.

They were nineteen. They were married. All was well with the world, and the world was theirs.

CHAPTER 7

THE REAL WORLD

Mrs. David Read Richards, the cutline under her wedding photograph in the *Waco Tribune-Herald* read. All those male names sound a little out of place, if not unacceptable, now. The more so in the case of Ann Richards, who, however much she was conditioned and willing to love, honor, and obey, was always more an Ann Richards than a Mrs. David Read Richards.

That wasn't readily apparent as the newlyweds moved into a small apartment immediately south of the Baylor campus and embarked on a marriage that would last almost thirty years. Ann worked as hard at being a good wife as she later would to be a good mother—or a good politician. As Iona had taught and as the feminine mystique demanded, she cooked, cleaned, and worked part-time to help make ends meet. She and David finished at Baylor and, with bachelor's degrees in hand, headed for Austin and the University of Texas. There, with David accepted in the law school, Ann earned her teacher's certificate and, after a mandatory semester of practice teaching, was hired to teach social studies at Fulmore Junior High School.

Fritz Sackett, now a systems manager for Advanced Micro Devices, in Austin, was one of Ann's students. Fritz comes from a political family, yellow-dog Democrats all, and grew up in an even more intensely political atmosphere than David had, listening to shouted arguments at the dinner table and being carried along to strikes and rallies. His parents and the Richardses became friends, and his mother, Dell, would connect with them again in Dallas some years later.

Ann was "ravishing," Fritz says. Of course, she was only eight or nine years older than he and his classmates, all of whom, the boys, anyway, were little more than collections of seething hormones run amok. She was his homeroom teacher in the eighth grade, and used humor to control the class, putting students in their place—not meanly—with jokes. She was also his social studies teacher, and if she did not have the same effect on him as Bob Reid or Ralph Lynn had had on her, that may have been because he was going through his Fonz days. In any case, she made social studies interesting for eighth-graders, he recalls, and kept her own political slant out of the classroom.

The teaching experience was important—Ann later said in her autobiography that teaching was the hardest work she ever did—but the hands-on political education she received was even more meaningful. "School" was Scholz Beer Garden, now as then on San Jacinto Street. The interior has not changed much, sort of a cross between a German *Bierhaus* and a Texas saloon, but the large, once-graveled outside garden has been paved and the folding chairs and old, graffiti- and initial-carved wooden tables have been replaced with heavy picnic tables and benches. There, students, budding would-be politicians, and jaded lawyers and government employees still gather to spin out the same old unresolved arguments deep into the night.

Given that connections are the stock in trade of politicians, it can be argued that Ann Richards's political career began at Scholz Beer Garden. Friday night was Scholz night. After Ann's week with the teenagers and David's with professors and books, they left their house on West Thirty-first Street and headed for Scholz's and the table where the Horses Association—usually appropriately abbreviated—met to weave intrigues, discuss the latest gossip, and once again solve the problems of the world.

Real, working politicians hung out at Scholz. The big battle between Lyndon Johnson's liberal forces and Allan Shivers's conservative wing for control of the Democratic party in Texas was in full swing, and the outcome seemed uncertain. David was active in the University of Texas Young Democrats, which spawned and was shot through with its own intrigues. That autumn, in a coup worthy of the best a banana republic had to offer, David was elected president and Ann, because she had taken a course in parliamentary procedure at Baylor, was made parliamentarian.

The fraternity-like group at Scholz Beer Garden could be said to resemble a surrogate family. Political intrigue added spice to life, and every day was a new world. At the same time, dark spots appeared. Ann was the president of the University of Texas Law Wives in David's senior year, 1956–57. In 1950, one Heman Sweatt had been the first black admitted to the law school, and Ann was shaken when it became apparent that some of the Law Wives would not tolerate a black woman in their midst. The situation was analogous to the one she had encountered in Pi Alpha Lambda at Baylor, and strengthened her commitment to judge people by themselves alone, not where they came from, or what their parents did, or the color of their skin.

A darker, more ominous spot was medical in nature. Ann and David had been married for well over two years and she had yet to become pregnant. Finally she visited a gynecologist and discovered that she had an ovarian cyst. An operation was deemed in order, and she took a leave of absence from her teaching job, and went in to the hospital. Happily, the operation went well and there were no complications. Late that fall, she learned at last she was pregnant.

David was due to graduate that next spring, and the scouts were on campus. He talked to none of them. "I never wanted to be a lawyer," he told us. Instead, he had harbored fantasies of becoming a sports reporter. Sports reporters, however, were not immune to the draft, so he had enrolled in law school, and once accepted, as the draft continued, stayed. Even as he neared graduation, he "had no intention of practicing law. I didn't know what lawyers did, didn't like what I thought they did."

Politics, with no intention of running for office, had been his love. Some of his Young Democrat friends at Scholz's were involved with labor, though, so he was intrigued when he noticed a note on a bulletin board announcing that a firm wanted a lawyer to practice labor law. "I didn't know what a firm did," he continued, but he thought, "Well, hell, that might be something I might be willing to do."

It was with some surprise, then, when the interview was conducted by Sam Houston Clinton, a former member of the Horses Association. The firm was Mullinax, Wells, Morris and Mauzy, a Dallas law firm known for its liberal stance. Deemed by Otto

Mullinax, one of the founders of the firm, to be "damn brilliant and very aggressive," David was hired.

The final months of the spring semester were a heady time. With David's first job pending and their first child on the way, everyone was excited, including Iona and Mom El. One might have thought *they* were having the child. They were so concerned that they convinced Ann that David should move to Dallas alone and that she should have the child in Waco, where she would have their support.

However Ann felt about it in retrospect, having Cecile in Waco made sense. Better that than cope with obtaining a doctor, furnishing a new household, and finding her way around town while on the verge of giving birth. Better, too, for David, who could then concentrate on his job without worrying—of course he did, anyway, only at long distance—about Ann's well-being. So we leave Ann for a moment in the capable hands of Cecil and Iona and follow David to Dallas and his new job there.

A great deal has been written—much of it true—about the ultraconservative mood of Dallas in the late fifties and early sixties. A tiny minority of liberals—progressives, they preferred to be called—insisted on fighting the good fight, but in Dallas and, indeed, the state, tradition and demographics were stacked against them. Socially, the city was antiunion. Segregation—separate schools, waiting rooms, drinking fountains, rest rooms, restaurants, and very nearly everything else—was entrenched. A small Hispanic minority lived on the fringes, mainly in West Dallas, and were ignored by the mainstream. Jews were excluded from the Dallas Country Club. The Citizens Charter Association, once described as a collection of dollars represented by men, ran the city like a plantation, with handpicked and rarely defeated city council and mayoral candidates elected at large, which in effect excluded all minorities and progressives.

Joseph McCarthy had been neutralized for almost three years by the time of his death in 1957, but his rhetoric and paranoia lived on. Progressives in Dallas were considered by most right-thinking people to be pinkos, and even Communists. Anti-Catholic propaganda, which grew in virulence when John Kennedy won the Democratic nomination in 1960, inflamed the ignorant with tales of

Catholic missionaries in South America leading natives to kill Protestant missionaries. Even Catholics, in an attempt, perhaps, to out-Caesar Caesar, tended to be conservative. A case in point, Betty and Mike McKool, whom Ann and David met shortly after moving to Dallas, were Catholic and progressive, and very nearly had to buy car radio antennas by the dozen because of the times they emerged from mass to find their antenna broken off.

David, when he moved to Dallas to join Mullinax, Wells, found himself a member of a very small, select group of exactly one progressive law firm in the city. Otto Mullinax was one of three young East Texas lawyers who moved to Dallas at the end of World War II to establish a law firm specializing in personal injury law. In the mid-fifties, shortly before David arrived, Nat Wells, the son of a Dallas preacher and a nationally known expert on labor law, joined the firm, which began specializing in that area, too.

Later the firm was retained by the Southern Region of the National Association for the Advancement of Colored People to advise its members on how to conduct demonstrations legally and, if possibly, safely. Soon black clients long used to ill treatment at the hands of police forces and sheriff's departments across the state were calling on Mullinax, Wells. So highly regarded was the firm that Martin Luther King Jr. once visited its offices.

In a button-down kingdom of large, conservative corporate firms, Mullinax, Wells "stood out like a sore thumb," Otto Mullinax recalled in his home in East Dallas. The firm's 7:00 A.M. Wednesday breakfast meetings convened in the coffee shop of the Continental Trailways bus station. The ambience, which left something to be desired, was hated by the younger members of the firm who aspired to a higher level of sophistication. Nonetheless, young law graduates with a liberal bent from Harvard, Yale, and other top schools around the country came, saw, applied, and stayed. Because of its clientele and its willingness to do what it believed in philosophically, the firm became involved in precedent-setting cases, and its national reputation grew.

"It was very rough training," Otto said. "Each lawyer was required to argue a case at the appellate level in his first year on the job. If they didn't work out [after three years], they were out the door. If they did, they were made partners." Sam Houston Clinton's assessment of David had been correct: He had what it took.

Meanwhile, Cecile Richards was born on July 15, 1957, and Ann joined David in Dallas some six weeks later at the beginning of September. They moved into a small stone house on Taos Street, a long two blocks north of Lovers Lane and just across the street from Sudie Williams Elementary School, and about five miles north of Mullinax, Wells' downtown office. The house was small, two bedrooms, living and dining room, and kitchen, and easily put in order. Cecile needed to be cared for, and there were the usual chores: washing, ironing, and making clothes for both mother and baby. However busy she stayed, however she filled her days with make-work, it was a far cry from preparing for and facing a day full of students, and time hung heavily on her hands.

Luckily, Austin was only two hundred miles south, a five-hour drive from North Dallas in 1957. Ann and David made frequent weekend trips there for Young Democrats meetings and raucous beer-drinking bouts with their old political buddies at Scholz Beer Garden. She did not want for friends in Dallas for very long. Soon, through a friend of David's mother, she met Virginia Whitten. Ann talks about Virginia and Sam Whitten in her autobiography as a couple with whom she and David "shared our babies, shared our dinners, shared our politics." More than that, though, Virginia became not only one of her closest friends but perhaps, in a way, the big sister she never had, and simultaneously a second, undemanding, nonjudgmental mother figure. Virginia did not insist that the floor be scrubbed on hands and knees. Nor did she particularly care if the floor was scrubbed in the first place.

There is a manic side, to which Ann Richards has not been immune, to the enormous energy level with which overachievers are endowed. She could pretend that taking care of Cecile, watching television, washing, ironing, and cleaning house were enough. She could tell herself that being a wife and mother, as she had been taught was proper, was fulfilling. In reality, she had been involved and active throughout high school, college, and in the early years of her marriage. Now there was nothing interesting to do, and she was going crazy with boredom. She fled to Virginia's house when the tension built to the breaking point. There, with their children running around banging pots and pans, in the midst of barely controlled bedlam, Virginia would give Ann a cup of coffee and sit and talk with her. The therapy worked. Soon both women were laughing, and Ann's sense of perspective was restored.

Formal politics soon became a second outlet. The conservative wing of the Democratic party in Texas, then, has been characterized as a Republican party in disguise. It had fought against Franklin D. Roosevelt, Harry Truman, and Lyndon Johnson, and it supported Dwight Eisenhower in the 1952 presidential election. Indeed, it was so "Republican" that Governor Allan Shivers, who for Ann and David personified everything bad about politics, had run again on both tickets in 1954 and had been reelected.

There were no gray areas in Allan Shivers's approach to the social issues of the day. After the high court in Washington issued the historic 1954 *Brown* v. *Board of Education of Topeka* decision that marked the beginning of the end of public school segregation, Shivers appeared at a political rally in Lufkin, deep in the piney woods of East Texas, and said, "All of my instincts, my political philosophy, my experiences and my common sense revolt against this Supreme Court decision. It is an unwarranted invasion of the constitutional rights of the states, and could be disastrous to the children and to the teachers of both races."

The governor's stance against the cause of organized unionism was specific as well. In his 1954 campaign against avid prolabor populist Ralph Yarborough, Shivers delivered a hard-line message. Yarborough's union sympathies, he declared, put his opponent in close company with "reds, radicals, Communists and goon squads."

Against the monolithic power that Shivers represented were arranged a loosely allied coalition of blacks, Hispanics, unionists, and liberally educated, usually affluent progressives. Lacking any real power, they brought the fierce determination of perennial losers in the fight to liberalize Texas's old south, mythic west, and segregationist politics and policies. Yarborough, their guru, was the favorite whipping boy of the conservatives, but all others were fair game, too. So when Henry Gonzalez entered the governor's race in 1958, he must have known he had no chance of winning. The principle, though, was what counted. And lose though he did, he garnered a quarter of a million votes, which would be utilized as a bargaining chip in future races.

Blacks and Hispanics were more closely allied then than they often are now, and one of the few places where interracial groups could meet was the NAACP headquarters in an old house in East Dallas. There, Ann went to stuff envelopes and work on Gonzalez's campaign, and there she was first involved in interracial politics, an involvement that would grow and become an integral part of her strength as a working politician. There, also, were planted seeds of frustration and dissatisfaction that, before too many years passed, would move her toward feminism, roles in the decision-making processes, and finally, her entrance into politics as a candidate.

Meanwhile, there were people to meet. Juanita Craft, one of the earliest persuasive female black voices in Dallas. George Allen, who later became Dallas's first black city council member. Pancho Medrano, a union organizer who worked with Walter Reuther and became an early Hispanic power in Dallas politics. And Dan Weiser, who over the years has been a quiet but key figure in Dallas liberal politics.

Dan came to Dallas in 1958, met Ann and David at an early Young Democrats meeting at their house, and before long was part of a small group that spent a good share of its time looking for suitable candidates to run for almost anything. The cards were stacked against the progressives. *The Dallas Morning News* was almost violently conservative, the *Times Herald* only marginally less so. There was no support from the Democratic party. Raising enough money for even the necessities—yard signs or flyers— became a Herculean task. And if that wasn't enough, the neighbors—or fellow students, in the case of candidates' children—could make life miserable. In short, one needed to have money to throw away, a masochistically warped ego, the tenacity of a saint, and the thick skin of a crocodile. As a result, Dallas wasn't crawling with people begging to run.

Business picked up during the 1960 Kennedy presidential campaign, which became a focal point for Dallas progressives. Barefoot Sanders was day-to-day executive manager of the campaign. Sarah Hughes, not yet a judge but already a role model for many young women, was a cochair, and a good person to know. Ann, pregnant with her first son, Dan, busied herself meeting people and learning the ropes from the ground up. She herself talks about distributing yard signs and bumper stickers, and Dan Weiser recalls that she and David "played a fairly major part" in making sure someone was at campaign headquarters to man the phones.

Dan Weiser reminisced about that campaign. It was a heady, emotional time. It was as easy to vilify Nixon as it was to idolize Kennedy. The anti-Catholics sometimes became vitriolic, and it took a certain amount of courage to knock on doors to hand out campaign literature. It was all well and good when hippies, blacks, Hispanics, Catholics, and Jews partied at the Richardses' newly purchased house on Coogan Drive, but when the party was over, care had to be taken not to assign a black to hold up a Kennedy campaign sign on a street in the wrong part of town. Merely to have a Kennedy sign in one's yard could invite nastiness: More than one round was pumped through more than one window during that campaign.

Nixon carried Dallas County by 149,000 to 88,000, but the Kennedy–Johnson win state-wide, not to speak of nationally, gave an incredible boost to the spirits of the so-often-defeated Dallas progressives. Like many others who now openly called themselves liberals, David asked what he could do for his country, and with Ann's support and the help of a friend on Vice President Johnson's Democratic Policy Committee, was offered and accepted a job as a staff attorney on the Civil Rights Commission. Visions of Camelot and the New Frontier danced like sugarplums in their heads. They moved to Washington in February 1961 and rented a row house on Seventh Street, N.E., on Capitol Hill.

David had cut his legal teeth in Dallas representing unions. Now, in a 180-degree turn, he found himself investigating them. He liked what he did, for a while, but he said, "I had never been around a bureaucracy and found functioning in it not a particularly enjoyable experience." In Dallas, he stood on the top rung of the ladder, and win or lose was in charge of his cases. In Washington, he was very much on a bottom rung. There was neither winning nor losing, only reports to be funneled into the system to later emerge dehumanized, depersonalized, and virtually unrecognizable.

Ann was not subjected to those frustrations. She was not invited to the Rose Garden to shake hands with President Kennedy, as she had been in 1949 with President Truman, but life was exciting enough. After Dan was born, she took both children to parades, art museums, the Smithsonian, the mall, and the monuments. On days when she had a baby-sitter, she went to the Senate to listen to the speeches. There, she was especially touched by Hubert Humphrey's passion, and one can to this day hear the influence of the great orator himself, Everett Dirksen, in her speaking manner. She could have had no better teacher.

The spark of liberal commitment notwithstanding, the experience for both Ann and David soon palled. The glossy spirit of adventure that characterized the early days of the Kennedy administration translated well on black-and-white television news and documentaries, but the backstage reality of actually living and working in Camelot was another matter. Their expedition to Washington had taken them to the foothills of power, not the mountaintop.

The time had come to beat a retreat. Egos intact, they did not care if they were not missed. Washington was overrun with other young lawyers more willing than David to be shoehorned into the constraining organizational boxes of bureaucracy, in which he felt trapped. Ann had enjoyed herself, but there was nothing to do for a wife of a low-level bureaucrat and a mother of two with a third on the way. Tired of sight-seeing and *kinder, küchen,* and *Kirche,* not to speak of the endless gossip and speculation, she was as ready as David for something to which she could commit herself. In February 1962, a year after they had arrived in Washington, they headed back to Dallas.

CHAPTER 8

THE DALLAS YEARS

Dallas, Texas, was not the greatest place in the world for Kennedy supporters and liberal Democrats in 1962, but where else might they have gone? They had friends there and David was welcomed back at Mullinax, Wells, Morris and Mauzy, where he could manage his own cases and, without the weight of a bureaucracy stifling him, make a difference. As for Ann, it was whither thou goest with a sigh of relief. Settling in quickly, she threw herself into house hunting, reestablishing old ties, and forging new ones.

Dell Groese, who had become a friend of the Richardses when her son, Fritz, was in Ann's seventh-grade history class in Austin, was now selling real estate in Dallas, and remembers showing them the house on Lovers Lane and Athens, in University Park. University Park, like its sister city, Highland Park, was then and still is a separate municipality that shares one border with Highland Park and is otherwise surrounded by Dallas. Wealthy, exclusionary bastions of the conservative elite, the Park Cities were, as they are today, two of the pinnacles of upward mobility in Dallas. A moat and drawbridges could not have isolated them more effectively.

Minorities were welcome as maids and gardeners, but none lived there, even in servants' quarters. The swift and efficient Highland Park and University Park police patrolled the streets with a suspicious eye for vehicles with occupants that seemed "out of place." It was widely believed that any black or Hispanic man seen driving through the Park Cities had better have gardening tools in the back of his pickup truck or evident in the trunk of his car lest he be subjected to police harassment.

The two cities maintained their own school district separate from, and certainly designed to be a cut above, Dallas's. In 1962, they were immeasurably proud of the fact that the number one ranked graduates of both Annapolis and West Point were products of Highland Park High School. To this day, minority students are a rarity at Highland Park High School, which is known in some parts of greater Dallas as "Honkie High." Not exactly where you would expect a young couple with deep liberal roots to settle, but the neighborhood was safe and the schools were academically better than those in the Dallas Independent School District, an important consideration, with Cecile about to begin kindergarten.

With two children and pregnant with their second son, Clark, Ann loved the house. David, however, was not immediately sure. He had been reared above the salt, but University Park was more high-rent than he had contemplated or believed they could afford. "David paced the rooms and groused about all the things he'd dreamed of doing," Dell Groese said, with a laugh. " 'I'll never be a sports reporter. All doors are closed,' " she recalls him saying. With those payments, he was doomed to be a lawyer forever.

There were challenges, for Ann. North Dallas—of which University Park was considered a part—was virtually totally white and preponderantly Bible Belt Protestant. Economically, its residents were solidly middle-class white-collar to lavishly wealthy, and were as a rule virulently segregationist and anti-Communist, which may be translated as anti-Catholic, anti-Kennedy, and, by extension, anti-liberal-Democrat. The rest of voting Dallas, basically a combination of blue-collar and redneck, was equally segregationist, antiunion, and anti-Communist. It was not a pretty scene.

David Richards has vivid recollections of "the insanity of Dallas," and recalls its conservative nature was "just horrible." Liberals felt themselves besieged and "found one another," to "gather around a damn fire when the wild animals were outside the perimeter." The darkest days began in 1963. Some incidents were highly publicized. In one instance, Adlai Stevenson was hissed and booed off the stage and spat upon. In another, Vice President and Lady Bird Johnson were mobbed during a downtown appearance by a street full of elegantly dressed viragoes seized in a frenzy of hate. One can only say that episode would have been described as a riot and put down forthwith if the participants had been black, brown, or poor.

Other incidents escaped widespread notice. The works of Pablo Picasso and Diego Rivera—known Communists, according to right-wing ideologies—were for a time removed from the walls of the Dallas Museum of Fine Art. The Dallas Theater Center on Turtle Creek received anonymous threatening letters and was picketed when it staged Howard Fast's *The Crossing*. The symphony worried about losing financial support if the Russian violinist David Oistrakh were invited to play. People—even Catholics, oddly enough—cut one-time friends to the quick for expressing the slightest sympathy for Kennedy, his administration, or his programs. People became so sensitive that the ultraright and their liberal neighbors coexisted only, in many cases, by totally avoiding names like McCarthy, Stevenson, Kennedy, and Major General Walker, and words or terms like "segregation" and "integration," "the Fifth Amendment" and "the United Nations," lest there be a violent reaction.

Warren Leslie, in his book *Dallas City Limits,* chronicles the unsavory nature of the Dallas political and social climate at that time. The Minute Women, John Birch Society, National Indignation Committee, Friends of General Walker, and H. L. Hunt's *Life-Line* radio show were busily finding Communists (always capitalized) and pinkos (usually lowercase) under beds and behind desks, and trumpeting the news far and wide.

The city was parsimonious and had little patience with or use for its less fortunate residents. A totally disabled person received sixty-nine dollars a month in welfare; an unmarried mother of eight, one hundred dollars. Some eight thousand homes had neither bathtub nor shower; some three thousand families had no running water. The mayor had proposed that private enterprise help alleviate the plight of the low-income aging and "Negroes," and when private enterprise could not or would not do so, sought federal monies. That plan was endorsed even by *The Dallas Morning News,* not known for leftist tendencies, but opposed by the Dallas Real Estate Board, which could not advise the administration how to provide housing for indigent aged and blacks for twenty-five dollars per month per person, but nonetheless advised the city to "say no to Washington." So notorious was the political atmosphere in Dallas and the state that the political writer Theodore H. White was quoted as saying, "...within Texas, the machinery of government...has been captured by a nameless Third Party, obsessed with hate, fear, and suspicion."

Ann Richards returned from Camelot to Dallas, a city the columnist Molly Ivins once called "so materialistic and so Republican it makes your teeth hurt to contemplate it." Wife, mother, and political dabbler, she became the magnet for a growing circle of friends. In a number of interviews over the years, Ann characterizes herself as first and foremost a wife and a mother. Those who knew her well in the years from 1962 through 1969, and remain her friends to this day, report that she indeed fulfilled those multiple roles admirably—a Supermom, more than one called her—but that while home and children were her vocation, politics increasingly became an ever more important avocation.

The year of political inactivity in Washington had whetted Ann's appetite for action, and she pitched in eagerly. For as long as anyone knew, politically involved women had been used as helpers and little else. The men were pleased to accept their time and effort when there were stamps to be licked or phone calls to be made. Women were likewise useful for distributing yard signs or bumper stickers, trudging door-to-door handing out leaflets, or driving voters to the polls. Once the campaigns were over and the votes were in, though, women were relegated to the back seat of the political bus.

The North Dallas Democratic Women seemed to be a solution of sorts. The Democratic Women of Dallas County had been in business for some years, but the North Dallas Democratic Women that Ann, Carolyn Choate, Ann Chud, Ruth Winegarten, and Joyce Schiff, among others, formed was geographically more focused, and more progressive in outlook. North Dallas was a tough sell, given the generally Republican sentiments of North Dallas women, but there were liberal pockets in places like the Northhaven Methodist and the Highland Park Methodist churches. Too, however ultraconservative Southern Methodist University remained, the Perkins School of Theology was progressive enough to have integrated, and there were growing numbers of liberal faculty, faculty wives, and students, all of whom could be recruited to pump up liberal, or progressive, numbers in local precincts.

The late Tip O'Neill, the Massachusetts Democrat and Speaker of the House of Representatives for ten years, became famous for his maxim "All politics is local," and that is where Ann and her friends concentrated their efforts. In Texas, people who voted in primaries were eligible to attend and vote at precinct meetings. The polls closed at 7:00 P.M., and the meetings started at 7:00 P.M.. A precinct chair was on the ballot, but since the votes had not been tallied, the election of a temporary chair for that meeting alone was the first—and most important—order of business.

It was a hard row to hoe, for the progressives. The Johnson liberal wing of the Democratic party, having prevailed over the Shivers conservative wing in the 1950s, had become the new conservative wing. From the precinct level on up, it was virtually unchallenged in Texas at the time and dominated the decision-making process. The only way for the progressives to chip away at conservative power, or even to have a modest voice in party decisions, was to control precinct chairs, because democracy went out the door once the chair was elected: From that moment on, the chair simply ran through whatever agenda he or she had without recogniz-ing the opposition or even, often, counting votes.

Precinct meetings at the time were "really wild," Mary Vogelson, one of Ann's old friends, told us on the phone. It was Democrat against Democrat—read conservative against progressive. The con-servatives connived to change precinct meeting places without notifying known progressives. If they could not do that, or if word spread and it appeared that some progressives would attend, the conservatives on occasion tried to arrive early so they could lock themselves in and the progressives out.

The dirty tricks, supposed to constitute some of the joy of playing politics, were not funny, but they were instructive, and one learned either to play or leave the game. Ann and David learned, at least enough for David to be elected to the chair in their precinct in 1964. The victory was little more than symbolic, but it was a harbinger, however faintly heard, of the eventual liberalization of the Democratic party in Texas.

To that end, the house on the corner of Lovers Lane and Athens was turned into a de facto headquarters of the North Dallas Democratic Women and the Council of Democratic Clubs, which Ann helped found. Most days, three or four of the cadre showed up with children in tow to talk politics, to lay plans, map strategies, address and stamp mailers, and do whatever else it took to keep the progressive movement alive and if not strong, at least viable. Most important, in the long run, they compiled files of three-by-five cards with the names and addresses of what Ann in her autobiography called their "growing network of women." In years to come, these women would form a widespread base of political power undreamed of at the time.

Ann was indisputably the leader. "I thought for years that she was my age or older [she is five years younger], because she was the leader," Betty McKool told us, "*and* the entertainer. It was like Mort Sahl. She could always find something funny about the worst things in the world. We had a hard time getting the work done." Work they did, though, and once they got started on a project, the ideas generally came from Ann.

The brightest and best-remembered idea was Political Paranoia. Strapped for funds, in large part needed to pay baby-sitting fees so more women could participate, Ann conceived Political Paranoia as a takeoff on the Press Club's Gridiron show. All proceeds went to the North Dallas Democrat Women. Ann, Carolyn Choate, and Ruth Winegarten wrote most of the scripts. Ann wrote most of the lyrics. Joy Parker served as the choreographer, and Betty McKool was the costumer. The cast was completely female.

"You have to put yourself back in those times before everything got so grim," Jay Vogelson, one of David's colleagues, told us, "and people laughed at themselves and they laughed at politics and they laughed at government."

And laugh they did. Everyone from city to state to national figures became fair game. Democrats and Republicans both were the subjects of Ann's "biting, satirical, devastating takeoffs," according to Mary Vogelson, who sang in some of the shows. They used radio promos, sent articles to every magazine and daily and weekly newspaper in the county, distributed flyers, and played to packed houses for three nights every spring for six years, from 1962 through 1968. Mary sang one of the songs in the 1968 show, a roast of Dallas to the tune of "More":

More than the other cities of this size,
More than a place or show, we've won first prize,

More than El Paso or old San Antone,
More than Fort Worth or Houston, Big D alone...
Stands at the top again in crime,
For the umpteenth time and so,
It is simply great to be assured that you're first rate,
So, each one of us must do her part, and more,
To see we don't lose that All-American City ribbon we all adore,
So steal from someone who's dear,
And rape anyone who's near,
First place, we can surely win once more.

To call integration the driving force behind liberal thought and politics in the sixties (before Vietnam, anyway) is a simplification, but perhaps not one that is completely unjustified since it so clearly characterized the changes that liberals thought needed to be effected in America. In any case, Ann's and David's political philosophies were very nearly identical, with David perhaps the more radical of the two, as is reflected in his work. Committed to the labor movement and integration, he represented, among others, the United Automobile Workers and the Teamsters at Chance Vought, now Vought Aircraft Company and, according to Otto Mullinax, "with the NAACP on the sit-in things, not just in Dallas, but all over the southern region."

The looming specter of integration became an increasing source of anxiety in Dallas at the time. As had the rest of the nation, the citizens of Dallas had watched the National Guard encircle Central High in Little Rock in 1957, seen the intensity of the rage that gripped the Old South when James Meredith enrolled at Ole Miss in 1962, and later witnessed the fury in Selma on that Bloody Sunday in 1965. Even the most deeply committed segregationists realized that Dallas could not forever remain insulated. The integration of the schools was not a matter of if, but of to what extent and when. The only remaining question was how—peacefully, or accompanied with bloodshed and tear gas.

Rufus Shaw, a black Republican and part of modern South Dallas leadership, theorizes that one of the reasons racial disobedience did not amount to much in Dallas in the sixties was because many of the blacks there at the time, unlike the urban blacks of Chicago, Detroit, Atlanta, and so on, were first-generation East Texans just off the farm and relatively unsophisticated. Nonetheless, Dallas and the Citizens Charter Association nervously watched as "their Negroes" were increasingly swayed by Martin Luther King Jr. and the NAACP, the Congress of Racial Equality (CORE), and the Black Muslims. The white power structure resolved to do whatever was necessary to keep the lid on, and Dallas's name unsullied.

"Money was disbursed," says Jim Schutze, a Dallas journalist and political historian, "by the white power structure—what I call the Dallas Board of Elders—for humanitarian purposes, with the tacit understanding that a group known as the Ministerial Alliance would endorse a passive course of integration to the black community in Dallas. And they literally handed it out in suitcases. Nobody in Dallas, then or now, would dispute that."

Pressure was applied to the Dallas Independent School District, and the schools were integrated with a minimum of disruption. "Colored" and "White" signs were removed from drinking fountains and rest rooms in public buildings. In January of 1963, *The Dallas Morning News* reported that "Negroes" finally became "acceptable as non-janitorial county employees."

From 1955, when George Allen was named to the Community Chest Trust Fund of Dallas, black leaders played increasingly prominent roles in the city at large, and politically, beginning with the Dallas Progressive Voters League, began to force the white establishment powers to accept at least some of their demands. The advent of single-member districts and the subsequent election of George Allen in 1964 to the Dallas Council was a monumental step forward.

The whites of Dallas grudgingly paid lip service to the idea of public integration, but they were appalled and threatened by even token changes and remained firmly segregationist in private. Thus the "Colored" signs were removed from public water fountains, but it proved much more difficult to convince privately owned enterprises to drop the color bar. Finally, disenfranchised and disappointed, Dallas blacks followed the lead of others around the country and staged their first sit-in, beginning on May 31, 1964, at the Picadilly

Cafeteria, located downtown on Commerce Street.

The protest began when eight black and three white demonstrators sought service at the restaurant, were denied, and, after refusing police requests to leave, were detained. *The Dallas Morning News* reported that "civil rights leaders said the demonstration was staged by the Dallas Coordinating Committee for Full Civil Rights," which was later reported to be composed of members of CORE, the NAACP, and the Black Muslims. Hecklers with Confederate flags appeared. Black lawyers represented the demonstrators. With the exception of some name-calling and a few shoving matches, cooler heads prevailed.

Ann's friend Betty McKool says David was "down there every day, morning to night, in case he was needed." David says he "wasn't really involved in Picadilly," but that most of his "involvement with black issues was more on the political level." Whether he was there, newspaper stories indicate that the black leadership was competent to handle its own sit-in, and neither wanted nor needed white legal assistance. Other than the few whites who actively participated in the sit-in, others, like Ann and Betty, limited themselves to being there, most days, to indicate their support.

———

Clark was born in early summer, 1962, after their return from Washington, and Ellen, by cesarian section, late the next November, 1963, shortly after President Kennedy was assassinated. Within days, Ann began to hemorrhage, and was immediately rushed to the hospital, where she spent New Year's of 1964. The next spring, she blacked out while driving a car full of children. Luckily, her friend Virginia Whitten was able to reach the brake and take the wheel, and bring the car to a safe stop at the side of the road. After two more such attacks in the following few months, Ann was diagnosed as having epilepsy. Dilantin, which she took for some fifteen years, controlled the seizures, and outside of a few petit mal seizures, she claims to have had no more major episodes.

As if all that were not enough, she was stricken with encephalitis in 1966 during an epidemic that raged through Dallas that August. Once again, this time in severe pain, she found herself in the hospital. It was almost as if those early childhood predictions of frailty had come true, but the encephalitis turned out to be the end of a string of bad luck. Her health regained, she "was raring to go," in her words. Within weeks, she was off with David and a dozen or so politicos and their wives on a canoing trip through the Boquillos Canyon on the Rio Grande River.

———

The Richards house on Lovers Lane had quickly become a mecca of sorts. Most old friends remember it as bright, sunny, and homey. The kitchen was spacious and equipped for a gourmet cook. Children could play safely in the fenced backyard. The party-sized living room, with a picture window looking onto Lovers Lane, was eclectically decorated with modern art and collages created by Texas artists she met at art shows, and with antiques and upscale country bought at the Wrecking Bar. Furniture did not seem to be overly important but was still thoughtfully selected, with much of it—something to do when the children were asleep—redone by Ann herself.

Other than when the women met to talk politics, compile their files, and plan campaign activities, leisure time was spent in family activities. When some of David's colleagues, with wives and children, dropped by on a Sunday afternoon, the men drank beer and watched football, the children ran in and out, and the wives prepared supper. It was not hard to attract a crowd, given Ann's growing reputation as a "Texas" gourmet cook. Not only did she prepare the "world's best fried chicken," according to David's colleague Aglaia Mauzy, but she was also "the first housewife that I remember preparing Mexican food from scratch."

As the children grew, there were Indian Guides, Campfire Girls, and Cub Scouts, with outings for each. When a group of the women got together to work on a campaign or their annual fund-raising event, Political Paranoia, they brought their children. There were Easter egg hunts and Halloween, birthday, and what-the-hell parties, a constant flow of people coming and going, eating, drinking, sleeping over, a nearly constant hubhub that the Richardses relished.

Ann and David were Methodists, but they went to the Unitarian church on Preston Road. The liberal, more intellectual than religious congregation was comprised mainly of severely coiffed women and men wearing tweed jackets with leather patches on the elbows. After services, which were highlighted by genteelly humanistic sermons, the congregants mingled over coffee, tea, and hot cider.

The Unitarian Coop, a progressive preschool, was located in the same building. It came with finger paints, a chicken or two, a rabbit, and a boa constrictor named Pete that was carefully kept away from the pet rats and hamsters. The children were urged to make as many of their own decisions as practicable. With only three teachers on staff, four or five parents were scheduled to assist each day and, a tough lesson for many, defer to another parent when one's own child got in a squabble. It was the perfect place for an active and liberal Supermom like Ann.

The family activity extended beyond Dallas. Committed campers, Ann, David, and friends canoed the Guadalupe River and the white-water canyons on the Rio Grande. Ann had learned to adapt her gourmet techniques to campfires, and the campers ate well. There were side trips to Austin, to Corpus Christi, San Antonio. They traveled to towns in South Texas where David advised, and both showed support for, labor unions or striking farm workers. There were fishing trips, on which, thanks to Cecil, Ann was as handy with a rod and reel as she was with a cast iron skillet, and often, Betty McKool says, the only one who actually caught anything big enough to eat.

Whatever the activity, it was supposed to be fun, but there were days when fun was the last thing anyone thought of. One such day was November 22, 1963. Excitement gripped Dallas as it prepared for the arrival of President John F. Kennedy, his wife, Jackie, Vice President and Mrs. Johnson, and Governor John Connally, among others. Democrats vied for tickets to the luncheon to be given in the president's honor at Market Hall, a huge marketing center just north of downtown on Interstate 35. The right wing was surly, and in an ugly mood. Indicative of the tension that gripped the city, *The Dallas Morning News* printed a black-bordered ad that declared the president "wanted" for a list of his so-called "crimes" against America.

Ann managed to find a ticket to the luncheon on the third level, well above the main floor. The guests had been served and had started to eat when the news spread that the President had been shot. Ann says in her autobiography that she remembers being "terribly afraid." The feeling was endemic, as the crowd rushed for stairs and escalators, anything to get out and home.

David was stationed on the corner of Ervay and Main, in the center of downtown. After the motorcade passed, he walked back to his office, where he heard the chilling news. He, too, rushed home, but the downtown streets were snarled with traffic, and he arrived after Ann. There, like nearly everyone else, they stared at television in numbed disbelief.

"Nobody even called," Betty McKool said of the next few days. "It was as if we all retreated to the safety of our houses. Nobody knew what to say." Finally, after two days, David broke the spell. He and Ann called their friends, the Whittens and the Holleys, and the three families went on a picnic together.

However frustrating the politics of Dallas, Ann learned there the basic campaigning skills that in later years would send her to the governor's mansion. More important than techniques, however, were the personal bonds established between groups and individuals.

During these years in Dallas, she formed strong political bonds with labor, African Americans and Hispanics. Later, in 1982 when she ran for state treasurer and 1990 when she campaigned for governor, no one could accuse her of suddenly adopting positions or opinions that were politically expedient. She had, over the years, worked too hard to increase voter registration, abolish the poll tax, further union causes, and elect African Americans and Hispanics.

As important was her ability to make friends. Ann Richards has her rough edges, can be short of temper, and doesn't always suffer fools gladly. She is a tough, pragmatic politician who can throw, and take, heavy campaign punches. The friends she made in Dallas in her nearly twelve years there, and who have become an important part of her political base, remember her differently, though.

They remember "a good mother," and an "indefatigable" worker. They talk about how "she cares about people," "she listens," and "she can laugh at herself." People, for Ann Richards, were more than names on three-by-five cards kept in a box in the guest bedroom.

In 1966, Dell Groese, the real estate agent who sold them the house on Lovers Lane shortly before she moved to Alaska, returned to Dallas after her elder son was killed in action in Vietnam. To her surprise, Ann and David met her at the airport and gave her a bottle of Chanel No. 5. Ann hugged and held her. "At least you'll *smell* pretty," she said.

Rusty Hoffman, née Regina Garrett, Sybil of old, remembers that "Ann sent a present when my daughter was born. It was a baby dress from Neiman Marcus, and a note, 'Every little girl should start life with a Neiman Marcus dress.'"

Jay Vogelson, Mary Vogelson's husband, a colleague of David's at Mullinax, Wells, told us that Ann was one of the first to visit Mary in the hospital after the birth of their son, and brought presents. "Ann understood people. It didn't take her very long to know where you come from, what's your perspective, what's the root of your concern."

Aglaia Mauzy, David's colleague at Mullinax, Wells, remembered, "Despite the intensity of most of the sympathies of Ann's neighbors in University Park, I can't recall any unpleasant confrontations. That had a lot to do with Ann's basic talent for tact, and because she was so personable and outgoing, and so active in the conventional school activities and neighborhood kid activities. It's my guess that nobody in University Park openly resented her because of her politics. They looked at her as the ideal mother, which was her consuming interest."

The one thing that everyone remembers were the Christmas cards that Ann and and her friend Betty McKool sent. They began at a flea market with the discovery of two pairs of eyeglasses that they were sure made them look "too funny for words," moved on to costumes pulled from a box of clothes Ann's children used to play dress-up. From there it was a short step to posing for some comic photographs taken in Ann's backyard, and the bright idea of incorporating them into Christmas cards.

Ann and Betty never signed the cards, but everyone quickly realized who had sent them. For the next seven years, a growing list of the lucky recipients waited to see what kind of a zany photo Ann and Betty would come up with. By the time they finished, some five hundred people were on their Christmas card list in Dallas. One way for liberals or members of the media to know he or she had made it was to be on the Ann Richards–Betty McKool Christmas card list.

—

By 1968, Dallas had become home, every bit as much as Waco or Austin. Cecile was eleven, Dan in second grade in University Park Elementary School, and Clark and Ellen attending the Unitarian Coop. Their life was "pretty decent," David thought, with "lots of kids around, a funny, funky house."

David and Ann, however, saw Dallas in a different light. David was thirty-five and, a senior partner at Mullinax, Wells, one of the most highly regarded labor lawyers in Texas. According to Aglaia Mauzy, he had become "discouraged, if not fed up, with the whole political and business climate in Dallas." He was not alone. Ann, too, was ready for a move. She did not like the vibrations in the community or the schools, and had begun to wonder about her sanity. She was tired of politics in general, and specifically of helping male candidates who used women during campaigns without listening to them, and who when elected gave them no positions.

They were not, at first, sure where they wanted to go, or what David would do. Both David and Ann had fond memories of Austin. They also considered Corpus Christi and San Antonio, both of which they liked, and where they had friends. Their weeks were spent in Dallas, where David was under some pressure to stay at Mullinax, Wells, which did its "damnedest to hang on to him," according to Otto Mullinax. On weekends, they often traveled to Austin to visit Sam and Virginia Whitten, who had moved there and whom they missed.

At last, David agreed to join Sam Houston Clinton, his old friend from Scholz Beer Garden who had later recruited him for Mullinax, Wells, in his Austin practice. An income assured, then, they put the Lovers Lane house on the market in the spring of 1969. And as soon as school was out, they packed and moved the two hundred miles south to Austin.

"We were by no means affluent," David said. "It was an economic gamble to go down to Austin." The gamble would pay off in ways that neither dreamed of at the time.

CHAPTER 9

HOME SWEET AUSTIN

It would be hard to find a city and a couple more in tune with each other than Austin and Ann and David Richards. Austin had hills, a river, and scenery, all of which the Richardses loved. Austin, capital of Texas and home of the University of Texas, was charged with intellectual and political energy. Austin was becoming a center of country and western music, and more so every passing year. Austin was famous for its bars where, from five in the afternoon until early the next morning, the interesting people met to plot and hobnob, the real work was done, and the deals that counted were cut away from the public eye. Austin, it has been said, was a city populated entirely by politicians, most of whom made their livings as cab drivers, CPAs, bartenders, and teachers. One noted activist earned a living of sorts selling roses on street corners.

Austin was also undergoing a sea change from traditional Texas conservatism to a new and fervent liberalism. The conservatives still held tenaciously to political power in 1969, but theirs was a losing battle. Austin, in the late sixties—and more so in the seventies, eighties, and nineties—was as laid back and as liberal as a place could be in Texas. Indeed, it would soon become the state's limit-case of liberalism and earn the conservatives' sobriquets of "la-la land" and "the People's Republic of Travis County."

Austin had become Dallas's political, social, and psychological opposite, and moving there, for Ann and David, was like returning to an ancestral home that one knows and loves. David called the move back there "like being transported to paradise." And Ann later said in *Straight From the Heart* that she had never "flown home to Austin that she wasn't glad to be there."

Ellen, their five-year-old and youngest, had just started elementary school when they found, bought, and moved into the house at 810 West Red Bud Trail in West Lake Hills in the southwest corner of Austin. David Richards recalled they soon discovered West Lake Hills was fiercely independent and conservative, a "red neck" section of town with little tolerance for liberal politics or views.

Living as one pleased was a West Lake Hills tradition. The early populace was comprised largely of cedar choppers, who kept to themselves and had their own ways. Well into the late 1940s and early 1950s, most of the roads, which as a rule followed deer and cattle trails, were unpaved. Water came from private wells, some as deep as one thousand feet. "Outsiders" started moving into the 2,800-acre area in the early 1950s, and West Lake Hills was incorporated in 1953 so its residents could maintain their independence from Austin. As late as 1966, residents were responsible for providing their own water, sewage, and garbage pickup. There were no municipal taxes. Instead, residents contributed what they wished to help defray the city's minimal expenses. As late as 1970, one could buy a lot with a view for $3,500.

West Lake Hills was a beautiful part of Austin. The land there rises in steep hills accented with limestone outcroppings. Scrub cedar predominates and poses a fire threat when summer bakes the earth. West Red Bud Trail, narrow and winding with blind curves and dead ends, runs off Bee Caves Road. The view from the rear of 810 and the balcony that overlooks Oracle Gorge was spectacular, especially at night. It was far enough removed from the bustle of town for the occasional deer to graze in the yard, a quiet and peaceful place for kids to roam and play. The houses were widely separated and one could live as one pleased. It was precisely the place for a woman who had said repeatedly that she wanted nothing more to do with politics.

Built as a retreat by a doctor, the Richardses' house was too small for a family of six, so Ann began to remodel it. Designed as she and the builder went, it was eventually expanded to twice its original size. Friends from around the state dropped in for a night or a weekend, and soon the Richardses' house became nearly a second home for their many friends. Sleeping bags lay strewn around on the floors, and the balcony was busy with barbecues and beer and loud arguments. Adding to the confusion were a dog for Dan, a couple of cats, and even, at one time, a few chickens.

———

For a while, Ann did remove herself from politics. Peggy Romberg, the executive director of the Texas Family Planning Association, has been concerned with women's and pregnancy issues since the early 1970s, and remembers Ann first as a mom. Their daughters, Margaret and Ellen, attended first grade in Eanes Elementary School together in 1969, and she and Ann became friends at PTA meetings and school fund-raising events.

Life was not all home and children, even during the first two or three years. David was frequently on the road. In Denton, Texas, he argued for students' voting rights. In two trips to Washington, D.C., he argued, and won, censorship and freedom-of-the-press cases before the United States Supreme court for *Notes From the Underground* and the *Rag,* respectively Dallas and Austin alternative newspapers. Ann, with Cecile and Dan, accompanied him for the *Notes* hearing. She also maintained ties with her many Dallas friends, both visiting and writing "long and absolutely hilarious letters," according to her old pal Betty McKool. One trip occurred during her first year in Austin when she returned to Dallas to help her former Political Paranoia friends mount a special performance for Women for Change. The show was designed, in part, to prove to *Ms. Magazine,* which they thought took itself too seriously, that women could be funny. In addition, there were side trips across the state to attend fund-raising events for old and new political allies, and a multitude of camping trips.

There were some who thought, later, when Ann was running for treasurer and governor, that her encyclopedic knowledge of Texas was a campaign ploy. Nothing could have been further from the truth. In Dallas, for party mixers, she grouped guests into teams. Each team was given a list of questions about Texas and Texas history, many of which were so arcane that only she and Betty's husband, Mike McKool, knew the answers. Her interest in the state continued with the river-running and camping trips she, David, and friends took. Later in the seventies, she and David invited friends to accompany them on what she called "Know Your Texas" tours.

Armed with maps, guidebooks, and historical sketches, the tours visited such places as the Big Bend Country, South Padre Island, the Big Thicket in East Texas, and Palo Duro Canyon in the Texas Panhandle.

For the first three years after their return to Austin, Ann for the most part did what she had long considered herself trained to do. Her top priority was rearing the children and getting the house in order. In the midst of the mess of expanding the house, she sewed curtains, washed clothes, ironed shirts, and mended jeans. Super-mom, she drove the children to and from school, where she volunteered in the library, reading stories to the students and designing and decorating bulletin boards. She kept food on the table, cooked for parties she hosted, and for a while taught a course in gourmet cooking. And, although she stayed away from what David called "the nitty-gritty of politics," she couldn't resist dabbling around the periphery.

Ann and David moved to Austin and West Lake Hills at the beginning of the biggest economic boom ever to hit the area. Land values skyrocketed, especially after the completion of the huge Barton Creek Mall and Loop 360, around the southwest quadrant of Austin. New subdivisions sprang into being virtually overnight, and the population exploded. And in West Lake Hills, the environment became the issue of the day.

West Lake Hills, and indeed, much of Austin and Travis County, where Austin is located, lies atop part of the Edwards Aquifer, which supplies dozens of municipalities with water. The land in West Lake Hills is fragile, with thin, rocky topsoil, and little to hold it in place. Malls, highways, new housing and businesses, threatened to destroy not only the peaceful serenity of the area but the physical environment as well.

Environmentalists sprang into action. Groups such as the Audubon Society, the Sierra Club, and the newer Save Barton Creek Association banded together to fight the developers. Siding with the environmentalists, Ann joined the Audubon Society and the Sierra Club and served on the activist West Lake Hills Zoning and Planning Commission.

Perhaps most hated by all the environmentalists were the new highways. How much growth—highways, malls, planned communities, and so on—could the land absorb without damaging the aquifer and destroying the natural beauty of the dry, hilly countryside was ultimately an issue of freeways. Freeways despoiled the land and hampered the natural recharging of the aquifer. They opened sparsely settled land to development, which meant more pavement for homes, schools, shopping centers, more sewage, air and noise pollution, and, of necessity, eventually, more freeways. The environmentalists became known in conservative, or pro-development, circles as "highway politicians." Soon Ann was given that label. It would stand her in good stead when, later, she ran for county commissioner.

Austin, as everywhere else in the country in the early 1970s, seethed with the Vietnam War issue. The University of Texas at Austin, a prime factor in the liberalization of the city, harbored a large, vociferous, and even radical antiwar student population. You could inject race, sex, family values, and abortion into a conversation and everyone would run to one side or the other of the Vietnam War line.

The Richardses, naturally enough, were opposed to the war. They were antisegregationist and sought the inclusion of minorities in politics, business, and the social life of the city. The Austin City Council would not allow students to march, and they were duly outraged. Both Ann and David were sympathetic with the women's movement and prochoice on the abortion issue. David was deeply involved with students and civil rights and redistricting cases. And because of the children, Ann became involved with the schools.

The Austin Independent School District was integrated. David and Ann quickly learned, however, that West Lake Hills was part of the Eanes Independent School District, which at the time was rapidly becoming a "white flight" district. Eanes Independent School District was established in 1957. At that time, it consisted of Eanes Elementary School, with junior high and high school students being bused to Austin schools. In 1960, Eanes I.S.D. opened a junior high school but continued to bus high school students. In 1967, Eanes I.S.D. was forced to choose between opening its own high school and becoming absorbed entirely by Austin I.S.D. It chose to open its own high school.

By the time the Richardses moved to Austin, the Eanes

Independent School District schools had a great deal in common with the University Park and Highland Park schools in Dallas. Minority students were rare, and the school board, administration, and staff were determinedly conservative. In one instance, the board tried to fire a teacher for asking students to compare *The Red Badge of Courage* with *The Catcher in the Rye*, even though the students who objected were given an alternative assignment.

"We were in constant conflict with Eanes Elementary School over one matter or another," David told us. The conflict led to one of them, usually Ann, heading for the school "to raise hell." Teachers and administrators *said* they wanted parents to be concerned and participate, but theirs and Ann's definitions of concern and participation didn't always match. Participation in both parties' eyes certainly included volunteering in the library but often differed when school policy and rules were concerned.

One can imagine the staff cringing when Ann strode into the office with a fiery look in her eyes. She "blew a fuse" when Cecile was not allowed to join the drill team because she was too tall. She "blew up," in her words, when Dan and some of the other younger boys were taken advantage of by being "allowed" to clean out varsity football players' lockers. Curriculum, too, became an issue, with the exclusion of women from history texts and lessons. Ann was incensed when Cecile's German language course was cut from the curriculum to save money while other, more trivial courses and, of course, sports programs were retained.

Ann and David would eventually decide to withdraw the three older children from the Eanes schools and enroll them in St. Stephen's Episcopal School. St. Stephen's was coeducational, small (fewer than three hundred students), and had been integrated since 1961. Tuition was high, Spencer Shropshire Jr., who was a classmate of Clark's, recalls, about $4,000 per year. Scholarships were available, but many of the minorities enrolled were the children of wealthy Mexican or Middle-Eastern families. Important to the Richardses, the school was academically far superior to Eanes High School. The children had to achieve high test scores in order to be accepted, and the school boasted that Clark's 1978 graduating class had the highest cumulative SAT scores in the country.

From the beginning, the bar scene played a crucial role in Ann's and David's lives. Austin is small enough—250,000 in 1970, 345,000 in 1980—for a relatively few bars to handle the in-groups. The bars, then more so than now, could be likened to clubs of another time or in other cities. They are remembered fondly and with nostalgia by those who lived there. It was "a kind of magic time," Big Al Ragle recalled wistfully. Eve McArthur, who moved to Austin in 1976, agrees. She remembers a night at Another Raw Deal, her neighborhood bar, at a table shared with John Kenneth Galbraith, Studs Terkel, Norman Mailer, and James Michener.

Ann was a "drawing card" long before she entered politics herself. She knew almost everyone and attracted interesting people. With Cecil's knack for telling a story and her own quick wit and innate sense of humor, she enjoyed a reputation of being "hysterically funny." People gravitated to her table, and many women secretly wished they could be more like her. She and David seemed to fit in wherever they went. They hung out at Scholz Beer Garden, which was frequented by politicians and, especially, the Young Democrats.

They often went to the Quorum, Nick Kralj's place. If you were not at the Quorum, Nick says, "you were out of the loop. Things happened between twelve and two A.M., you missed it, you missed the train. People made friends with others they normally wouldn't have had anything to do with because they were so far apart politically. Ten guys you'd been trying to see all day long in their office, you'd meet them there in five minutes."

The Cedar Door, the Capitol Oyster Bar, Silver Creek Saloon, the Short Horn, and the Stallion, renowned for its greasy chicken-fried steaks, were stops on any given evening. From the early 1970s, the famed Armadillo World Headquarters was packed with country and western aficionados who came to dance the two- and three-step and listen to a succession of big-name pickers and singers. Eddie Wilson, who started the Armadillo World Headquarters, opened the Raw Deal, a cramped place where liberal political folks and the literati gathered. A sign over the door said No Dogs or Guitar Players Allowed, and Eddie showed he meant it by ejecting the western singer Jerry Jeff Walker more than once.

The bar scene was wilder when the legislature was in session. David might be off to one side telling good stories quietly, Ann on the other side of the room "entertaining a whole bunch of people." Political arguments broke out, with sides changing as freely as the drinks flowed. Hookers appeared, and the parties got out of hand. Marijuana was as popular and ubiquitous as alcohol, and the wrong look or ill-considered phrase in a bar packed with drugstore cowboys looking for a fight could lead to the arrival of the Austin police. The police also patrolled aggressively for drunken drivers, and David, whom Big Al Ragle described as "always a lawyer for the common man," more than once went down to bail friends out of jail.

Ann became the honorary secretary-treasurer of Mad Dogs, Inc., a loosely knit collection of media, political, and entertainment "characters" known for their rowdy antics. The Mad Dogs were a perapetitic group, in and out of town, there one day and gone the next. Musicians like Jerry Jeff Walker, Willie Nelson, and Steve Fromholtz dropped in. So did actors like Dennis Hopper, Sissy Spacek, and Tommy Lee Jones, when they were not on location somewhere else. Molly Ivins, the political humorist who wrote for the *Texas Observer*, among many other publications, was a regular.

Other writers included Jap Cartwright and Bud Shrake, and their wives, and Billy Lee Brammer, a Lyndon Johnson staffer until he published *The Gay Place*, with a thinly disguised Lyndon Johnson as a protagonist, and became persona non grata in the White House. "Billy Lee usually got the ball rolling," after which, Big Al says, the party "sort of revolved from house to house, joint to joint, nothing planned."

Alcohol has been described as the rocket fuel of Austin politics. Daytime work, it was said, should never interfere with what you did at night. There was just enough truth in both those sayings to put a romantic patina on the deeper truth, that ideas were the real rocket fuel, and a lot of work was done day and night. David partied hard, but he was also a respected lawyer who tried cases both in and out of town. Ann could make a roomful of people laugh until their sides hurt, but she also stayed busy bringing up four children, running a household, and, from 1972 on, working on political campaigns. Nonetheless, Friday nights when they were in town and not busy with children and friends, they contributed their share to the making of the myth. And Ann, unknown at the time, was drinking her way toward very nearly devastating political repercussions on down the road.

Wife, mother, camper, hostess, partier, environmentalist, gardener, PTA member. Ann had energy to spare. She was everywhere, busy all the time, and as she said in her autobiography, "I mean, you have here a tossed salad that's bigger than most bowls."

But there was no real focal point, as 1971 wound to a close with the traditional elaborate Richards Christmas party. The children were all in school. David was arguing important cases and becoming a name to be reckoned with even as he avoided the limelight. Ann was in her mid-thirties, a name herself, to be sure, but more as a socialite without portfolio, with neither the temperament nor the money to follow the traditional paths of Women's League, garden club, symphony board.

There had to be more. Cecil had raised her more like a son than a daughter. She could hold her own with men—outcuss, outjoke, and outthink most of them—and all around her men were making the decisions. Men were the movers and shakers, and the women were wives, mothers, and housekeepers. Playing the role of jester and clown in a court where men ruled was fun, but it also proved to be frustrating.

Ann had said that it had never occurred to her to be anything other than a wife and mother. She had said she was tired of politics. One senses, though, that she protested too much. What she said was true enough as far as it went, but there was a conflicting truth. She needed more, a project that had a specific goal. She hungered to compete on a new level and make a difference to which she could point with pride.

That challenge was only a phone call away.

CHAPTER 10

IN THE RING

"It was a kind of magic marriage, because Sarah was desperate for someone to tell her what to do, and I was desperate for somebody who would let me tell them what to do," Ann said on the 1979 oral history tape cited earlier. The quote contradicts what she says in her autobiography. There, she recounts receiving a phone call in late December, 1971, from Caryl Yontz, inviting her to lunch with a friend who was considering running for the Texas legislature in Travis County's District 37-B. After Ann explained that she was no longer involved with politics, she quotes Caryl as saying, "Just come and talk with her. . . . We really need your advice. Her name is Sarah Weddington."

Sarah Ragle had been twenty-one and unmarried in 1967 when, a third-year student at the University of Texas Law School, she and Ron Weddington, her husband-to-be, went to Piedras Negras, Mexico, for the abortion that she could not obtain in Texas. The experience had scarred her emotionally, and she had been involved ever since in the women's movement in Austin. A volunteer at the Problem Pregnancy Center, and with the Austin chapter of the Clergy Consultation Service on Abortion, she was a dedicated advocate of change in Texas's strict antiabortion laws and of a woman's right to manage her own reproductive process. She was a student of abortion history, law, and politics, and had argued for the plaintiff in *Roe* v. *Wade* before the Supreme Court of the United States.

Like Ann, Sarah had smarted under the limits described in *The Feminine Mystique*. Interviewing for a job during her third year of law school, she was told by one Dallas law firm that they would not hire her because she was married and would have to leave the office early to cook her husband's dinner. She had been denied credit when she declined to have Ron sign her application for a credit card. Not much had changed since the early 1940s when Ann's father, Cecil, had convinced the Lakeview school board not to fire that third-grade teacher. Sarah Weddington knew teachers who had been forced to resign because they were pregnant. And, of course, she had been subjected to the terror of undergoing a dangerous and illegal operation at the hands of a stranger in an illicit abortion clinic. As a result, she was, unlike Ann, an unapologetic feminist.

It was a time when Texas women were becoming politically bolder. Frances "Sissy" Farenthold, from Corpus Christi, was elected to her first term in the Texas House of Representatives in 1968 and won again in 1970. She was one of the leaders of the notorious "Dirty Thirty," a House reform coalition fueled in large part by the angry reaction across the state to the Sharpstown scandal. Sharpstown was a complicated maze in which officeholders profited by trading stock in the Bankers National Life Insurance Company of Houston. Many old-line politicos had been caught up in the scandal, and all were quickly voted out of office. Now, waiting only for Ralph Yarborough to clear the way by deciding to run for the United States Senate instead of for governor of Texas, Sissy, with the avid support of women and progressives, was about to declare her candidacy for the governorship. She, more than any other woman, spurred the hopes of other potential female candidates.

Which was one reason why Sarah and a small group of activist friends thought they should run a candidate, too. Since Sarah was a lawyer, which after all most legislators were, and because she was known, they decided that she should be the guinea pig. Four days before the deadline, she withdrew one hundred dollars from her savings account, paid the filing fee, and became a candidate for Travis County's District 37-B seat in the Texas House of Representatives. The next step, given their inexperience, was to find someone who knew how to get her elected. And for that task, Patty McKool, now Patty Rochelle, a Dallas lawyer, who was Betty McKool's daughter-in-law and had known Ann for years, suggested they call her. Answering Caryl Yontz's call became the first step on the long political road that would lead, nearly two decades later, to the governorship of Texas.

Ann had read Sarah Ragle Weddington's name in the papers and knew she had argued *Roe* v. *Wade* before the United States Supreme Court earlier that month. She had not met her, though, and so accepted the invitation. They met for lunch at the Alamo Hotel. To Ann's surprise—she expected to meet a much older woman—Sarah was only twenty-seven, ten years younger than Ann, and pretty. She was also all business, her credentials were impressive, and she was forcefully persuasive when she asked Ann to manage her campaign.

Quickly, Ann said she would, with but one caveat. She would manage Sarah's campaign providing Sarah listened and did what she told her to do. When Sarah agreed, the deal was struck. Ann Richards was in politics on her terms.

"We were not thinking about women's rights, empowerment," Ann's longtime friend Betty McKool had said, speaking about the Dallas days. But that is where Ann had been heading. She later declared on the oral history tape that she was tired of helping male candidates who used women during campaigns without listening to them. Betty McKool recalled she had said, more than once, "Well, here we are working for the men again."

It was not that Ann did not *like* men. She did. She was just tired of being treated condescendingly, patted on the head, told thank you, and sent home where, according to the men, she belonged. Still, at the time she agreed to manage Sarah's campaign, she by no means thought of herself as a "feminist" in any politicized sense of the word. That would come five years later. For the time being, she took care not to let the campaign consume her life to the point that her roles as wife and mother were eclipsed.

However much she energized women and progressives across the state, Sissy Farenthold's coattails were not long enough for Sarah's election in Travis County to be a foregone conclusion. Until then, according to David Richards, Austin had sent "the worst damned old know-nothings you ever saw to the legislature." No woman had ever represented Travis County in the legislature, and the gender barrier would be difficult to break. Sarah and her friends were all young, and, though most had worked in campaigns, their experience was as menials. No one really took them seriously. Her name was known, but having argued *Roe* v. *Wade* could be counted on to draw as much opposition as support.

Ann and Sarah and their friends had not talked to the city leaders, or any men in the legislature who might have been sympathetic. They were, in short, simultaneously way out on a limb and in over their heads, and did not really expect to win. What they *could* do was learn the ins and outs of running a campaign themselves and bring before the electorate issues in which they were interested.

And potent, emotion-arousing issues they were. At first, they almost exclusively involved women's rights. Rape law reform, equal access to credit, pregnancy leave, and employment equity headed the list. (Texas ratification of the national Equal Rights Amendment and the inclusion of an ERA in the Texas Constitution were early priorities, the former coming to pass that summer, the latter passing in the November general election.) Ann, however, convinced them that women's issues alone were not enough, and that the list would have to be expanded.

Together, Ann and Sarah's group identified issues germane to a wider and more varied constituency. To tap the enormous wellspring of the inherently progressive teaching staff and older students on the University of Texas campus, they allied themselves with the powerful anti–Vietnam War sentiment there. They generated their own mailing list of nonteaching staff at the University of Texas, a large pool of voters who had not received a wage increase for years, and implied that Sarah would work for them. They promised to fight for men's *and* women's rights in child custody cases. They reached out to the environmentalists, a rapidly increasing number of Austin voters who were concerned about water and air quality. Although Sarah's district was predominantly white and middle-class, they sought the support of blacks and Hispanics, who were relegated for the most part to the fringes of the electoral process.

The Weddington campaign opened the door to a new world for Ann. Sarah's campaign was staffed entirely by women, and Ann has said in various places that the experience of working cooperatively with like-minded women was a thrill. She met Cathy Bonner, Jane Hickie, and Mary Beth Rogers, a trio who would become long-term friends and supporters, key players in her political rise. Women were running the campaign for women, not for men, and David, for the first time, was involved because she was, and not vice versa. Notwithstanding the cooperative nature of their venture, Ann was the grand strategist and tactician and ultimately called the shots.

Not autocratically but, since she was ten to fifteen years older and vastly more experienced than the others, more like the teacher, the mother who knew best, the seasoned campaigner. She was, in short, according to Patty Rochelle, "the driving force behind the campaign."

Ann provided a certain professionalism, political savvy, and the organizational abilities Sarah and her friends lacked. She brought a wide circle of friends and acquaintances. She possessed contacts in the black, Hispanic, and environmentalist communities. Most of all, she brought a level of energy that matched Sarah's, and knew how to raise money.

Financially, theirs was a catch-as-catch-can campaign. Primary support came from the fledgling Texas Women's Political Caucus, even then being assembled by Sissy Farenthold's and Sarah's people, who became allies. They held open houses at campaign headquarters—Sarah and Ron's house. They held five-dollar suppers featuring chili, chips, and beer. Ann and David, children, dogs, cats, all running in and out, held fund-raising parties at their house on West Red Bud Trail.

They scrimped, saved, and cut corners. The campaign stationery and stickers were printed at a union print shop, but everything else was done as inexpensively as possible. They designed the logo, a purple-and-white stylized flower that was easily identifiable, and used it on yard signs, campaign literature, bumper stickers, and larger signs that Ron made to be affixed on car roofs. Sarah passed out brochures downtown and worked state office buildings to solicit support. They delivered literature throughout the district by way of a home-delivery service, a relatively new idea at the time and cheaper than the mail. Ron wrote, produced, and directed the few radio and television spots they could afford to air.

One idea of Ann's was to hold a Democratic fair where voters could meet Democratic candidates from across Travis County. There, to carry the campaign giveaways offered by better-funded candidates, Sarah handed out cheap white paper sacks on which they pasted bumper stickers. When they ran out of bumper stickers, she autographed the bags. They even "taped leaflets on the mirrors and over the toilet-tissue dispensers in every ladies' room in town," which was new to the annals of Austin campaigning, Sarah related in her book, *A Question of Choice.*

Whatever they did, it worked. On May 6, 1972, they won a place in a primary runoff with Hugh Hornsby, one of the three other candidates in the race. The war was not over, but they had won the first round.

All the odds were in Hornsby's favor. He came from an old, well-established Austin family, and Sarah was a newcomer. His campaign was relatively well financed, and Sarah's was anemic. He was a man, Sarah was a woman. Hornsby charged that Sarah was a transient because she came from Abilene, in West Texas, had lived in Austin while earning her law degree from the University of Texas, moved to Fort Worth, Texas, to be an assistant city attorney, and then returned to Austin. Sarah turned this to her advantage at the University of Texas and other Austin colleges. Hornsby complained that Sarah tried to confuse the voters by wearing her hair down one day, in a bun the next. Sarah and her supporters explained that women were not required to arrange their hair the same way every day, and turned the charge into a joke. Mostly, Hornsby asked whether a woman could do the job. The voters answered with a resounding yes on June 3, 1972, when Sarah Weddington soundly thrashed him 47,620 to 37,713. In the aftermath, Hornsby's supporters wondered bleakly how he had outspent "that sweet little girl" two to one and lost.

A woman could win, and though Sarah had so far won only the primary, she had run on the Democratic ticket, which in 1972 was tantamount to victory in the general election. And indeed, with a side trip in October for a rare reargument of *Roe* v. *Wade* before a full court (only seven justices had been present for the first hearing), Sarah sailed through the general election with 84,373 votes to her Republican opponent's 34,970. The results came in early, and there was jubilation that night at Sarah's house. Sadly, though, on that same November 7, 1972, Sissy Farenthold lost, some said dooming a woman's chance to be governor of Texas for the foreseeable future.

Ann had "her" first victory. Win or lose, she had stipulated that she was finished when the election was over, and as she had promised herself, she returned to being a wife and mother full-time. The problems with the children at the Eanes schools continued, as did the river-running trips, Know Your Texas tours, and fund-raising jaunts around the state. David was doing well enough for them to buy a place on the North San Gabriel River, where the family and an ever-growing circle of friends gathered on weekends to camp out, sit around a bonfire at night, drink, and in true Texas tradition, spin yarns, political and otherwise.

In January 1973, Sarah was seated in the Texas House of Representatives and began learning how to navigate through the labyrinth of legislative procedures and protocol. Quickly she introduced bills that addressed the issues on which she had campaigned. She and Eddie Bernice Johnson of Dallas, who later became a member of Congress, passed a state law requiring school districts to retain pregnant teachers on their payrolls. She and the four other women in the legislature sponsored and saw passed a bill allowing married women to have separate credit. She advocated, and the legislature passed, changes in the Family Code which gave fathers and mothers equal consideration in child custody cases. She and State Representative Kay Bailey, now United States Senator Kay Bailey Hutchinson, cosponsored an amendment to revise Texas's rape statutes to provide greater protection for victims of sexual assault. And Sarah and a rapidly growing network of women and women's organizations, fought successfully to defend the Texas Equal Legal Rights Amendment.

The call for Ann came next in 1974 when she was asked to help Wilhelmina Delco run for the Travis County District 37-A seat in the House. No Travis County legislative seat had ever been held by a black, either male or female. That Wilhelmina, a black female, even considered running or might have a reasonable chance of winning was due to two mutually reinforcing factors.

First, there was a change in the voting age and laws. Eighteen-year-olds, for the first time in Texas, were enfranchised, and an old law that required students to vote in their parents' hometown was declared unconstitutional (in a case David argued in Denton, Texas). This created a fresh pool of young, liberal voters, many of whom were still galvanized by America's role in Vietnam.

Second, minorities and liberals had begun in earnest to flex their political muscles as never before in Austin. Richard Moya, for example, a Hispanic, had recently become a county commissioner. In addition, Sarah and four more women were in the legislature, and, though Sissy had lost, more and more women across the state were running for elective offices.

The Delco race was far different from Sarah Weddington's. Unlike Sarah, Wilhelmina was already known in Austin. She had been on the Austin Independent School District school board. She knew the issues—education, discrimination, teenage pregnancy, and so on—in detail. She had an extensive and long-cultivated network. Her own people were in charge of the campaign. The last thing Wilhelmina's campaign needed was a white woman from West Lake Hills in a high-profile position. Ann was able, though, to help with organization, strategy, and the ever-important fund-raising. The result, when Wilhelmina won, was a second notch on Ann's political belt. In addition, by helping both Wilhelmina and Gonzalo Barrientos, who was elected to the House that year, she cemented racial ties that would be crucial when she herself became a candidate.

After Sarah Weddington's first term, Caryl Yontz, who had become her administrative assistant, resigned to accept a job in Washington, D.C., and Ann agreed to fill her post. Managing the office proved as instructive as managing a campaign. Ann had been a casual student of the legislature. Now she became intimately involved in the legislative process. She helped Sarah design a legislative package and session strategy. They conceived, drafted, and followed bills as they made their way through the legislative mill. She hired staff and directed the work of five interns from the Lyndon Baines Johnson School at the University of Texas.

Ann managed the office while Sarah spoke around the country. And she learned the importance of doing her homework, how essential it was to ferret out what a representative wanted and why. She made lists of supporters and opponents of bills important to Sarah and herself. She learned to negotiate the compromises necessary to win a key opponent's support. Later she would observe that there was "nothing pretty about watching either laws or sausage being made."

The process, however, proved to be as fascinating as it was ugly, and Ann loved the role she played in it. She was, she discovered, a good negotiator and a good manager. She enjoyed the planning, the networking, the give-and-take, the homework, the pressures of time and compromise, and the manipulations that made the process work. She had the best of two worlds, home, where her need to be wife and mother was fulfilled, and the office, where she had become a player in the political arena.

The next step was an office of her own.

CHAPTER 11

A RACE OF HER OWN

You take your repressions home and funnel them into recipes just so long and then you are going to erupt somewhere. The timespan for total housewifery isn't lifelong.

—ANN RICHARDS

"Ann Richards to Run for County Commissioner." The headline in the *Austin American-Statesman* sounded unlikely in light of Ann's repeated avowals that she had no desire to hold office. It was true, though. Her hat was in the ring.

Her decision to run had not been made lightly. The story has it that David was first approached in the spring of 1975 by a group of the Richardses' old Young Democrat friends who were interested in getting liberals elected. The liberals were gaining ground in Austin, the thinking went. It was a time of political change. The student movement was in full swing, and elections were being won by liberals, ethnics, and women. There had been breakthroughs in the legislature and in city government. If ever there was time for liberals to take firmer control of county government, it was then.

Ann, in her autobiography, says she felt David would have made a superb officeholder but not a good campaigner, because he did not have the temperament for the long grind—lunches, suppers, meetings, door-to-door calling, and the never-ending organizational effort that keeps a campaign working smoothly and on track. Some acquaintances thought just the opposite.

John Collins, a Dallas attorney who, like David, received his undergraduate degree from Baylor and his law degree from the

University of Texas, was hired by David for Mullinax, Wells, David's old firm, in Dallas. "David had tried a lot of important cases and was highly regarded," John told us. "My sense, though, is that he worked hard to avoid the limelight." Eve McArthur, who spent time with the Richardses at the Raw Deal, said that Ann would make a statement and David would nearly always carry it "one step further." Others spoke of him as being too much a loner and too unwilling to compromise to be a good officeholder. In any case, David appeared to be more a behind-the-scenes player who, never having wanted to hold public office, declined. At which point, the now aging Young Democrats with whom Ann and David had partied and connived for the past twenty years, approached Ann.

The thought of running for office, even one as low level as county commissioner, was tempting, if for no other reason than the challenge. The dangers for Ann, however, seemed great. She and David were forty-three years old. They had four children who needed her attention in school and at home. More important, she had watched Sarah and Ron Weddington's marriage disintegrate as Sarah's public life eclipsed their private lives, and she feared the same pressures would tear apart her own marriage.

"I had worked in politics so long," she was quoted as saying in *Third Coast,* then an Austin monthly, in February 1984, "I knew what the personal sacrifices really were....My greatest fear was that it would be the end of my marriage." And then with a smile, because, by then, she had made that sacrifice and was within months of a formal divorce. "I was born married."

David's response, when she expressed these fears, impressed her. "Don't do that," she quotes him as saying in her autobiography. "Don't tell them no. You will wonder all your life whether you could have done it or not. And in the end, you'll probably be good at it." Her voice on the 1979 oral history tape, made after their marriage had, indeed, begun to fail, thins wistfully as she quotes him further. "You cannot," he said, "turn down this opportunity."

It was a defining moment in Ann Richards's life. She and David had been married for twenty-two years. He had been around politics and politicians long enough to know the dangers as well as she. He also realized that not running could prove as corrosive to their marriage as running, because she *would* always wonder. If her deep-seated prefeminist values demanded that she get her husband's permission, he was willing to give it.

The question remained, *could* she win the office of county commissioner? Precinct by precinct, Ann researched the election results of the last city council election, in which Margaret Hoffman had won a seat, and from Gonzalo Barrientos's winning House race. These would give her an idea of the viability of "nontraditional" candidates in her precincts. As she had for Sarah, she talked to friends to get a feel for her strengths and weaknesses, and those of the county commissioner she would run against. Then, in the summer of 1975, she, David, and the children drove to South Padre Island deep in South Texas on the Gulf of Mexico coast for a month during David's vacation. There, after poring over the numbers and spending hours discussing the pros and cons, Ann and David decided she could win, and began plotting a campaign that would put her in a county commissioner's seat.

"How's she going to do that?" Peggy Romberg, who had worked with Ann on Sarah Weddington's campaign, says she wondered when she heard Ann was going to run. A woman county commissioner? A woman in the legislature was one thing. Entering the knock-down, drag-out backroom political arena of the good-old-boy road-and-bridge crew was another.

Traditionally, the county commissioners' court was seen as a group of men in charge of carefully guarded fiefdoms. They built and patched rural roads and bridges, and held on to their power by keeping taxes low and doing favors for a handful of important citizens. That image persists in many rural areas but had changed in urban areas like Austin by the 1970s.

County government in Texas is a local entity created to execute state policy on a local level. It is comprised of elected officials like the sheriff, constables, justices of the peace, district attorney and all district and county judges, the county treasurer, tax assessor-collector, and the district and county clerks, among others. Appointed officials include county health officer, human services director, public works director, and many more, all of whom are named by the commissioners' court. The court is an elective body of four commissioners, one from each of four precincts, and a county judge elected at large. A great deal of the commissioners' clout and importance derives from their budgetary powers: They approve the annual budgets for each of the county's elected and appointed officials and their departments. In 1976, the Travis County budget was some twenty-two million dollars.

Ann's campaign would not only serve as a model for her later campaigns for state treasurer and governor, but in revised and expanded form become a plan offered to women candidates elsewhere in Texas and, indeed, around the country.

The first element to consider was her opponent, and Ann's analysis of his strengths and weaknesses. The Republican party in Austin, as elsewhere in Texas, was still weak, and the tough campaign would be against her Democratic opponent in the primary, the incumbent Johnny Voudouris. Voudouris's strengths mirrored those of Sarah Weddington's opponent, Hugh Hornsby. Voudouris was a businessman who owned a sizeable building maintenance company and enjoyed the support of the business community. County commissioners tended to hold their offices for some time. Mike Renfro and Bob Honts, two of Ann's colleagues on the court, replaced men who had held office for thirty-one and twenty-four years respectively, and Voudouris had been Precinct 3 commissioner for over ten years. Finally, the public thought the job suitable only for a man because of the emphasis given to building and repairing roads and bridges.

Voudouris's weaknesses were few but telling. He had plastered his name on every piece of county property in his precinct and was perceived by some as vain. If being a businessman helped, it also hindered, especially on the heavily antibusiness University of Texas campus. He had earned a reputation for not returning telephone calls and for ignoring his constituents. Finally, and perhaps most importantly, he assumed he would win. Ann believed his weaknesses outweighed his strengths and that he was vulnerable.

The urban nature of Travis County was an important element of Ann's analysis. In 1970, the city of Austin, with its population of some 250,000, comprised 85 percent of Travis County. That percentage had decreased a few percentage points by 1976 as the city spilled over its traditional borders. Generally, however, the people who left were affluent and city-dependent. The city dwellers did not care if the ditches along Farm Market Road X needed cleaning. They did care about how the county jail was run and how the parks were maintained and policed. They were interested in the availability and quality of emergency medical care, transportation planning, fire protection, pollution control, waste disposal, and clean water, to name only some of the services the county delivered. They cared how they were taxed for those services and how efficiently their tax dollars were spent.

In an urban setting, county commissioners functioned primarily as administrators. They were ombudsmen, direct links between the people and their government on that basic level where people and government most interacted. They were lobbyists, and protected and promoted county interests vis à vis city and state interests even as they helped coordinate the efforts of all three. They did not need to know how to build or maintain bridges or roads, rather how to hire people who did. More and more so, as the 1970s went on, urban county commissioners also had to represent minority interests, which, in Austin, had been at best mollified and at worst ignored.

The third important element was the burgeoning women's movement in Austin. Frances "Sissy" Farenthold, Sarah Weddington, and Wilhelmina Delco had energized large numbers of women. Women's rights had become a national issue and rallying point as women had learned to cooperate and make themselves heard. More and more women were assuming roles previously reserved for men. Women were meeting and talking, and a "good old girl" network had begun to take shape. Already, the Texas Women's Political Caucus, Citizens for Parenthood by Choice (which later became Texas Abortion Rights Action League, or TARAL), Planned Parenthood, the Austin Women's Center, and the Austin Rape Crisis Center were active in Austin. Ann knew most of the women involved in these organizations. Given the impact a woman county commissioner could have on county budgeting, she could count on their support, both financially and with the day-to-day physical demands of a campaign.

Fourth, and perhaps most important, Ann had declared her candidacy after she determined she *could* win. She did not, however, *expect* victory simply because her name was on the ballot, or because she was a liberal or a woman. Better than anyone, she knew she would have to work long and hard, and was prepared to do so. She looked first at Precinct 3 as a whole, roughly the southwest quadrant of the county from the center of Austin to the county limits, and approximately eighty-five thousand inhabitants, mostly white and middle-class to affluent upper-middle-class.

She could discount the rural vote, which amounted to approximately 11 percent of Precinct 3's population. Those voters were solidly conservative, knew Johnny Voudouris, and were loyal to him. The labor vote, due to her and David's long advocacy of unions, was hers virtually automatically, as was the liberal vote. Travis Country was redistricted that year to more closely reflect population shifts as North Austin grew. In the process, Precinct 2 Commissioner Bob Honts relinquished two boxes, or voting precincts, on the University of Texas campus to Precinct 3. Honts, who was considered middle-of-the-road to conservative, said he "wasn't sorry to lose them" because any liberal who ran against him would win those boxes by an eight-to-one margin. Finally, she could count on the "enlightened" women's vote.

She began by dividing her voting precincts into thirds. She wrote off the rural and conservative third that she considered hostile. She would canvass the third she thought to be friendly before she decided how much time, effort, and money she would have to spend to win those votes. She would campaign hard in the remaining, undecided, third.

From voting records, she compiled lists of voters in school board, bond, and other off-elections. These diehards who *always* voted heavily influenced any election. To them, especially, she mailed flyers pointing out that she was a graduate of Baylor University, a mother of four, and a former teacher at Fulmore Junior High there in Austin. She had also served on the board of the Unitarian Church of Austin, was a member of the Laguna Gloria Art Association, Common Cause, the Sierra Club, the Audubon Society, the Eanes Civic Association, the Texas Women's Political Caucus, and the St. Stephen's Mothers Club. Ann was, in other words, a concerned and committed citizen who cared about and worked for her community, as she would for her constituents.

As they had for Sarah Weddington, her friends in the Old Girl network volunteered for the phone bank she organized. She produced and aired radio commercials: In one, referring to Voudouris's reputation for ignoring his constituents, a phone rang repeatedly without being answered. Then an announcer said, "The least you can expect from your county commissioner is that when you need help, at least he'll return your call."

She lobbied community leaders, lawyers, judges, bank presidents, and business and union leaders and solicited their opinions— what did *they* want from a county commissioner? She called on radio stations and local weekly publications to seek their endorsements. In one incident, she spoke to Sam Woods, who, as editor of the *Waco Tribune-Herald*, had employed her uncle Jimmy, the photographer, and who was presently editor of the *Austin American-Statesman*. "What do you think would happen to this newspaper if we endorse you, a woman, for county commissioner?" Woods asked.

"Well, Sam," Ann responded, "I don't know. The whole building just might collapse, but why don't you try it and see?" It was vintage Ann Richards, and it worked. The *Austin American-Statesman* endorsed her the next week.

She campaigned hard in the precincts where University of Texas students lived. One flyer directed toward them trumpeted, "Things to know about Ann":

- Administrative Assistant to State Representative Sarah Weddington
- Secretary of West Lake Hills Zoning and Planning Commission
- Representative to the Austin Transportation Study
- Member of Common Cause
- Endorsed by AFL-CIO, COPE, and local building trades unions

Day after day, Ann walked the areas where she sought support. She soon discovered that her initial assessment of the third of her precinct that she thought to be friendly was correct. Those voters were solidly behind her. She concentrated on the third that were in doubt by going from door to door. If she found someone at home, she identified herself, explained that she was running for county commissioner, asked what he or she wanted in a county commissioner, and then left some literature. If no one was home, she left literature and a card that said she had been there. Before she went to the next house, she made a note to herself on some aspect of the house. Later, near the end of the campaign, she mailed postcards to each home, mentioning a salient fact about the house.

Early on, Ann learned how important money was in a campaign. She and her friends worked the phones soliciting funds. They held fund-raising events at her home, at the Raw Deal, the Quorum, and elsewhere. For one affair, on April 4, the invitation read, "Liz Carpenter and Friends Invite You to an Afternoon with John Henry Faulk." The names were impressive. Few candidates for the ground-level office of county commissioner could expect to run with the assistance of Lady Bird Johnson's former press secretary and a nationally known humorist.

At the same time, she was accused of compromising her environmentalist stance by accepting contributions from, among others, Gary Bradley, a prominent South Side land developer. Robert Spellings, now her confidant and bridge-playing friend, was a Voudouris supporter and involved in West Lake Hills real estate ventures, which made him, too, suspect in the envronmentalists' eyes. He met and got to know Ann one night in a whiskey-drinking session with the flamboyant and often controversial chairman of the University of Texas Board of Regents, Frank Erwin. Spellings says that he decided Ann was "as comfortable with who she is, as a person, as anybody I have ever met." Before the evening ended, she won him over to the extent "that I decided I had to support them both."

Taking a cue from a well-known television commercial, Ann measured ballots one voter at a time. No detail, no potential voter, was overlooked or ignored. David said he helped put up yard signs, which Voudouris's supporters removed as rapidly as they could. There were a few television commercials, and more radio commercials. The phone bank worked overtime. Peggy Romberg recalls not noticing that five registered voters shared the same telephone number. The fifth time she called that house on the same night, someone told her, "We were *going* to vote for Ann Richards, but if we get one more call..."

The pace picked up as May 1, primary day, neared. On that

morning, a Saturday, women walked the precincts urging people to vote. Peggy and a friend were two of the faithful. Peggy laughed as she recalled approaching one door. Before she could knock, the man who lived there walked down the stairs completely nude. He jumped aside when he saw her, reappeared wearing a pair of trousers a moment later, answered the door, and apologized profusely. "That's okay," Peggy told him. "The least you can do is vote for Ann Richards for county commissioner."

Whether Ann got his vote isn't known. If not, she and the rest of the volunteers at least had a good laugh when Peggy regaled them with the story as they waited for returns later that night at the South Lamar Street campaign headquarters.

A few hours later, the results were in. Ann had won her first race, with 13,002 votes, 63 percent of the total, to Johnny Voudouris's 9,498. With the victory in the Democratic primary, she was virtually assured of another over her Republican opponent in the November general election.

As indeed happened. November 2, 1976, Ann handily defeated the Republican candidate, Paul Pederson, 27,538 to 15,978. Travis County had elected its first female county commissioner.

CHAPTER 12

COUNTY COMMISSIONER

James Hyde Sr. is an assistant road foreman in Precinct 3, Travis County. In 1976, he was an equipment operator who drove water trucks and graders, helping to patch and build roads and bridges. James is fifty, a trimly bearded man of average height who wears tinted glasses to protect eyes scorched by asphalt fumes and Texas summer sun. He and his wife, Melba, live in a house he built himself just outside the southern city limit of Austin. He is instantly friendly, with no pretensions.

You can see in his face and hear in his voice that he both adores and respects Ann Richards. He has snapshots that show her playing Santa Claus at a Christmas party just before she took office on January 1, 1977. No one could tell by just looking at the photographs that Santa Claus is the governor of Texas, but James sees her there, and cherishes the pictures.

Ann replaced Johnny Voudouris, whom the men liked. Johnny wanted everything done yesterday and his name posted everywhere. However, he occasionally went out on a job, and talked to and took an interest in what the men were doing. When Ann defeated him, it was rumored she would force everyone to join the union, and fire their foreman, James Weir, who was tough but fair. Fire half the others, too, they said, and replace them with minorities or women. It was a man's world, and the crew wondered what the world was coming to.

So everyone thought it was hilarious when Rufus Johnson, a old water truck driver who didn't much care what he said to whom, started calling the mangy, tick-infested mongrel bitch that had taken up residence outside the barns and office Miss Ann or Miss

Richards. Nobody guessed, of course, that the new county commissioner would even notice the dog, much less ask its name.

County Commissioner Richards made her first appearance at the precinct office in December, a month after she had been elected, and a couple of weeks before she took office on January 1. The weather outside was cold, the room steamy. The commissioner was predictably upbeat and outgoing, the men quiet and almost surly. She made her pitch, assured them that no one would be fired and that the rules would not change. Then, perhaps a bit desperate when no one said anything, asked about that dog, and was told its name.

"I don't remember who finally told her," James said, "but it kind of broke the ice when she kind of laughed."

Ann quickly established herself as one of the guys. She and Jane Hickie, her administrative assistant, made everyone laugh with their antics at the Christmas party. She played quarter-limit poker with the men and was a good bluffer.

"Let's put it this way," James Hyde said. "She talked like a sailor. It wasn't a put-on thing. Wasn't just snowin' guys with dirty talk. You either took her as she was or you didn't take her. What you seen is what you got."

Ann was the last county commissioner in Precinct 3 to take much of an interest in the men and their jobs. She was the last one to visit a job site, James said, and ask, "Why you doin' this, why you doin' that?" And after a big job well done, she was the last commissioner to buy the beer and sit and drink, and joke with the men in the little park across the road from the office and barns.

The work was hot in the summer, often freezing in winter, and parties were the spice of the road crew's life. At Christmas, small gifts were exchanged. Ann gave the men funny T-shirts or a bottle of good liquor. The men went together to buy her gag presents—once, a huge box of condoms. They could not embarrass her. When she resigned to run for state treasurer, the gift was more substantial, a hundred dollar pair of cowboy boots.

Johnny Voudouris and Ann give different views of her victory and his loss. In her autobiography, Ann says he "took it hard" and cleaned out his office when he left, leaving her nothing but empty file cabinets.

To talk to Johnny now, one gets the sense that he could not have cared less. "She just plain beat me," he said. "I have nothing against her. She simply ran a good campaign and beat the pants off me." He even sounds grateful. "In retrospect, she made me a multimillionaire because she got me out of politics and let me focus on making money."

The commissioners' court has not been, traditionally, a stepping-stone to higher office in Texas. If Johnny Voudouris saw politics as a hindrance to making money, Ann may have seen it in a different light. She says she did not, but the opinion of others varies. Raymond Frank, Travis County sheriff from January 1973 through December 1980, thought it was apparent, as time passed, that she aspired to higher office. According to Ed Kirk, a retired U.S. Navy Master Chief with thirty-one years in the service, and a constable during Ann's term as a commissioner, "We all knew she wasn't going to be there long." James Hyde, from the road crew, remembered more than one person saying "That woman won't rest until she's the president of the United States."

On the other hand, Bob Honts, Precinct 2 commissioner, agrees with Ann, and does not think she had aspirations to higher office until 1981, when she learned that Warren Harding, the Texas treasurer, was under investigation for using his office and employees to further his reelection, providing Ann with a window of opportunity.

In any case, Precinct 3 was a small fiefdom to use as a conscious or unconscious stepping-stone to the office of state treasurer, much less the governorship. It was comprised of some eighty-five thousand constituents living along five-hundred-plus miles of streets and roads, many of them inside the Austin city limits. Twelve men worked on the road crew. Neither the commissioners' offices nor much of county government was computerized when Ann took office, and would not be until after a study that started in the summer of 1976 and ran well into 1978.

While not traditionally viewed as a stepping-stone to higher office, the county commissioner's job proved to be a superb school for an ambitious politician. Ann was a keenly interested student. She had promised honesty and a judicious husbandry of county funds, as had her political hero, Harry Truman, when he was a county judge. She had promised to listen to her constituents—indeed, had said she could not imagine an officeholder *not* listening to constituents—and kept the promise.

In marked contrast to Johnny Voudouris, she returned phone calls. She made herself available to virtually any organization that asked. She attended meetings held by PTAs, environmental groups, Rotary Clubs, churches, and chambers of commerce. She attended dozens of breakfasts, lunches, and dinners that crowded into her datebook and schedule. If a meeting involved labor or unions with which David was acquainted, he sometimes accompanied her. Otherwise, as he had agreed before she ran for office, he took his turn, after twenty-three years of marriage, watching over and caring for the children and the house.

Networking was her strong suit. Ann was never shy about asking for help when she did not know enough about something. If she did not know, a friend did. If no friend knew, she turned to a friend who had a friend who did, or simply started calling around. When the Capital of Texas Highway, a loop around southwestern Austin, was in the planning stage, she and others became concerned that a proposed bridge that crossed the Colorado River would only be utilitarian. Ann brought in architects and environmental and arts groups and, going beyond the usual role of a county commissioner, met with the State Highway Department. The department's engineers were not willing to work with the architects but did take the hint, and in the end designed a bridge that blended with the countryside and enhanced the view of the Colorado River.

The addition of Ann to the court strengthened its commitment to the delivery of human services in Travis County. Her vote, with Judge Mike Renfro's, Precinct 4 Commissioner Richard Moya's, and often Precinct 2 Commissioner Bob Honts's, constituted a solid majority, with Precinct 1 Commissioner David Samuelson, who was more rurally oriented, often being in the minority. Renfro's knowledge of the law, Moya's of everyone in the courthouse, Honts's of city management and budgeting, and Ann's ability to capture the media and speak, brought the county government more in line with its urban constituency. Taking advantage of federal revenue-sharing monies, they increased the funding for programs for the deaf, for Down's syndrome families, and for abused children.

Years earlier, Austin had accepted responsibility for Breckenridge

Hospital, which delivered care for indigents in the city. Now, however, the burden had become too great for the city to bear alone. Consequently, upon request by the city, the commissioners' court agreed Breckenridge should be at least in part a county hospital, so, according to Bob Honts, they "threw in their lot and accepted responsibility." Not only for the Travis County indigent but, under contract with ten outlying counties, for their poor as well.

Women were making themselves heard, and women's issues were coming to the fore. Founded in 1977, the Austin Center for Battered Women, one of the first in the state, operated out of a house donated by the city, and desperately needed funds. The county's power to fund such an organization seemed questionable, and the court was initially unwilling to do so. Ann argued forcefully that the Texas Constitution charged counties to provide for the needs of "imbeciles and idiots and indigent," and that battered women almost invariably became indigent the moment they fled their homes. She prevailed. ACBW's first funds, $18,000 were granted by the court.

Debby Tucker began her social service career as a volunteer for the Austin Rape Crisis Center when she was a student at the University of Texas. She first met Ann in Sarah Weddington's office when Ann was Sarah's administrative assistant, and became more closely associated with her through the Austin Center for Battered Women. In Debby's mind, the formation of the Travis County Social Policy Advisory Committee (SPAC) was one of Ann's important contributions to the delivery of social services in Travis County.

Previous to SPAC, social service organizations had to approach separate entities for funding. SPAC was comprised of representatives from the city, county, the United Way, and the school board. Sitting as a single entity, it was designed to obviate the necessity of social service organizations' preparing budgets for, filling out forms for, and lobbying each of the participating organizations.

Making SPAC a reality was easier said than done. The county, city, United Way, and school board each worried about losing budgetary control. The social service organizations feared that general funds would be cut back and that as a result their individual slices of the funding pies would diminish. Debby credits Ann with much of the fence-mending, cajolery, and mediation that overcame these objections. Finally, in 1978, after more than a year of negotiations, the first budgets were presented and the first funds disbursed. At last, Debby said, "We could concentrate on doing all of that only once." It saved everyone involved time, energy, money, and, most of all, "reduced a lot of political game playing."

Successes notwithstanding, there was no pleasing everyone. Ann led the fight for the court to raise all wages on county jobs to union rates, according to Bob Honts. The workers were happy, but others complained that her munificence cost too much. With the proliferation of fire ants across Texas, the state implemented an eradication program that made the powerful insecticide Amdro, one of the few agents that would kill fire ants, available to the counties. Ann took the environmentalist side and argued against the use of the chemical.

As one person who was glad to get the Amdro said, "It's easy to be against it until you or one of your kids gets bit by about a hundred of them boogers. They don't call 'em fire ants for nothin'." Those who wanted Amdro got it.

Vested interests, as always, tended to oppose change. Ann had scrimped and saved as a young housewife and knew that buying two of anything when one was sufficient was a waste of money. As a county commissioner who visited job sites, she frequently saw equipment sitting idle. Her suggestion that the court adopt a unitary system of heavy equipment purchasing and usage was not accepted, even after a study conducted by a University of Texas Business School student showed that the change would save the county tens of thousands of dollars. To Ann's mind, that money could be better spent elsewhere. Later, when she was no longer a county commissioner, her plan would be adopted.

There were other examples of criticism scattered over the years. In April 1978, the *Austin Citizen* reported on complaints about a questionable sandblasting and painting contract pushed through the commissioners' court by Richard Moya and approved by Ann. In late 1979, the *Citizen* reported on the 57 percent raises the commissioners had given themselves over the past two years, while giving other county employees much lower increases. In September 1981, the *Austin American-Statesman* reported that commissioners were being criticized for not spending enough on the county criminal justice system, while at the same time spending $42,000 to

Election Night, November 1982. Ann Richards, right, enjoys a relaxing moment with her dear friend Virginia Whitten. *(Photo by Tad Hershorn)*

Ann Richards with Geraldine Ferraro at a "Breakfast for Ferraro" at the Fairmount in Dallas in September 1984. The Old Girl Network raised some $179,000 for Ferraro at this function. *(Photo by Robert Cabello)*

Ann Richards with her friend and colleague Barbara Jordan.
(Courtesy Ann Richards Committee)

Jim Mattox, the "pit bulldog" of Texas politics,
whom Ann defeated after a tough and wearing primary campaign in 1990.
(Courtesy Dallas County Democratic Campaign Headquarters)

Clayton "Claytie" Williams, looking like a governor even though
he lost the general election to Ann in 1990. *(Photo by Gray Hawn)*

Election night, 1990, at the Hyatt Regency in Austin. Ann holds the famous "A Woman's Place Is in the Dome!" T-shirt. *(Photo by Tad Hershorn)*

Inauguration. Ann is sworn in on the steps of the Capitol, January 19, 1991.
Left to right. Governor Ann Richards, Clark Richards, Cecile Richards,
Texas Supreme Court Chief Justice Tom Phillips, Dan Richards.
(Photo by Karen Dickey)

Iona and Cecil Willis at Ann's
Inaugural Ball.
(Photo by Karen Dickey)

Ann at her Inaugural Ball, flanked by Bud Shrake, at her righ
and son, Clark, at her left. *(Photo by Karen Dickey)*

Ann the adoring grandmother, with Cecile's
daughter, Lily. *(Photo by Karen Dickey)*

Ann in the House of Representatives for her
1992 State of the State address. *(Courtesy Ann Richards Committee)*

remodel their offices and increasing their travel budget from $5,700 to $21,500 that year.

Harsher criticism of Ann revolved around her presence, or nonpresence, and her involvement, or noninvolvement in the daily affairs of the court. She has said in her autobiography that serving in public office demands the officeholder's "full-time attention." That she invested enormous amounts of time in the business of the court and county is indisputable. However, she did not give the job her full-time attention, especially after the first year.

County Judge Renfro and Commissioners Moya, Honts, and Samuelson were men whose view was, in the main, limited to Travis County. Ann's view extended beyond the county's borders to include the state. After the National Women's Year Convention in Houston in 1977, and her inclusion on President Jimmy Carter's Advisory Committee for Women later that year and into 1978, her network of women grew exponentially, and she looked more and more to the nation at large.

Many people did not know how they should perceive their county commissioner. In person, she came across as utterly charming, persuasive, and genuinely caring. She fought hard for projects she believed in, such as the Center for Battered Women, the Social Policy Advisory Committee, and union wages, among others. They were proud of the wide exposure she enjoyed. Many women, as the 1970s wore on, were grateful for her commitment to women's rights.

At the same time, she was often absent, speaking around the state, attending conferences throughout the country, busy in Washington, D.C., on the President's Advisory Committee for Women. Some complained that she spent more time during county court meetings "wisecracking" with Precinct 4 commissioner Moya than paying attention to details. Men carped about her focus on women's issues. Bob Honts saw himself, Renfro, and Moya as dominating the court in issues like budgets and the hiring of judges, with Ann as an ally. Otherwise, she concentrated more on political agendas, leading to the belief that she had higher office in mind all the time, and did not get bogged down in things like how well Precinct 3's roads were being maintained.

Ann herself did not see that as a problem. She was an administrator, an ombudsman—or -woman—a connector of people. She did not claim to know how to build a road or bridge. Her job was to make sure that the people who *did* know were informed, had the wherewithal to do what needed to be done, and were happy in their work.

Likewise, during virtually all of 1977 and into 1978, when the court was moving to a county-wide computerized system, she did not get bogged down in the minutiae. Indeed, looking through the minutes of court meetings, her name is conspicuous by its frequent absence. She agreed that they needed to computerize. She did not, however, need to know bits and bytes. That was the job of the experts the court retained, and she would not waste time second-guessing them. She accepted whatever system the court bought, as long as it was up-to-date, efficient, and cost-effective.

———

"As much as anybody I have ever met, she has a true sense of who she is," Ann's bridge-playing friend Robert Spellings has said. That opinion is shared by many of her friends, going all the way back to high school. But at least during one period in her life, she did not feel at all confident that she knew exactly who she was and what she was doing.

The years 1977 and 1978 were tumultuous ones for Ann. It was as if, at age forty-five, she was being reborn. She had never contemplated holding public office, and suddenly she did. She had been reared believing a woman should be wife and mother, and suddenly she was less of both than she thought she should be. She liked and got along with men better than most women did. More and more, however, she found herself in the company of dedicated feminists and, especially after she attended a National Women's Educational Fund conference in Aspen, Colorado, in 1978, was swayed to their point of view. She had never shied from responsibility, but now the decisions she made helped determine policies that affected thousands of people and the expenditure of millions of tax dollars. She had long been an insider to political goings-on, and now she was almost painfully aware of how much of what she had heard had been the "beer talk" of men with their own agendas.

It was a confusing time. David had been the one to travel. Now she found herself on the road more and more often. She said she had always felt David was smarter than she, and the decision maker. Now she knew things he did not know and made decisions without his help. As a result, their marriage of over twenty-four years had become strained. Adding to the confusion was the fact that while that change in their relationship frightened her, she could not—indeed, did not want to—stop herself.

Her life was extraordinarily hectic. School functions with the children. County commissioners court meetings. Women's conferences. Fund-raisers for political allies in Dallas, Houston, San Antonio. Meetings of the Advisory Committee for Women in Washington. New friends, new connections. New ideas, new horizons. The phone rang off the hook. They were off on a Know Your Texas tour, running a stretch of the Rio Grande, traveling as far as Georgia to run a new river. This weekend camping with the family, the next a busy travel schedule of Leadership Texas speaking engagements with women's groups in Houston or Tyler or Lubbock, wherever she and her cohorts, Jane Hickie and Mary Beth Rogers, were asked. A Rotary Club meeting, a supper at a black church, a *Cinco de Mayo* festival, an evening of hard drinking at the Quorum or Another Raw Deal.

Who was Ann Richards? Travis County Precinct 3 commissioner provided only a partial answer.

CHAPTER 13

THE OLD GIRL NETWORK

Ann Richards's election to the "brotherhood" of Texans serving on the 254 county commissioners' courts in 1976 was not unprecedented. According to statistics compiled by the Texas Women's Political Caucus in 1975, Ann joined a widely scattered group of 18 other Texas women who had been elected to the same post. The remaining 997 county commissioners were men, meaning that Ann's election elevated the percentage of women on Texas county commissioners' courts to almost 2 percent.

That figure was comparable to the percentage of Texas women serving in other government posts in the mid-1970s. Of 31 state senators, 1 was a female. Of 150 representatives in the Texas House, 7 were female. Of 235 state district judges, 2 were female. Even in the realm of public education, where women were traditionally expected to participate, the number of females with geniune clout was amazingly small. Of the 7,058 seats on school boards around the state, only 525, just 7.4 percent, were held by women.

These numbers came as no surprise to the women who comprised the Texas Women's Political Caucus. Indeed, the very existence of the caucus was due to the growing number of women who resented their sex's underrepresentation in the bodies that governed them. The short shrift given women was pervasive. Government, business, and even history were male dominated. Ann had been irritated by the paucity of women in her daughters' school history books. The lesson was brought home more sharply when she and her family visited the Texas Institute of Cultures in San Antonio on one weekend in 1977. There, they watched a slide presentation that depicted a procession of Texas heroes.

"One after another the images of early Texans flashed by," Ann recalled. "The adventurers, the settlers, the soldiers, the statesmen. These were our forefathers. Face after face. But only two were women. One was an opera singer, the other a sculptor. Out of the thousands of early Texans, only two were mentioned. I wondered what my daughters were thinking."

Later, Ann would write that if her daughters were to select their role models from a textbook, their American examples would range from "an ax-swinging prohibitionist in a saloon to Rosie the Riveter in World War II who did the work of men, but only in the name of national defense." There had to be a way for them, and all contemporary Texas women, to connect with their past.

Back in Austin, Ann discussed the matter with her friends in the Texas Women's Political Caucus. The result was a decision to find a way to illustrate Texas women's role in the history of the state. Money was collected, and Mary Beth Rogers, Ann's friend and political ally, who owned and operated a public relations firm in Austin, agreed to direct the project.

Four years later, the exhibit, *Texas Women: A Celebration of History,* opened on May 9, 1981, and embarked on a two-year tour of the state. The Honorable Ann Richards was listed in the program for the Opening Activities Celebration Luncheon as a "major contributor." Today, the exibit is housed in the special collections section of the library at Texas Women's University in Denton, in North Texas.

Texas historical machismo, presented in the context of a museum cultural exhibition, revived Ann's feelings of impatience with "the way things were." They had been that way for as long as she could remember. At Waco High in the late 1940s, the Kuder Preference Test she and the other students took was presented as a guide to career planning. The test, however, was rigged. "In those days, the girls were given tests different from boys, so the choices were predictably limited," Ann has written. "Even if your answers indicated an interest in people and their problems, the vocational choice was social worker or nurse, never a politician. But what better way [than as a politician] to serve people?"

From high school on, Ann had been involved in a love affair with politics. Because of gender constraints throughout the 1950s and 1960s, however, her involvement was limited to the role of a menial. "Women were not allowed roles of responsibility beyond stamping or mimeographing, no matter how much experience or education we had," she said. When Ann and David moved from Dallas to Austin in 1969, she made a "personal vow after about eleven years of that kind of devotion to the cause that I would divorce myself from licking another political stamp."

Things did not work out that way, of course. "A political junkie," as she's been described, she was drawn to politics in spite of her vow to concentrate on being a wife and mother. It was as if she *had to* get involved in very nearly anything that touched her or her family's life in any way. By the time she ran for county commissioner, she had been a member of the PTA, St. Stephen's Mothers Club, the Sierra Club, and the Audubon Club. She had been a representative to the Austin Transportation Study and served on the Unitarian Church board and the Westlake Hills Zoning and Planning Commission, among others.

Everyone, it seemed, wanted chunks of Ann Richards's time and energy, especially after her return to "real" politics as Sarah Weddington's campaign manager in 1972. The demand continued through her assistance on Wilhelmina Delco's campaign and increased after she was elected to the county commissioners' court in 1976. The court met formally on Mondays, but Doris Shropshire, the county clerk at the time, recalled that there were informal meetings nearly every weekday, and Ann was expected to be there. Lieutenant Governor Bill Hobby named her to a special committee on the delivery of human services. Ann was responsible for assembling an overview of services available for Texas children through the age of seventeen.

More and more, Ann left the city to attend conferences. She was in Houston for the National Year of the Woman Conference in 1977. In the fall of 1978, she attended a conference for women elected public officials held in Aspen, Colorado. In 1978 and 1979, she traveled back and forth to Washington D.C., to serve on President Jimmy Carter's Advisory Committee for Women.

Along the way, she met a succession of women who were passionately interested and involved, or wanted to be involved, in politics. Their common goal was to elect women to positions at all levels of government. They were dedicated to the proposition that women, not government, should control their own bodies. And they were committed to the task of creating organizations and passing laws designed to break deadly cycles of violence that most often harmed women and children.

These women, many of whom became Ann Richards's associates and lifetime allies, understood they needed to become unified, then organized, and then funded in order to force the system to accommodate them and women's needs. Each seemed equipped with a hidden antenna that tuned them to a common frequency. Most of them, like Ann, were wives and mothers. Most, if they were not already dedicated feminists, were, like Ann, moving toward a definite feminist stance. One and all, they shared the notion that "what you are seeking is you." Before long, they functioned much as the Old Boy network that was the source of so much of their frustration, and against which they railed. It is this loosely knit, widely spread sorority, that some now call the Old Girl network, that comprises, in large part, Ann Richards's political power base.

The Old Girl network was no mistake, and did not just "happen." Austin alone was a gold mine of politically active women. Ann knew most of them by the time she was elected county commissioner. Her network, even then, stretched back to the Dallas years when she was the motive force in the North Dallas Democratic Women and began her file of three-by-five cards holding the names of "our growing network of women." Added to the catalogue were the hundreds she met and worked with on committees and boards, on the Weddington and Delco campaigns, and during her tenure as Sarah's administrative assistant.

The network, already well established by the time she became a county commissioner, increased exponentially during the years that followed. A letter writer, she stayed in touch with the original Dallas cadre. She maintained lines of communication with women in the legislature. Putting friendships and connections to use, she made it her business to know who was interested in what, and was able to alert friends whose programs might be facing cuts or changes, or point them to legislators or agency heads who were willing to help further a cause. The names of all these women and the organizations to which they belonged would fill a small book of its own. One of the women—and one of the organizations—is illustrative.

Debby Tucker, as a student at the University of Texas, volunteered at the Austin Rape Crisis Center during its formation in 1974 and continued on staff after her graduation that year. In 1977, she was instrumental in the founding of the Austin Center for Battered Women. In 1978, when the need for a statewide umbrella organization for shelters for battered women became apparent, Tucker was one of the founders of the Texas Council on Family Violence, of which she is presently the director.

Tucker met Ann in Sarah Weddington's office. She had gone there to discuss how child protection services would not offer assistance to children who had been abused by someone outside the family, only inside the family. She had fallen asleep in a chair in the outer office and was awakened by Sarah and Ann.

Tucker is a feminist who, like Ann, likes men. She is forceful, knowledgeable, and has lobbied for shelters for battered women, the Council, and a wide range of women's issues in both houses of the Texas legislature and in the United States Congress. And she is an unabashed admirer and supporter of Ann Richards, to whom she occasionally refers as "our Ann."

As well she might. Ann argued forcefully for the Austin Center for Battered Women's first grant of $18,000 from the county commissioners' court. She was instrumental in the formation of the Travis County Social Policy Advisory Committee and worked closely with Debby in the process of allocating SPAC funds for human services delivery. When Tucker began lobbying for all women's shelters in Texas, Ann helped her devise a strategy and then, with her knowledge of who supported what and to what degree, pointed her to key legislators.

The two women know each other well enough to have had their differences. At a Social Policy Advisory Committee meeting in 1981, Ann entered and angrily confronted Debby. "Have you lost your mind, asking [the legislature] for an increase from $200,000 to $1 million?" she asked. "Everyone knew," she went on, "that you requested no more than a 5 percent to 10 percent increase." Tucker was taken aback, but countered that the Texas Council on Family Violence was trying to keep sixteen shelters in business and she thought you asked for what you needed. Ann told her they were being too pushy and would lose their credibility but in the end sent

Tucker to "the senator who would do them the most good." Ann was wrong about Tucker losing her credibility but right about the senator. The Council got the money.

Tucker's job has grown, with the Council now representing sixty-two shelters that help and protect some thirteen thousand women and nineteen thousand children a year, and having a biennial budget of over $18 million. It has lobbied for and seen passed laws that, for the first time, in 1993, protect Texas families from stalkers, give police the authority to arrest wife batterers without warrant, and require an arrest if a protective order is violated in an officer's presence. Additionally, a law was passed that required training for police and judges in the areas of battered women, batterers, sexual assault, and child abuse.

"You wonder how any legislator might be opposed to measures like these," says Christina Walsh, now on Tucker's Council staff. "But there were and are plenty of old-line folks in the Texas legislature who maintain the attitude that a man's home is his castle. But we've managed to accomplish a lot at the legislative level gradually over the years, and lot of that had to do with the advice and guidance of Ann Richards."

Tucker seldom sees Ann these days. Ann's crowded calendar and the necessity of her, as governor, having to address a panoply of state-wide issues limit access. Still, according to Tucker, Ann has "made a real point of getting things to me through her people that I need to know." She remains committed to the agenda, and the relationship in which Ann helps make possible the delivery of services that both women believe are vital continues. For her part, Tucker is at the center of a network of hundreds of women whom Ann does not know personally, and can energize and activate them on the governor's behalf.

———

"Activism is here, but you have to be practical about it," Ann said, in late July, 1976, when she was in Dallas for that year's Texas Women's Political Caucus convention.

Practical was what the whole women's movement was about. Becoming pragmatic was both cause and effect of the Old Girl network. Women in Austin, as elsewhere, were organizing in new ways in the 1970s. The groups they formed were a far cry from the usual garden or cultural clubs with which women had been associated for years. A list compiled from a cursory reading of newspaper clipping files, arranged approximately in order of their organization, would show: Planned Parenthood (actually late 1960s), Texas Abortion Education Committee, Texas Family Planning Association, Austin Rape Crisis Center, Texas Women's Political Caucus, Texas Abortion Rights Action League, Austin Women's Center, Austin Battered Women's Shelter, Tarrant County Social Policy Advisory Committee (not solely women's issues), Texas Council on Family Violence, and Texas Foundation of Women's Resources. There were others, addressing a range of concerns as varied as women themselves.

The directorships of these organizations tended to be interlocking. The members knew each other well and had worked together on campaigns and various projects. They can be said to have come together in the Texas Women's Political Caucus, which became a clearinghouse for the many voices, programs, and projects that collectively comprised the women's movement in Texas, whose members formed the Old Girl network.

The Texas Women's Political Caucus was an offshoot of the National Women's Political Caucus, which was founded in July 1971 as a "political action arm of the women's movement." Bonnie Lesley, Texas Women's Political Caucus president, 1976–77, described the national caucus as "a unique organization that devotes its energies to recruiting and supporting feminist candidates for public office at all levels of government and to lobby for women's concerns."

According to a September 7, 1973, article in the *Texas Observer* The Texas Women's Political Caucus was born, "amid factious anarchy in November, 1971," with the same stated aims. The original membership numbered some 150 and two years later had increased to 1,500. Those first two years were not easy.

Both the national and Texas caucuses were marked by power struggles that, because women were involved, the male dominated press characterized as "catfights." By whatever name, the "factious anarchy" spawned battles about whether men should be allowed to vote, whether Chicana or black groups should have permission to set up their own local caucuses, the caucus's stand on lesbians, and so on.

Mary Lenz, in a February 12, 1973, article about a National Women's Political Caucus convention written for *The Dallas Morning News*, noted that "Sunday was like something written by Lewis Carroll. But 'Women in Wonderland' did not even have a Red Queen to give it a semblance of order, as delegates issued contradictory motions, reconsidered business that had been taken care of earlier, voted and revoted the same issues.

"One female reporter from a liberal Texas publication could only shake her head at all the disorder and comment, 'We're not ready for self-government.'"

The Caucus would not remain mired in an anarchic swamp forever. By 1976, the Caucus helped Irma Rangel of Kingsville and Ernestine Glossbrenner of Alice, both Democrats, win seats in the Texas House of Representatives. Increasingly, the goal of both the national and Texas caucuses turned to getting women elected at every level of government. To further those aspirations, Mary Beth Rogers, Ann's ally since they had worked together on Sarah Weddington's campaign, created a slide show for the National Women's Educational Fund. The show, designed to teach women how to run effectively, used Ann's campaign for county commissioner and other women's campaigns as examples. Then, as other women did across the country, Ann, Rogers, and Jane Hickie played the show and spoke to women's groups across the state, all the while adding names to their list of politically enlightened women who would work for change.

Jane Hickie was typical of the women in the Texas Women's Political Caucus, and to women like her go the credit for establishing the Old Girl network and maintaining Ann's ties with it. Hickie has a reputation of being smart, funny, innovative, incredibly loyal, and politically astute. There are those who add that she also is neither very nice, warm, nor caring. Hickie comes from the West Texas town of Stephenville, and is fifteen years younger than Ann. The two met during Sarah Weddington's campaign and have been friends and colleagues ever since. Hickie worked on Ann's campaign for county commissioner and was Ann's administrative assistant after she was elected. Hickie played key roles in Ann's decision to run and in her campaigns for state treasurer and governor. She was also concerned and brave enough to be one of those to arrange intervention when Ann's drinking got out of control. Celia Morris, in her book *Storming the Statehouse*, says, "For years, Jane Hickie had focused with almost tunnel vision on Ann Richards' political future."

Jane Hickie has been consumed by the mission of advancing the role of women in politics since her high school days. She was one of the founders of the Texas Caucus and was formulating assertive and even pugnacious strategies for the Caucus before she graduated from the University of Texas in 1971. One "position paper" stated, in part, "the greatest factor in women's reluctance to run [for public office] is a lack of self-confidence. To overcome this psychological barrier, women are urged to start considering a campaign at least a year in advance of the first election, and to go watch the incumbent and his colleagues in action every time the women candidates feel they aren't qualified. One of the side benefits of mobilizing women to lobby the Texas Legislature is the look of shocked recognition that passes over the faces of the women who are seeing the good old boys at play for the first time. It is always a confidence builder." In Jane Hickie, Ann quickly recognized a young woman who could not be intimidated by anything or anybody.

By 1973, Hickie, at age twenty-four, was elected chairwoman of the Texas Women's Political Caucus at its state convention in San Antonio. In 1976, she won the Caucus's Woman of the Year Award. She attended the International Women's Year Convention in Austin in 1976, the National Women's Year Convention in Houson in 1977 (all while attending the University of Texas Law School from 1974 to 1977). She managed Ann's campaign for state treasurer in 1982, and in 1985 was a founder and member of the board of dirctors of the Texas Foundation for Women's Resources.

Connections were everything. Men had been "connected" for years in business and politics, and women very deliberately set out to do the same. The same names crop up over and over again.

Frances "Sissy" Farenthold, whose close race in the Democratic primary for governor aroused the feminist spirit around the state in 1972, connected women in the Corpus Christi area, on the Gulf Coast, to Texas women across the state. When she became chairwoman of the National Women's Political Caucus in 1973, she connected Texas women to the Bella Abzugs, Gloria Steinems, Betty

Friedans, and others elsewhere around the country.

Her keynote speech at the 1973 Texas Caucus's convention echoed the philosophy of politically active women everywhere. "I know," she said, "that when you start thinking about getting into the political arena, you will start to wonder if you are really qualified. Because all your life, you've heard people say, 'I'd vote for a woman if she were really qualified,' or 'I'd vote for a black if he were really qualified. Or a Mexican American.' Well, when I look at the competition that's in the political arena now, I just wait for the day when unqualified women, unqualified blacks, and unqualified Chicanos are in there competing with unqualified white males."

The connecting web of the Old Girl network now covers the country. Many of the names that stretch back to Ann's early days in politics remain part of that web, which in a real sense is Ann's power base.

Jane Hickie, as the director of the office of State Federal Relations, represents the State of Texas before Congress and federal agencies. She is basically a state lobbyist, and she connects Ann to Washington circles.

Mary Beth Rogers, who was Ann's chief of staff during her first nineteen months in the governor's office and recently compeleted a year's tenure as visiting professor at the University of Texas's Lyndon B. Johnson School of Public Affairs, is managing Ann's 1994 reelection campaign.

Cathy Bonner is described by Ann as having been the guiding light behind Leadership Texas, a broad-based program to help women be better acquainted with government, business, and educational leaders and institutions. Bonner was Texas Director of Commerce until she resigned to become director of communications for Ann's 1994 gubernatorial reelection campaign.

The list goes on. Liz Carpenter, Lady Bird Johnson's former press secretary, who has campaigned for Ann. Former congresswoman Barbara Jordan, University of Texas professor. Lily Tomlin, the comedienne. Erma Bombeck, the humorist. Aurora Sanchez, who ran the personnel office when Ann was treasurer. Molly Ivins, the political commentator and humorist. Geraldine Ferraro, for whom Ann campaigned in the 1988 presidential election campaign. Betty McKool, who goes back to the Dallas years, the Richardses' house on Lovers Lane, and those early three-by-five cards with the names of "our growing network of women."

The Old Girl network has become a potent political force over the course of the past twenty-five years.

The Texas Women's Political Caucus, after its 1975 survey, knew exactly how many women held elective office in Texas. Today, in 1994, the numbers have increased significantly, but a representative of the Caucus says it no longer keeps track. That in itself seems an indication of how far the Old Girl network has brought women in government in Texas in recent years.

Indeed, it would be safe to say that many women holding elective office in Texas—and in other states as well—owe their positions to the Old Girl network. As does Ann Richards, who was one of the early members.

CHAPTER 14

Taking the Cure

Conspiracies are the spice of politics and, as the autumn of 1980 began, Ann Richards was the focal point and subject of a conspiracy. The people who designed the conspiracy were opposed to calling it that, but they were acting in secret with the goal of intervening in Ann's growing dependence on alcohol. When the conspiracy unfolded on September 27, 1980, the effects were devastatingly traumatic. Later, Ann would thank the conspirators. To this day, she remains grateful that they dared to be so bold. Indeed, had they not, she would very likely still be drinking, and just as likely not be the governor of Texas.

In Sam Houston's memoirs, the patron saint of Texas mystique dismisses United States President James Knox Polk as "a victim of the use of water as a beverage." Some suggest that Sam Houston's legendary affinity for bottled spirits established a legacy that would endure and prevail for generations of those in positions of power in the Lone Star State. Few of the political players who gather daily and well into the night at Austin's Quorum Bar would admit they needed Sam Houston to lead the way.

Nick Kralj, an Austin entrepreneur and latter-day product of David Richards's old University of Texas Kappa Sigma fraternity, opened the Quorum in 1970 with the premise that politicians in the state capital needed a central watering hole where they could gather and iron out their differences. Kralj, a political enthusiast himself and staffer for the colorful former lieutenant governor Ben Barnes, a central figure in the Sharpstown scandal in the late 1960s, had the right idea.

"Other than Dolph Briscoe [democratic governor, 1972–78], I

can't think of any Texas politician of consequence who I didn't see in the Quorum in the dozen or so years that I owned the place," Kralj says. "We didn't serve food. No live music. This was a place for serious talking and drinking. This was where the deals were made. This was where people who were the bitterest enemies on the floor of the Texas House or Senate could sit down and have a civil conversation. If anybody ever got out of hand or lost their temper, which was rare, they were tossed out. The place would start filling up about 11:30 in the morning and didn't slow down until 2:00 A.M. [the closing time mandated by state law].

"Mostly, the crowd consisted of politicians and lobbyists," Kralj goes on. "A smattering of media people, but not many. Then there was a constant flow of celebrity types. Sissy Spacek, people like that. Hardly anybody was ever seen drinking beer or white wine. They drank hard liquor."

Kralj remembers Ann Richards vividly. "Ann was one of the favorites," he said. "A standout. A setting like that was a natural stage for her. When Ann was on the county commissioners' court, she would come in there and conduct a lot of 'official' business, like everybody else. People liked to sit at her table. She told great stories and could talk that 'man talk' better than most men could. Ann was kind of a group leader in the Quorum." The Ann Richards that Kralj and a legion of others have described would have been welcomed as a regular at the fabled Algonquin Round Table. Her drink preferences were vodka and gin.

In the mid-1970s, in her middle forties, the time in Ann's life that she described as "a tossed salad larger than most bowls," her visits to the Quorum and other Austin bars like the Raw Deal offered respites from the pressing demands of maintaining an elective office, intense involvement with a half dozen women's social action agencies, and a household. She traveled extensively from the time she was elected county commissioner until the fall of 1980, not only in Texas with the Leadership Texas project, but out of state as well, including the trips to Washington, D.C., to attend meetings of President Jimmy Carter's Advisory Committee for Women.

Ann was, in many ways, a woman on the edge. Many of her friends attributed her behavior to a heavily overloaded schedule. Most did not know that underneath the fun, laughter, and honors underlying the hectic pace, her marriage was in trouble. As she had watched Sarah and Ron Weddington's marriage disintegrate as Sarah rose in the political world, so she found herself and David drifting apart. Her worst fear during the days she was trying to decide if she should run for county commissioner was coming true. She was frightened, even terrified. Because, as she says in her autobiography, "the relationship was simply beyond reclaiming. We had grown so far apart." Under those conditions, alcohol was more than a respite from a busy schedule. It eased the pain. It was an old and valued friend. And more and more, a necessary friend.

Ann's old Waco High School chum Bill Dosher, who was in her debate class, remembers that Ann would drink a couple of beers on double dates, "when we could manage to buy some." David had drunk heavily at the University of Texas and, though he had returned to Waco to "dry out," certainly had not stopped drinking. Alcohol was a given on the weekend parties during Ann's and David's junior and senior years at Baylor University, both before and after they married. They drank, too, sometimes heavily, at least on weekends when they lived in Austin during the three years David attended law school and Ann was first in graduate school and then teaching.

Life was lived from party to party, the way many people live from paycheck to paycheck. Everyone in the Richardses' circle drank. Drinking was fun; it made everyone funnier, wiser, and wittier. The participants at the weekend parties that the Richardses hosted in the backyard of the house on Lovers Lane in Dallas were as liberal with their drinking habits as they were with their politics.

"Of course we drank," says Betty McKool, a companion of the Dallas years. McKool especially remembers a fishing excursion into the interior of Mexico. The party had been told there would be food on the train, but there was none. "Everything possible went wrong," Betty laughed, "and we survived on peanut butter sandwiches and margaritas. So Ann drank in those days, but I can honestly say that I don't remember her ever having been drunk or behaving outlandishly."

The family's move to Austin in 1969 placed Ann and David in a freer and more relaxed social environment than was found in Dallas with its prevailing stuffy atmosphere. David seemed intent on seeking out and surrounding himself with penurious writers, guitar pickers, and other heroes of Austin cabaret society, none of whom were given to bringing up the rules of civil procedure in their versions of polite conversation.

Journalist Richard West, then a charter member of the writing staff of the promising new magazine *Texas Monthly,* recalls, "It was a group of folks who didn't take himself or herself very seriously and was not inclined toward inhibitions. David and Ann Richards had quite a few Austin friends who might be termed philosophic or creative, but not the sorts of people who are asked to serve on banking committees or grand juries." These eighty-six-proof think tanks, echoing with insight and laughter, offered a natural setting for the wit and wisdom of Ann Richards.

Few of Ann's friends or associates can pinpoint when her drinking habits, or the manner that alcohol influenced her behavior, began to change. But they did, apparently at about the same time as she began her tenure on the Travis County Commissioners' Court.

Former legislator and Ann's longtime friend Bill Kugle spoke, in a *Los Angeles Sunday Times* article, of one of the frequent river rapids canoe and rafting trips in which the Richardses participated. "This was sometime in the mid to late 1970s and a group of us piled into a big Winnebago motor home for a trip to Georgia," Kugle said. "We all drank beer the whole way to Georgia and back, except for Ann. She drank straight vodka. But on a deal like that, when everybody's drinking, nobody pays that much attention to how anybody else acts."

Others, however, did pay attention, and stories abound. In one, another longtime friend remembers the time Ann approached him at an out-of-town political fund-raiser in 1978. "Ann was pretty loaded, and she tied into me, right there in front of a bunch of people, for divorcing my wife, who was an old friend of hers, too. She called me a 'no-good S.O.B.,' among other things. David was right there and I felt bad for him, because he was embarrassed."

Like so many others, Ann's friend did not know how strained her and David's marriage had become, how his divorce must have threatened her. "It's clear now," he said, looking back. "If my marriage could break up, why couldn't hers? I've seen that happen lots of times."

Dan Weiser, the Democratic progressive who met the Richardses in the early 1960s, recalled a trip to Austin in the late 1970s. Ann was thinking about running state-wide, and Weiser had driven to Austin to discuss that possibility with her and David. Until then, he said, he had not been aware that her drinking had become a problem. On the way to dinner, he dropped her off at a reception she needed to attend for an hour or so. She went in sober and came out drunk. Later, as he had with a number of male friends, he talked to her about it. The conversation was private, but Weiser is not a man who minces his words.

Weiser was not the only friend to be concerned about Ann's drinking. Friends and family, all too familiar with her time-honored practice of identifying problems and attacking them with an "Is there a better way to do this?" approach, had collectively decided that alcohol dependency had become a threat to the woman many regarded as "a national treasure." No one talks now about who said what first—this was an intensely private affair—but Jane Hickie, according to Ann in her autobiography, was the person behind the first consultation with chemical dependency specialists John and Pat O'Neill. University of Texas law professor Mike Sharlot and his wife, Sue, were old friends and beer-drinking buddies of Ann's from the late 1950s Sholz Beer Garden days. The Sharlots and Ann's son Dan were early recruits in the intervention process. David was reportedly reluctant to participate at first but finally agreed to do so after Mike, Sue, and Dan talked to him.

John and Pat O'Neill, according to the biographies in their book *Concerned Intervention*, are licensed chemical dependency counselors and nationally certified addiction counselors. Based in Austin, Texas, they have worked as a husband-wife team since 1973. They "have led interventions for many notable entertainment and sports personalities, high-level political figures, and leaders of business and industry."

According to the O'Neills' book, intervention often entails a meeting in which the chemically dependent person (known as the CD in clinical terminology) is confronted by the people nearest to him or her. If intervention is handled correctly, the CD is first made aware that a problem indeed exists, and then is told in crystal-clear terms that professional assistance should be sought to overcome that problem. Obviously, a session of this nature offers the potential for an emotionally wrenching experience for everyone involved.

It is important that the participants in the confrontation phase of the intervention not appear or sound self-righteous. The O'Neills wrote:

> The goal of the intervention is to break through the wall of delusion surrounding the CD person long enough to get him or her to accept help. Intervention is a nonantagonistic effort done with the absence of judgement and packaged in concern. Sometimes, but not always, the intervention [takes] the form of a confrontational meeting with the CD person.
>
> Intervention is not a case of proving the CD person wrong and you right or getting him to admit to being an alcoholic or drug addict.... Whenever possible, intervention is not based on fear, coercion or threat of consequences but derives its power primarily from love and concern. An intervention effort conducted by a properly trained individual or group has little danger of backfiring.

In Ann's case, the intervention was as effective as it was dramatic, for the simple reason that she was already beyond the stage of denial and acutely aware that she had a problem. James Hyde, one of the road crew in Precinct 3, said she had mentioned at a party that she was thinking of getting some help to dry out, and some of the men had wished her well. In an interview printed by the *Austin American-Statesman* in 1985, Ann said that she had considered help well before the intervention and had consulted a doctor about the problem. "I told him I was worried about how much I was drinking. He asked me how much I was drinking and I think I was pretty honest when I told him. He said, 'You don't have anything to worry about. I drink that much myself.'"

She added, "Alcohol for me was the thing you did; after you got off work, you go to the club. And alcohol was part of the political system. I drank a lot. But the people around me drank a lot, so I didn't see myself as any different. Of course, alcoholics never do. My saving grace was that I couldn't stay up very late. I did all my drinking between 5 and 9:30 P.M. By and large, when I drank, I went straight to bed and fell asleep."

Her other saving grace was her friends, who cared enough to put themselves and her through the ordeal of the confrontation. Even if she had been thinking of getting help, that morning was "a painful, emotional" time.

It might have helped had she read Betty Ford's book, *Betty: A Glad Awakening,* in which she recounts the story of her intervention and treatment. The book had not yet been written, though, so Ann had to face that day and the weeks that followed alone.

The ordeal started when Sue Sharlot arrived at Ann's house with a trumped-up story about her father being ill, and asked Ann to go to her house with her. Ann did, and when she entered, found her old friends the Korioths, the Whittens, the Sharlots, and the Meachams waiting for her. With them were David, Cecile, and Dan, and a pair of strangers, the O'Neills. Immediately, she thought something must have happened to either Clark, who was in school in Japan, or Ellen, who was at Middlesex, a girls' prep school in Massachussets. When she asked, they told her the children were fine, offered her a seat, and turned the meeting over to the O'Neills.

The O'Neills had rehearsed all the participants except Ann. Each had prepared a short speech outlining something embarrassing or hurtful that Ann had done while she was drinking. One by one, they read their statements. Each ended by telling her that she probably would not have done what he or she had described had she not been drinking. There were no recriminations. All the descriptions of events were factual and to the point. Each person spoke of how much he or she cared for and loved Ann. In the *American-Statesman* article, she muses that it was at least as hard on them, too, because "they were terribly afraid and I'm not exactly a weak sister."

This gentle brutality, Ann says in her autobiography, was "overwhelming. Unbelievable. A trauma beyond any that you can imagine, and with a dozen people speaking for three or four minutes each, it went on for a while."

She was staggered, humiliated, frightened, angry. Some of the people pointing out her faults had drunk with her for years. Especially David. She wept, and so did everyone else, except the O'Neills, the professionals. The tears were an important part of the process. As the O'Neills point out in their book, "There appears to be a correlation between the amount of tears shed and the impact of the statements."

Finally, Ann asked what she should do, and learned the next step was arranged if she wanted to take it. They had signed her up for treatment at St. Mary's Alcohol Treatment Unit, now called St. Mary's Chemical Dependency Services at Fairview Riverside Medical Center, in Minneapolis. David had already bought airplane tickets for himself and Ann. Their flight was at three o'clock that afternoon. Ann agreed to go. Later, she said, "It was a great relief for me to know that I could do something about it," but initially she was so angry with David that she did not want him to go with her. Finally, back home and packing for the thirty-day stay, she relented, and he accompanied her and stayed with her while she was admitted.

There are few secrets in the political community in Austin, and that Ann had gone off to "take the cure" was soon common knowledge among her friends and colleagues. Few were surprised, given the occupational hazard of alcohol among politicians. One or another of them was always "drying out" somewhere. The papers played along. "County commissioner Ann Richards missed her fifth consecutive commissioners' court meeting Monday," said one story that appeared on October 18, 1980. "She had been undergoing treatment for an undisclosed medical problem since September. Richards has continued to draw her $2,472.83 monthly salary and $300 monthly car allowance. Commissioners do not have to answer for their hours because they are considered at work or on call 24 hours a day."

The report continued, "Nancy Cannon, Richards' administrative assistant, said, 'The treatment is something her doctor said she couldn't put off any longer.' Neither Cannon, nor Richards' husband, attorney David Richards, would say what the commissioner is suffering from or where she is hospitalized."

The program at St. Mary's at the time lasted four weeks. Ann spent the better part of the first week simply sorting things out. Still traumatized and frightened, she went about in a state of shock. She worried what would happen when she returned to Austin. Worried if she would ever be funny again. More than anything, she worried about David being there. Thankfully, unlike many other patients, she did not have to be detoxified. Gradually, through individual and group therapy, lectures, and assigned readings, and by putting her thoughts in a journal, she began to realize that the confrontation and her hospitalization were a rare gift, and that she would make of it as much as she could.

Alcoholism is defined in different ways by different people. The definition accepted by the National Council on Alcoholism and Drug Dependence and by the American Society of Addiction Medicine, which was that used at St. Mary's, reads: "a primary, chronic disease with genetic, psychosocial, and environmental factors influencing its development and manifestations. The disease is often progressive and fatal. It is characterized by continuous or periodic: impaired control over drinking, preoccupation with the drug alcohol, use of alcohol despite adverse consequences, and distortions in thinking, most notably denial."

The treatment gave her knowledge of alcoholism, and of herself. The patients listened to outsiders who came to tell stories similar to theirs. There were lectures and films explaining the intellectual aspects of alcoholism. There were Alcoholics Anonymous meetings each night. In therapy and class sessions, Ann and the others explored their alcoholism, recalled when they had first drunk alcohol, tried to determine how much they had drunk over the years and what it had cost, and remembered the times they had harmed themselves while under the influence.

St. Mary's treated patients addicted to prescription drugs, heroin, cocaine, uppers, and downers, in addition to alcohol. But however varied the treatment from individual to individual, each patient was introduced to the Twelve Steps of Alcoholics Anonymous. Over and over, in their book *Concerned Intervention,* the O'Neills stress the importance of the Twelve Steps for people with all kinds of compulsive behavior. Ann, too, found what the O'Neills call "a practical pathway to spirituality in the Twelve Steps of Alcoholics Anonymous."

The Twelve Steps have helped her, she says, to take each day one day at a time. In speeches and interviews, she relates how she learned to accept "a spirit and a power greater than myself." No matter what happens to her politically or personally, she remains grounded in that spirituality.

One of the most difficult times of her four-week stay at St. Mary's occurred during the third week, called Family Week. St. Mary's program was instituted at the end of 1968. At that time, family therapy was limited to one day, which the patients dubbed Terrible Tuesday, and usually only the patient's spouse attended. By 1980, the program had been expanded to four days, and whole families commonly participated.

David and all four of the children flew to Minneapolis to take part in this phase of Ann's treatment. The idea of facing her family in the therapy sessions during which they confronted their own codependency was terrifying. In Ann's case, she relates that, among other things, they played a game called Sculpting, in which each family member arranges the family in a pose that reflects how that member sees the family. "My children placed me in a chair with my arms upraised and my hands in fists," she wrote. "In their eyes I had succeeded in what I had worked so hard to be, and that was Superwoman."

In a later interview with a reporter for *The Dallas Morning News,* Ann expanded. "I remember being so shocked to hear that my children saw me in superhuman fashion," she said. "And yet, I'm sure that's what I tried to be. It was a real revelation to learn that I didn't have to be a super chef, chauffeur, nurse, teacher, and everything else. It was kind of tough on them. It's hard to get next to a strong woman. And it's hard to grow up knowing Mom can do anything—and will whether they want her to or not."

In the aftermath of the treatment, Ann said, "I'm much closer to my children now in the fact that we like each other. I've learned to let them be them and me be me. I just want people to know that there is life after drink and it is a wonderful life indeed."

Eight years later, on Sunday, December 11, 1988, Ann returned to St Mary's. This would be a happier visit, for she was the honored speaker at the Twentieth Annual Alumni Celebration and Banquet, St. Mary's Chemical Dependency Services.

Surprisingly, for some, Ann continued to keep the home liquor cabinet well stocked for friends. Surprisingly, too, she continued to be seen at Nick Kralj's Quorum Bar upon her return to Austin from Minneapolis. "She was right back in there, holding court as usual," Kralj said. "The fact remained that a lot of important political business was still being transacted in that bar, and she realized that. Only the drinks Ann was drinking didn't contain any alcohol. But her personality stayed absolutely the same. Still laughing. Still funny. Still telling those stories. Nothing, on the surface at least, seemed to have changed at all."

But Ann had changed, and deeply. The woman who seemed to have the ability to be everywhere at once had added Alcoholics Anonymous meetings to her schedule. Two years later, her friend, Robert Spelling, who was still drinking heavily, told Ann that he, too, was going to take the cure. Upon hearing the news, Ann hugged him and wept. When he returned from undergoing a treatment similar to hers in California, Spellings started attending Alcohol Anonymous meetings, too.

Spellings says, "You're not supposed to talk about who shows up at AA meetings, [because] the anonymity is the core of the program, you know. But, yes. Ann Richards still shows up at AA meetings in Austin and that's important to anybody's program of recovery. The more AA meetings you attend, the more bricks you add to your foundation and the stronger you become. You'd think that a person of Ann's notoriety would be kind of conspicuous at an AA meeting. But she's not, really. You see all kinds of high-profile personalities at AA meetings in Austin. I'll never forget the first one I attended. I looked around the room and I recognized maybe a dozen, half of whom were judges."

—————

Ann considered being sober, not even wanting to drink, a blessing. Even so, there was a price to pay, and it would prove substantial. Shortly after her arrival home, in October, she invited Jane Hickie, the Korioths, the Whittens, the Sharlots, and the Meachams to the house on West Red Bud Trail for an accounting of sorts. She told them about the treatment, how much it meant to her, how much *they* meant to her. She was grateful to them and needed to tell them that they did not need to treat her with kid gloves, that their drinking would not bother her.

They talked politics that day, too. Betty Ford had drawn praise for being open about her hospitalization and treatment for her addiction to alcohol and prescription drugs, but she was a politician's *wife*, not a politician. Ann's friends counseled her not to reveal where she had been and why. A male politician might be able to survive that sort of revelation, as had Ann's friend Bob Bullock, the state comptroller and, later, attorney general. But what in Texas was acceptable for a man, would be political suicide for a woman. Ann reports that she thought trying to keep the secret was "pretty silly," but agreed to follow their advice. The strategy would prove to be costly less than a year and a half later when she ran for state treasurer, but no one at the time could see that far ahead.

David had been home when she returned. Sheila Taylor profiled Ann a little over a year later in *The Dallas Morning News*. During the interview, Ann told her, "I think my relationship with David, which had been so totally intense, underwent a dramatic change. We had been so totally bound to each other that [my getting into politics] was very difficult for him." Their relationship was still strained, but she was better able to cope with her new one-day-at-a-time outlook and a measure of serenity given her by her newfound spirituality.

They carried on, but the drift apart continued. Ann may still have frequented the Quorum, where she did business and held court, but she no longer chose to spend her evenings hanging out with the beer drinkers. Alcoholic wisdom, in her new sobriety, was simply too inane, and the more so the longer the evening wore on. She and David had been drinking partners for nearly thirty years, and now he drank, if not alone, without her.

Ann and David separated for the first time near the end of 1980, only two months after Ann's return from St. Mary's in early October. Christmas, with the children there, brought them back together. Nothing had been solved, though. Ann was still a politician; David still drank alone. There were no fights, just the dismal realization that the marriage no longer worked. When David left again that summer, 1981, and moved into an apartment, the word spread rapidly.

The Richardses had been more than a couple. For nearly thirty years, they were perceived as the perfect couple, made for each other, happy together as few others were. They were an institution, and many of their friends were devastated by the breakup, which came as a shock to most. Typical was Betty McKool, who had been their friend since their early days in Dallas. "I was losing sleep over the breakup of David and Ann," she said. "So many people were so close to them, and they felt the same way."

For such a public couple, the breakup and subsequent divorce were intensely private. David, who freely speaks about their lives in Waco, Austin, and Dallas, their political involvement, their children, and so on, demurred when the subject of the divorce arose. "I don't like to get into that," he said.

Ann's and David's friends similarly limit themselves to expressions of how shocked they were. "We couldn't believe it. Not Ann and Dave!"

Ann herself has said, "Getting a divorce was the hardest thing I have ever done. Harder than alcoholism, harder than treatment, harder than politics." Perhaps because it was so traumatic, so difficult, she has needed to speak, to try to explain, as much for herself as for others.

"I thought I would die if I were not married to David Richards," she said later. Now, married in name only, her worst fears had come to pass. Not only was David gone, but the children were, too, for the most part. Dan had an apartment in town and visited. Cecile was working as a labor organizer in New Orleans. Clark was in and out of town, in and out of the house, and Ellen had returned to school in Massachussets.

Some time later, Ann said, "The impact of divorce...is enormous. But out of it there is a really positive side. I've never lived alone before, ever. To me, it's an enormous accomplishment."

Life did not stop. She was busy with commissioners' court business, went to parties, continued speaking to women's groups for Leadership Texas. There was, however, time to be alone for very nearly the first time. There was time to read, or simply to sit on the deck and look out at the lights of Austin. And there was time to learn to be comfortable with herself, to better understand and tap the spiritual resources she had discovered at St. Mary's.

Finally, as she began life anew, there was time to find "contented loneliness" and to cement her faith in a higher power, which would carry her, with equanimity, through the political battles that lay ahead.

CHAPTER 15

THE RUN FOR THE TREASURER'S OFFICE

Ann Richards and her inner circle had discussed her running for a state-wide office for months. In early July, 1980, she announced plans to run for lieutenant governor in 1982 should her friend and the incumbent Bill Hobby decide not to seek reelection. When he did, the question became, which other office, and when?

The answer came suddenly on Tuesday, January 26, 1982, when the *Austin American-Statesman* reported that file cabinets in State Treasurer Warren G. Harding's offices had been seized and subpoenas served on several of his employees. The story revealed that investigators were looking into Harding's relationship with bankers who had contributed to his campaign funds, allegations that bankers had worked with Harding's son, Glen, who was in the bond business, allegations that Harding had not taken bids on interest rates paid for state money on deposit in certain banks, and Harding's use of state employees in his reelection campaign. No indictments had been handed down at that time, but Harding was immediately under a cloud.

Ann tells a truncated and matter-of-fact version of what then led her to run for Harding's post. Others recall that the atmosphere and events that took place during the next few days were much more highly charged and dramatic.

The calls started early that morning. Bob Armstrong, who was running for governor, told her to read her paper and get back to him. Liz Carpenter, Lady Bird Johnson's former press secretary and a longtime friend, called. So did Cathy Bonner, one of the leading lights in the Texas Women's Political Caucus. The phone kept ringing, and each caller had the same message: This was her window of opportunity.

Ann was not sure. She did not even know what the treasurer's duties were. She feared her drinking history and her marital status, shaky at best, would make her too vulnerable for a state-wide race. She called Bill Hobby, the lieutenant governor, and Jane Hickie, her closest political adviser, who had long wanted her to run state-wide. Austin's "quintessential couple" had now been separated and living apart for over a year and a half, but she phoned David, for she would not have dreamed of running without consulting him or, indeed, being assured of his support. She called her oldest, best friends, Claire Korioth, Mary Beth Rogers, Virginia Whitten, among others. All told her she should run.

Time was of the essence. The filing deadline was on February 1, less than a week away. Finally, a decision absolutely necessary, an informal meeting of the inner circle was called for Saturday morning, January 30.

By 9:00 A.M., the house on West Red Bud Lane in the wooded hills of West Austin began to fill with Ann Richards's dearest comrades-in-arms. Mary Beth Rogers and her husband, John, were first to arrive. Others followed quickly. Claire Korioth. Jane Hickie. Cathy Bonner. David Richards, who was still attempting to adjust to what he called his "apartment thing" and who was now a visitor in his own house, was conspicuous by his presence.

The occasion on this January Saturday morning provided a peculiarly similar setting to the friends-and-family intervention confrontation that so dramatically enabled Ann Richards to confront her alcohol crisis. This time, though the spirit of the moment was no less purposeful and intense, the small convention of friends and allies gathered with her blessing and under much brighter circumstances.

A "feeling of urgency among Ann and her friends to go forward" makes the gathering one of Mary Beth Rogers's most vivid memories.

"I'm the world's worst when it comes to remembering dates," laughs Mary Beth Rogers. "Ruth Winegarten told me that she'll never correct me in public as long as I'm within a hundred years of what I'm talking about. But I remember that Saturday morning meeting at Ann's just about as clearly as any event in my life.

"We all really wanted now to demonstrate that a woman *could* get elected [to a state-wide office] in Texas, [and were] acutely aware that no woman had won one in fifty years," Rogers continued. "We all felt that it was possible and now we wanted to prove it. Everybody was hoping, on this memorable and unusual weekend, that the decision would be made to push forward. The thinking was that Ann was ready and certainly well versed enough in Austin politics to warrant a bid for the job. From the standpoint of talent, savvy, political know-how and so forth, Ann was primed and ready. And Harding was in trouble," she emphasized. "That presented the opening that Ann and her people were looking for.

"There were no campaign plans or strategies laid out. No itineraries. Nothing like that. Just the simple decision to run or not to run."

The decision was not as simple as it might appear at first glance, or to the uninitiated. Many factors came into play. As mentioned, no woman had successfully run state-wide in the Lone Star State in the last fifty years. More and more women held elective office, but at no higher a level than the legislature. Conventional political wisdom held that, even in the enlightened 1980s, vast areas of Texas were too conservative to vote for a woman.

Was the leap from county commissioner to state treasurer feasible? Harry Truman, whom Ann admired, had begun his political career as a county judge. Thanks to the Pendergrast machine, he went from the county courthouse to the United States Senate. Later, of course, he became a Vice President of convenience for a powerful President who barely knew him, and backed into power only when President Roosevelt died. The comparison was not particularly helpful.

On the positive side, this was to be the culmination of two and a half decades of labor and preparation that began with the Young Democrats meeting in Scholtz Beer Garden in 1957 and ran through a nearly flawless campaign for county commissioner in 1976. Her experience ran from women's workshops in small Texas towns to the White House in Washington, D.C. She was a consummate and articulate speaker, capable of holding audiences spellbound. As a result, perhaps no other woman in Texas was as admirably poised to run for a state-wide office.

The invitations to the political skills workshops read, "This workshop is designed to introduce the basic skills involved with the planning of a political campaign—how to decide whether to run; who are your potential voters; how to develop a campaign theme and use it; and strategy, planning and timing." Ann and her inner circle now had to practice what they had preached, beginning with the issue of timing.

It has been sarcastically suggested that the most influential individual in Texas politics is Ronnie Earle, the Travis County district attorney since 1967. Earle, through his office's Public Integrity Unit, which is funded by the state to search out crimes committed by officeholders, exercises considerable authority as to whether to indict and prosecute high-profile officeholders on a wide range of misdemeanor and felony charges, and thus cripple or destroy political careers. With the pending indictments of State Treasurer Harding, Earle's power was confirmed.

Harding was outraged and called the action taken against him "politically motivated." In a statement issued on March 24, he charged that "one of the three grand jury commissioners who picked this grand jury is the Travis County Democratic chairman and a close personal friend of one of my opponents.

"The courthouse crowd hatched this setup when it appeared that I would have no opposition for reelection.... It was no accident that one of their number was ready and primed to file for office as my opponent within 48 hours of the so-called 'investigation.'"

Harding referred to Ann and Democratic county chairwoman Barbara Vackar, who indeed was her friend and contributed one thousand dollars to Ann's campaign. Vackar, when called on by the *Austin American-Statesman,* declined to comment. Ann, who was campaigning in Midland when she heard the story, called the charges "ridiculous." "When you're in public office and have been indicted, you want to come back and lash out at something," she said.

The "Yes you did, no I didn't" continues to this day, but in any case, Ronnie Earle's affinity for the spotlight, some said, was insatiable, and he did not need Ann Richards or anyone else in his zeal to ferret out wrongdoers. Nor did party affiliations concern him. In time, he proved to be an equal opportunity prosecutor as, in 1984, he indicted Democrat Jim Mattox, the attorney general. Later, in 1989, he brought charges similar to those he'd brought against Harding against the Democratic Speaker of the Texas House, Gib Lewis, and in 1993 against newly elected Republican United States Senator Kay Bailey Hutchinson. Treasurer Warren Harding thus became an unfortunate pioneer in the annals of District Attorney Earle.

Harding's misfortune became a challenger's good fortune. Faced with the distraction of possibly having to defend himself on felony criminal charges, Harding's energy was dissipated. Predictably, his funding dried up: During the next two months, his campaign received only $1,175. The possibility of conviction colored his every move, for a convicted felon cannot take office in Texas. With Harding under this cloud, the timing to send Ann Richards into the vast wilderness of state-wide Texas politics appeared to be ideal.

Unfortunately, Ann and her friends were keenly aware that she was vulnerable, too. Her drinking had been legendary, and her "drying out" at St. Mary's Hospital was no secret. Stories about "that old drunk Ann Richards" would recirculate, and her recovery might well be questioned. Of concern, too, was her and David's separation. Some 50 percent of Texas marriages ended in divorce, but the myth of the family was part of a powerful political rhetoric, and much might be made of a woman who left husband and children to try to take a "man's" job. These were double-edged issues in the sense that no one could reliably predict how the electorate would respond to them, or how Ann herself would handle the subjection of these aspects of her private life to public scrutiny, how she would hold up to the rigors of the challenge.

For the present, however, Ann's loyalists congregating at the house on West Red Bud Trail gave little thought to their champion's vulnerabilities. Emotions ran high. The primary election was three months hence, and if Ann ran, those months would be some of the toughest and most exciting politics in which any of them had been engaged. If Ann won, not only would their dream of a woman in a state-wide office be realized, but their own political careers, taken along for the ride on the Richards wagon, would be enhanced.

Still to be discussed was an ingredient that Ann had always deemed of primary importance: money. When the topic was broached, John Rogers, Mary Beth's husband, who had been sitting quietly, watching and listening, stirred.

John was a former newspaperman turned political campaign consultant. His main client was the American Federation of Labor and Congress of Industrial Relations, for which he selected candidates sympathetic to labor concerns and approached them about issues important to the AFL-CIO. His reputation as a political savant was impeccable. He could be blunt, was not one to sugarcoat reality, and was a man to be listened to.

Warren Harding, he had learned, had bankrolled $300,000 in anticipation of an uncontested bid for reelection. Once indictments were handed down, as it was virtually certain they would be, he would be hard pressed to raise any new funds. At that time, Ann's campaign could expect to receive some of the funds that would have otherwise gone to Harding. In the meantime, she had to establish a travel, expense, and promotional budget. John Rogers suggested a minimum of $200,000.

"If you can't raise $200,000 over a weekend," his wife, Mary Beth, remembers him telling them, "then you have no business being in politics."

"It all came down to finances," Mary Beth says. Targets and goals, which were among the basics that Ann and her friends taught, were quickly established.

If, by sundown on Sunday, the people working the phones on West Red Bud Trail and in other homes had collected pledges amounting to $200,000 for the Ann Richards for Treasurer campaign, Ann agreed she would place her name on the ballot for the May 1 Democratic primary. If not, if the fund-raising effort fell even a nickel short, their attempt to elect a woman to a state-wide office would be shelved for another time and place. That position agreed to, John Rogers wished the group well and departed. Mary Beth stayed behind and wrote a check for $1,000, which she handed over to a hastily named Ann Richards for Treasurer Committee. The race was on.

There were not enough phones at Ann's house, so lists were made up and passed out, the group split up, and the telephoning began.

For the rest of the day, the women hammered the long-distance circuits. The project was etched with a rare quality of passion. Many of the phone workers, after all, had devoted ten years or more of often-discouraging toil on committees and support groups that sought to make Texas a better place for women. They had fought long, uphill battles for funding and legislative support for women's issues the male-dominated power structure had ignored and even ridiculed. John Rogers's one-sentence pep talk had served its purpose. The $200,000 *had* to be met.

The work, as Mary Beth Rogers remembers, was not an around-the-clock effort. People came and went. Not all the calls were outgoing: One phone was reserved for women working in their own homes to call in reports on pledges they had received. Someone started a bridge game. Someone else sent out for food.

Despite the stakes involved, Ann maintained a measured calm. That might have been a bit of a facade, for, at age forty-eight, she sat poised on the edge of an historical effort. Later, she told *Third Coast* magazine, "My adrenaline really flows during that period of pursuit. Something happens from the time of the inception, not to the end but seeing the end. That's when the sadness sets in. That's the kind of drive I have. The process is what excites me."

By late afternoon on that Saturday, January 30, 1982, the returns were promising. Ann and her friends' trips up and down and across the state to speak to groups that sometimes numbered no more than a half dozen in Texas outposts like Comanche and Cisco were bearing gratifying fruit. Ann had crossed the paths of so many who now remembered and gave. David did his share, calling lawyers and labor groups and gaining promises of their support. Mostly, the solicitation targets were simply Ann's old friends. A regiment of those pals responded wholeheartedly.

On Sunday morning, the cars once again filled the circular drive in front of the split-level house on West Red Bud Trail. Inside, tile and hardware floors polished to a glitter that would have earned the approval of Ann's mother, Iona, waited, as did the phones. The figures on the total board rose. So did the level of excitement.

Around noon, amid "an atmosphere of relief and celebration," the numbers—cash, pledges, and loans—added up to, and then surpassed, $200,000. The hay, as they say in Texas, was in the barn.

The challenge met, Ann Richards would run! Now, the real work would begin.

———

The filing deadline was 6:00 P.M., Monday, February 1. Ann filed on time and said, as quoted in the next day's *Dallas Times Herald*, "I'm shocked that the allegations are so harsh, and I deeply regret his position as a friend, but as an officeholder, this needs to be looked into." Later that day, Ann and her fledgling team, headed by the consummate pragmatist Jane Hickie, gathered to devise strategy.

Hickie, a lawyer, would serve as Ann's campaign manager. Her credentials and range of experience were impressive. She was a cofounder of the Texas Women's Political Caucus, and active in the National Women's Political Caucus. She had worked with Ann on Sarah Weddington's campaign for the Texas House of Represent-atives. She had labored in Ann's campaign for county commissioner, and served as her administrative assistant after she won. With Sarah Weddington, she had coauthored a book entitled *Women in Texas Politics*. According to the people who know Hickie well, her training and instincts are those of a lawyer and she is a specialist in analytical reasoning. She practices little law, though, for her first love is politics.

One of the first jobs at hand was to analyze the opposition. The Democratic ballot included, as expected, the beleaguered incum-bent, Warren G. Harding, state representative Lane Denton of Waco, a friend of Ann's, and one John Cutright, who they quickly determined was too obscure to be a factor. They began with Harding.

Harding appeared to be in trouble, but he was still a threat due to his financial muscle. A $300,000 war chest put him in the armed-and-considered-dangerous category. With that much money at hand, it was entirely possible that he could prove himself innocent in a television campaign rather than be forced to stand in a court of law.

Part of his strength lay in the nature of the office he held. The treasurer's duties are so nonpolitical that more than one candidate has vowed to work to abolish the job as an elective post and have the treasurer be appointed by the governor. Perhaps because the office generates so little controversy, the treasurer, once elected, historically has expected a lengthy and comfortable tenure. Harding's predecessor held the post for thirty-six years, a considerable accomplishment considering that his name was Jesse James. In fact, Jesse James was so securely ensconced that he was replaced by Harding only after he died, in 1977. Harding was appointed interim treasurer by then Democratic governor Dolph Briscoe, elected to the post in 1978, and expected to be reelected in 1982.

Harding was a "known quantity" among the state's bankers, after having been treasurer of Dallas County for twenty-five years prior to his appointment to the state treasury. A former Dallas fireman and furniture salesman, he had entered politics after a stranger approached him and said, "With a name like that, you ought to run for something."

Political pros realized that Harding was a natural. He fostered a keen sense of self-preservation, and many voters automatically assumed that he was a relative of the former President Warren G. Harding. He was not, but the treasurer took care not to disabuse the electorate of the error. In fact, he relished telling how he was once introduced to a man who claimed to have served as President Harding's personal valet, who informed him that he "was the spitting image of his grandfather." Plus, at six foot one and 225 pounds, Harding *looked* presidential. That he plucked a guitar and sang a stirring rendition of "Help Me Make It Through the Night" did not hurt, either.

David Richards had long been familiar with his wife's soon-to-be-adversary. He told a reporter for *Third Coast* magazine in Austin that "Harding came out of a different tradition. He was Dallas County treasurer when Ann and I lived there. I'd go around to the courthouse, and there he'd be, standing in the hallway, backslapping, punching arms and telling jokes. He moved down here and did the same damn thing.

"They're all gone now," David continued. "Virtually all gone in state politics and yet, they so dominated it for generations. Texas has changed. What the hell. You can't let a place grow like this and expect to run a danged old patronage system, a system that seeks out the most mediocre people in society and lets them run the store."

Ann articulated identical sentiments in her own vernacular in the months to come. Calling Harding a troglodyte, however, did not change the fact that she had prevailed in only one real campaign of her own, and that over the ill-prepared, lukewarm Johnny Voudouris in a county precinct of some 85,000 voters. Warren Harding, on the other hand, pending indictment notwithstanding, was a veteran in the state-wide arena, and a successful one at that. In addition, he had friends in each of the 254 county courthouses, and virtually all the banks, in Texas. He would be no pushover.

Lane Denton, the second name on the Democratic ballot, was of even greater concern to the Richards forces. Denton, like Ann, was a Waco native. He had been elected to the Texas legislature and had compiled a solid reputation there. He styled himself as a progressive, and his voting pattern on the floor of the Texas House bore him out. He was an advocate of most of the causes involving organized labor and appeared sympathetic to the legislative advocacy of women's rights. Like Richards, Denton was in the race because he felt that Warren Harding was prime for the quick kill. "Of all the state officials," he had said, "the one who absolutely cannot afford a loss of public confidence is the state treasurer."

Ann and her growing Old Girl network were convinced that a woman's chances of winning state-wide were enhanced by the women's movement. Neither Ann nor Jane, however, could clearly predict how Texans as a whole might respond to a female candidate. With that unknown to contend with, Denton posed a further, discomforting problem. An examination of his platform and political philosophy could lead voters to conclude that he was Ann Richards in male attire, which made it even more difficult to guess how a female candidate might fare when a similar male was available. Texas law dictated that a primary be won by a majority of the votes cast. If no candidate received a majority, a runoff election was mandated. With one candidate facing felony indictments and the other two philosophically nearly identical, the gender issue could influence enough votes to throw the election into a runoff, with the third-place finisher locked out.

The gender issue was doubly important because Texas was clearly in a state of political transition. Governor Bill Clements, Texas's first Republican governor since Reconstruction, had defeated Texas attorney general John Hill in a resounding upset in 1978. Clements, a man with a perpetual snarl, was not a person of overwhelming charm. His old-money, conservative sympathies had spoken to the wallets, not the hearts, of the voters. Thus, Ann and Jane had to consider that anyone, and especially a woman, seeking a state-wide office might be better positioned to win if she fostered a conservative, "run the government like a business," no-frills approach.

The primary would take place on May 1, only three short months away. Time was short. The campaign Ann and her staff put together would have to be vastly different from when she ran for the Travis County Commissioners' Court. Then, it could safely be said that she stood on the front steps and rang the doorbells of the majority of the thirteen-thousand-plus residents in her precinct who voted for her. That would be impossible in a state-wide campaign. The grassroots, blanket-the-precinct approach that worked in Travis County simply would not work across a state that was larger than many countries and demographically more diverse than most.

The field for the treasurer's race was intact, and Ann's campaign was taking shape. Early on, they decided Ann would tour as much of the state as possible. Her son Dan, twenty-two years old, agreed to be her traveling companion and serve as her administrative assistant on the road. Her daughter Cecile took a leave of absence from her job in New Orleans to join the campaign as a roving ambassador. At age twenty-four, Cecile was a veteran campaigner. She stayed in the homes of Ann's friends in the Old Girl network in order to save money. She appeared on every radio and television station that would give her airtime, and in one town, unnamed by Ann in her autobiography, garnered a newspaper editorial endorsement.

As the Old Girl network shifted into gear, volunteers from across the state flocked to the cause, to set up and work phone banks, print and distribute flyers and yard signs, all the "little" things that Ann knew made the difference between winning and losing. With part of the first $200,000, they bought mailing lists by the dozen and sent the volunteers out to raise more money. Lists of banks and bankers were compiled; eventually, Ann would visit many of them in person. Newspapers, television, and radio stations received individual attention, with Ann herself calling on them to tell them how she planned to modernize the treasury, to ask their opinions, and to seek their endorsement.

As the campaign got under way, Ann busied herself learning

exactly what the treasury did and what the treasurer's responsibilities were. The treasury was, in effect, a bank. It accepted deposits for taxes and fees, and paid the state's bills. Unused monies were kept in checking and savings accounts spread around to give virtually every bank in the state a piece of the state's fiscal pie. In 1982, some $40 billion to $50 billion passed through the treasury, neatly itemized in a 160-page fine-print annual report issued by the office of the Texas Comptroller of Public Accounts.

The treasurer's responsibilities, on the surface, appeared simple enough. The treasurer oversaw some one hundred employees in the treasury building in Austin. A politician's touch was required for dealing with the state's bankers, mostly all hidebound conservatives, but the job was mainly one of management, both of money and people.

Harding, Ann's sources told her, was managing both badly. His employees were unhappy and unproductive, and he was accused, behind doors, of sexual harassment of employees. More open to public scrutiny, his campaign boast that he had taken the management of such funds out of "the horse-and-buggy era" was demonstrably an exaggeration. In fact, it often took days for state money to be deposited in a bank. Worse, some fourteen hundred banks across the state each held state money on which they were paying no interest.

Ann and her staff anticipated that Harding would dismiss these charges as simple solutions from an outsider who just didn't know how things worked, and attack her from the trite angle of being "a woman who didn't know how to balance her checkbook." If that was his plan, however, he never had a chance to implement it. On February 27, the *Austin American-Statesman* reported that formal indictments were "on their way." That same day, John Cutright, whom Ann and her staff had dismissed as being of little substance, brought the sexual harassment allegations into the light of day in a press conference.

Finally the other shoe dropped, and Harding's direst (and Richards's and Denton's fondest) expectations materialized when, on Tuesday, March 23, 1982, two third-degree felony charges were filed against him for using two separate state employees in his reelection campaign. No charges had resulted from the allegations that he had sought favored treatment from bankers for his son, or that he had accepted campaign contributions from bankers, or that he had not taken bids on interest rates. He had avoided the most serious charges. Neither had he been subjected to the ignominy of being booked and jailed, for however brief a time. Nonetheless, the felony filings placed him even more on the defensive, in the eyes of the public, for the remaining five weeks of the campaign.

Harding was not, however, on the defensive with a second and equally important constituency, the state's bankers. To reach and win this constituency's support, Ann had to step beyond the established perimeters of the Good Old Girl network and the cozy parochialism of county-level politics. She had to meet and favorably impress the power brokers in Texas banking circles, many of whom, according to an *Austin American-Statesman* story in late March, had earlier made one-thousand-dollar contributions to Harding's campaign.

This campaign within a campaign was waged largely backstage, out of the public eye. Ann's bridge-playing friend and political ally in Austin, Robert Spellings, arranged a series of private receptions at which Ann would be introduced and make her pitch to a number of carefully selected heads of Texas banks. Spellings, in his post as chief deputy of then-state-comptroller Bob Bullock, knew most of the key players. The first of these sessions was scheduled in the most treacherous of political territories possible for Ann, the perfectly horizontal expanses of West Texas, where the people were as consistently conservative as the landscape was flat.

In 1982, the time-honored Texas mystique of oil and cattle still controlled the economic heartbeat of West Texas, where Ann met the heads of banking communities in cities like San Angelo, Midland, Odessa, Amarillo, Lubbock, and finally Fort Worth, a city that prides itself as being "where the West begins." People who have spent their lives in these regions are inherently skeptical of change and new ideas, and the concept of a female running for the office of state treasurer amounted to a radically new idea in the minds of many.

Robert Spellings recalls that the atmosphere at some of the early get-acquainted sessions between Ann and the West Texas bankers was "thick" and lacked cordiality. "In fact, in a couple of cities, the mood was full of hostility," Spellings says. This was not necessarily due so much to the fact Ann Richards was a female as it was to the liberal reputation that preceded her. "These fellows all presumed that Ann was a card-carrying Communist," Spellings continued.

Ann quickly convinced them that a social liberal could be a fiscal conservative. "What they discovered, and discovered rather quickly, was that Ann was a pay-as-you-go fiscal conservative," Spellings says. "I guess it was a financially conservative approach that she probably inherited from her parents during the Depression." Her ease with the men and her straightforward technique as a communicator also impressed the no-nonsense prairie bankers.

"We were in Lubbock, and Ann had talked for about ten minutes," Spellings recalled, "and one of the genuine heavyweights out there, Joe Milam, who did *not* like the notion of Ann becoming treasurer at first, walked up to me as we were leaving and said, 'Well, I'm gonna support your girl,' and stuffed a check in my suit pocket. It pretty much went that way from city to city.

"Oh, sure, Warren Harding had been indicted and all, but Ann still couldn't have won the race, I don't think, if the mainstream of the state banking establishment had chosen to actively oppose her."

Ann and her staff had predicted that her alcoholism and broken marriage would eventually boil to the surface in a tough, three way contest. They were prepared to face those issues openly. When the attacks came, however, they were mounted in a form and fashion that they had not foreseen, because Denton, as Hickie expressed it, "decided to take the low road. He got down."

The vitriolic nature of Denton's attack caught the Richards group off guard. "We looked at Lane Denton as a capable candidate and a good legislator," recalls Mary Beth Rogers, "but for some reason, when the campaign for the treasurer's office finally got rolling, he went totally ballistic on us." Traveling from town to town, scheduling himself to arrive a day before Ann said she would, he painted the public and private life of Ann Richards as something straight out of *The Days of Wine and Roses*.

Ann Richards, according to Lane Denton, was not only a drunk but a mean one at that. She had been known, he charged, to bat her children around. Her treatment program, he contended, was a colossal smoke screen. He alleged that Ann had a mental disorder and was drinking now as heavily as before. Furthermore, he cited her high absentee rate from county commissioners' court meetings and charged that her tenure on the court had been rendered ineffective by her drinking.

Ann was stunned by the brutal nature of Denton's attack, not only because she had considered him a friend, but also out of concern for her parents and her children. Nobody was more appalled by Denton's tactics than Dan Richards. He said to Austin reporter Roberta Starr, "Mom told us, 'You know, it really knocks you out that we could lose this thing over this.' She had *quit* drinking. And who can fault you on that? It's ironic that doing the right thing screws you around. I'd never seen Mom scared before."

She did not stay scared for long. It was true that Ann had missed more sessions than the other commissioners, and Denton would have been justified in suggesting that she had used her post as county commissioner as a staging area for broader ambitions. Placing the blame on alcohol, however, even before her stay at St. Mary's Hospital, was a mistake that Ann turned to her advantage. Not only was she proud of where she had been and what she had been doing during all those absences—Denton, after all, had not served on a White House committee—but she was an eloquent speaker on alcoholism. Among other points she made, she told voters that "somehow public officials are supposed to be perfect. The public desperately hopes that they are perfect. But politicians are like every other human being out there. There's the good side and bad side. We were not anointed by God."

Ann maintained that approach on the podium, but ultimately her greatest strength was her ability to work a crowd, and to connect individually with those who had come to see and listen to her. Austin television newsman Neal Spelce, who served as her speech coach prior to the keynote address she delivered at the Democratic National Convention in Atlanta in 1988, defined the quality.

"Watch how most politicians operate as they work a crowd," Spelce said. "I don't care who it is, Ted Kennedy or Bill Clinton or any of them, and watch their eyes. They sort of glaze over, and while they're shaking hands with somebody, they're always looking ahead to the person they'll shake hands with next.

"Ann, on the other hand," Spelce continued, "approaches each person in an absolutely direct fashion, looks them directly in the eye and focuses 100 percent on the individual, whether friend or stranger. It's a technique that you can't teach and you can't coach. She comes by it instinctively, I guess, and it's tremendously ingenuous and effective."

The openness and individual focus that Spelce described proved to be a marvelously winning technique as Ann toured Texas in the springtime, gripping hands, air-kissing cheeks, and offering a personalized greeting to thousands of voters. The rapport she established with her audiences was real because she was real and genuinely liked them. Once having actually met her, voters were hard-pressed to identify her as the woman described by Lane Denton.

In Ann's favor, too, was the tendency of Texans to admire and respect the reformed alcoholic who with sheer determination successfully beats the problem. The person who gets knocked flat but won't stay down consistently wins high approval ratings in the Lone Star State. If Ann's staffers initially feared the damage Denton's attack could cause, they grew more confident as election day approached that their candidate had transformed the situation into a plus.

The 1982 primaries lacked colorful races at the top of the ballot (the Democratic governor's primary race between Attorney General Mark White and East Texas lumber magnate Buddy Temple Jr. was hardly inciting riots in the streets), and a light state-wide turnout was predicted for the May 1 vote. As usual in Texas politics, bizarre events would begin to crop up in the final days before the vote. Most of the headlines were devoted to Reagan Brown, the incumbent candidate for state agriculture commissioner.

On Tuesday before the Saturday vote, Reagan addressed a group of vocational agriculture teachers in the East Texas city of Palestine. As the teachers looked and listened in astonishment, Brown referred to Booker T. Washington as "that great black nigger...er...I mean...great black educator." A TV news camera recorded the event for posterity. A spokesman for Brown's campaign, Rick Henderson, explained that his candidate's slip of the tongue was due to "too much campaigning, or perhaps the effects of food poisoning."

Everybody on the ballot could sympathize with the aspect of dangerous side effects derived from "too much campaigning" at this point. Everyone, perhaps, except Ann Richards. After rebounding from the Denton attacks and easily weathering the aftershocks, she decided that the demands of campaigning on a state level had proved, on the whole, a stimulating rather than daunting experience.

The early returns justified her high spirits. While the evening was still young, she was clearly in the lead, with Harding well back and Lane Denton a distant third. When the votes from all 254 counties were tallied, the results showed that Ann Richards had gathered over 466,000 votes, as compared to 362,000 for Harding and only 139,000 for Lane Denton.

Denton's tally proved large enough to force a runoff, but the results were foregone. "We did very, very well," Ann told her campaign workers and the press on election night. "The indictment [of Harding] helped. But it made a difference that I am a woman and the electorate is ready for a woman in state-wide office." Within two days, however, Warren G. Harding decided that it was futile to continue in the face of his legal problems. Before the runoff campaign could start, he contacted Ann Richards and informed her that an election would not be necessary. He was conceding.

The Republican candidate, Millard Neptune, had run unopposed in the primary but was judged so lackluster that he was induced by the Republican powers-that-be to resign. He was replaced on the ballot by West Point graduate and ex–Green Beret veteran Allen Clark. Republicans felt that Clark, who had lost both legs in Vietnam, would make a stronger candidate against Richards in the general election (the move triggered a rewriting of Texas campaign law to make the summary removal from the ballot of an elected nominee illegal). The change, however, made little difference. Allen Clark's campaign consisted of little more than ceremonies at which he placed wreaths on the graves of Vietnam casualties while his wife walked behind his wheelchair playing a tape of "The Ballad of the Green Berets." His candidacy and campaign proved to be no serious threat for Ann.

In November, Richards was swept into office by a huge margin. She gathered 1,433,000 votes to Clark's 899,000, and Texas, for the first time in fifty years, had a elected a woman to state-wide office. Ann and her staff, all the women who had worked so hard for her, were euphoric. The results for Ann Richards, though, were doubly significant.

"I don't think I could have made the race without going through that [alcohol] treatment," she would say. "It wasn't like going somewhere and not drinking. You go through all the periods in your life in that thirty days. It's pretty dramatic. You spend all that time assessing what really matters. The feelings you have from that are entirely positive, because you have met yourself and accepted yourself. Few people have that chance. It's a tremendous luxury...a rebirth."

CHAPTER 16

STATE TREASURER

At high noon on New Year's Day, 1983, several hundred onlookers gathered on the steps of the state capitol building in Austin. Most huddled beneath of a forest of umbrellas protecting them from a cold, foggy drizzle. All had come to watch the top figures in the new administration take their oaths of office. The short, prestigious list included a woman's name for the first time in fifty years. Alone among the men, Ann Richards was sworn in as state treasurer by Jack Pope, chief justice of the Texas Supreme Court.

David Richards stood in the crowd near the capitol steps. He was there not only to see Ann sworn in but also to watch his new boss, Jim Mattox, take the oath as attorney general of Texas. David had been hired by Mattox to "run the office for him." His job consisted of overseeing the work of some two hundred lawyers employed by the attorney general around the state. A close, longtime friend of the Richardses, Mattox espoused a political philosophy as liberal as theirs. Eight years later, he would emerge as Ann's mortal political enemy.

The adage that "politics is fun; government is hard work" was about to become a reality for Ann. She had promised the bankers and the electorate that she would implement productive reforms in the treasury if she was elected. The time had come to deliver.

The treasury offered little room for the headline-grabbing posturing associated with most elective posts. The treasurer was a manager, first and last. "There's nothing cutesy about this job. It's just a big bank," Ann told an Austin reporter.

Weeks before she took office, she began to assemble her staff.

The question, "Is there a different or better way of doing this?" had become an Ann Richards trademark. To answer it, she began by conducting what one former employee of the treasurer's office termed as "a giant talent search. She was not a financier, so she went out and interviewed and then hired as many men and women as she could from the world of finance who knew things that she didn't. Ann's never been threatened by those kinds of people."

She named Mary Beth Rogers her Chief Deputy Treasurer. She tapped Paul Williams to be her chief aide. Williams, only twenty-five years old, had been a CPA for one of the Big Eight accounting firms. He had been a controller of a $30 million bank and had audited two of the big Dallas banks. Ann, Mary Beth, and Williams searched for and recruited young people early enough in their careers to work for the notoriously low wages the government paid. Mike Arias, a whiz kid from an Austin bank, was recruited to "help get things set up." Mary Pilney, who worked for Arthur Anderson Accounting, was hired to overhaul the computer system. Jorge Gutierrez, a bright young lawyer from the Railroad Commission, would head the legal department of the treasury.

The treasury employed approximately one hundred people at the main Austin office. Some had been there for thirty-five to forty years and so distrusted computer reports that they added up and checked the figures by hand. A few were asked to leave; most retired voluntarily. In their stead, the brightest of the young employees were promoted and given new responsibilities and a chance to "broaden and grow."

The treasury had long been geared to operate at a pace more suited to the days when bookkeepers wore eyeshades and sleeve garters. When the new team took possession of the premises, they discovered systems and procedures reminiscent of the 1950s. Checks were processed by hand, and payments for taxes and fees often languished for days before being deposited in interest-bearing accounts. Some two thousand banks around the state held non-interest-bearing accounts of up to $5,000. Even office hours mitigated against efficiency: The doors opened at 7:50 A.M. and were locked at 4:50 P.M. Monday through Friday. On days when sales taxes or franchise taxes were due, the receipts that inundated the system stacked up and often waited to be processed until the next week. The inflexible schedule caused estimated interest losses of up to $4 million a day!

The first order of business was to modernize and streamline the system. All those $5,000 accounts—a total of some $10 million— were restyled to bear interest. Banks holding state monies were paying interest at a negotiated rate that was lower than market rate. That policy was changed, with an immediate increase in interest income for the state. The legislature granted emergency funds that allowed the treasury to purchase check-processing technology, like automated encoders and reader-sorter equipment that the banks had had on line for a decade. Ann later declared that the purchase paid for itself within weeks in increased interest income.

The changes continued at a rapid pace. Office morale was abysmally low. The portraits of dour, frowning former treasurers dating back to the Civil War were removed from the walls. "All of those guys were dead and their photos were black and white, expect for Warren Harding, who had a color photo," says Paul Williams. "I wanted to leave Harding's on the wall, just to see if the photo would turn black and white when he died." The walls were repainted, and decorated with works of art borrowed from state archives. Individuals were allowed to decorate their work spaces as they liked, and there was even a monthly contest for the best office door decoration.

According to a Dallas-area bank executive who describes himself as a thirty-year veteran of the industry, "Ann Richards, in her first year as treasurer, received high marks from the state business community and the banking community for the element of professionalism and efficiency that she brought into the office. She modernized it and automated some things that needed automating," the banker went on. "But what she also did was bring about some dramatic changes in the way that things had been for decades that, at first, kind of made some bankers mad.

"Here's the way it works. It's simple really. It is the job of the state treasurer in Texas to bank and invest all this money that the state brings in via taxes, and earn $100 million or $200 million in interest that becomes state money that the taxpayers don't have to pay. The way it had been done for years, throughout the tenure of Treasurer Jesse James and on back before him, would be to set an interest rate that was attractive to the banker, and the banker would often stay, or attempt to stay, on good terms with the treasurer in hopes of getting more than his share of these state deposits.

"Some cozy arrangements came about because of this policy. The state treasurer's job has attracted some colorful characters in the past," says the banker, "and in the modern climate, the way prosecutors and journalists go about their jobs, some of those old-time treasurers probably would be charged with a crime."

There were no "cozy arrangements" in the new regime. Paul Williams, her chief of staff, explained, "When Ann got there, the only thing the treasurer could put dollars into was bank certificates of deposit. Starting with the 1983 and during every succeeding legislative session, we broadened the investment authority of the agency to include, principally, all forms of United States government securities."

As a result, many smaller banks were upset with Ann because they suddenly lost a source of cheap funds. Those banks' irritation, however, was more than offset by the approval of the business community, which applauded the tactics that earned millions of dollars for the state. Also, Ann and the treasury won the respect of the large banks because, according to Paul Williams, "all we did was ask them to treat us like any other major customer." The large banks also appreciated the changes because, with modernization, the treasury sought them out to provide new services.

One such new service was the treasury's use of lockboxes. Williams explains they were employed when an agency received daily payments, such as for automobile license renewals. Under the old system, receipts were held for up to a week, then mailed to a regional field office, then to the Austin office, and finally to the treasury. With the new system in place, the agency deposited money each day at the bank closest to its field office. Then, "our main bank would sweep those accounts on a daily basis and bring that revenue directly into Austin," where it started earning interest that night. The fees the state paid the banks for handling the money was more than offset by the increased interest revenues to the state.

The benefits accrued to the state by the changes Ann and her staff effected at the treasury were not limited to the more than $1 billion in new interest income. The treasury became increasingly aggressive in attaching unclaimed, abandoned property that the state claimed after an appropriate waiting period during which no owner could be found. New computers increased record-keeping abilities and accountability. Dear to Ann's heart was her campaign promise to hire women and minorities in numbers proportional to the state's population. When Ann entered office, the staff was 65 percent male and 35 percent female. Six years later, those numbers were reversed. Of the total, 14 percent were African-American, 27 percent were Hispanic.

Later, in a speech to the state convention of the Texas Democratic party, Ann was able to crow, speaking of the treasury, "We got rid of the deadwood, we used new technology, and helped people excel at their jobs. And as a result, we earned two billion dollars for the taxpayers. Eight years ago it was quill pens and green eyeshades. Now the Texas Sate Treasury is a model for the nation."

During Ann's first campaign for county commissioner, she had noticed that constituents were disgruntled because her opponent, Johnny Voudouris, rarely returned phone calls. She won that race, in part, because Voudouris had not convinced his constituency that he was *their* commissioner. He had not kept his political roads and bridges in good repair, and the lesson was not lost on Ann. The office of the state treasurer was not a forever job. There was always another election, and elections are not won by shrinking violets. She was careful to keep the electorate informed. As Paul Williams said, Ann spoke "at every flea market in the state. She hit every Rotary, every Chamber of Commerce, every civic-type thing you could think of." The voters were well informed about her accomplishments, the changes she had promised and had effected.

Other changes were of a more private nature. Nine months after she took the oath of office, she turned fifty. For many, as the first half century passes, horizons appear to contract. Ann felt the opposite. Her job was challenging and stimulating. Her service was of value to the state—value that could be quantified in dollars earned and in occupations for women and minorities. As demanding as she found the job, she continued to travel and meet new people. Her world had widened enormously.

Another energizing change involved her freedom from alcohol. Friends who saw her occasionally, like Eve McArthur, who knew her from the Austin Center for Battered Women and from Another Raw Deal, said she seemed less contentious than when she was drinking. Robert Spellings, who had introduced her to the state's bankers, said she was "the same old Ann. Just as funny as ever." She had said she knew from the time she was at St. Mary's that she would never drink again, and she felt good about not drinking.

Troublesome, and simultaneously freeing, was the changed relationship with her children. Ellen, the youngest at twenty, was attending St. Edward's University in Austin. Clark was studying in Japan. Dan had his own apartment in Austin and was back in law school at the University of Texas. Cecile, the oldest at twenty-six, had returned to her job as a union organizer in New Orleans. After twenty-five years of being Supermom, there were no more car pools to drive, no PTAs to attend, no battles to fight with school boards.

The most disruptive change Ann had to deal with was the ending of her marriage. She and David were not yet legally divorced when she took office. They remained friends and confidants, but the marriage was essentially over. So much so that David later characterized the finalization of the divorce in February 1984 as "a formality and nothing more." In fact, he now says he does not remember the month or even the exact year.

Ann continued to live in the house on West Red Bud Trail, but it was too big and too empty. Shortly after New Year's, 1984, she began to look for a new home, and finally found, bought, and moved into one on Shoal Creek Boulevard near the end of the year.

—

Leading separate lives, David and Ann Richards occupied front row seats at one of the most turbulent events, other than the assassination of John Kennedy, to buffet Texas in the latter half of the twentieth century. The "New Texas" was a universal theme preached by politicians during the various campaigns of the early 1980s. Few dreamed that the new Texas would be a poorer Texas, or that the state's economy would be reduced to a shambles.

The troubles could be traced to 1973 and the oil embargo mounted by the newly formed Organization of Petroleum Exporting

Countries. Designed to raise the price of oil and increase OPEC income, the strategy had been successful. Too successful, as the years passed, for the high price of oil made production elsewhere profitable. By 1985, OPEC's receipts had dropped precipitously, and regimes were in political trouble. Thus it was, in midsummer of that year, Sheik Yamani, speaking on behalf of OPEC, announced that the price of oil should be determined by the dictates of a free and open market so that Saudi Arabia and OPEC could "maintain their market share."

At the time, the life support system of the Texas economy was directly connected to the stability of the price of oil. Within the span of approximately 120 days in late 1985, as Mideast oil flooded the market, that price plummeted from $48 to $11.25 a barrel. No natural disaster or act of God could have wreaked a more cataclysmic effect on the Lone Star State. In Dallas, Robert Allen "Monk" White, who is annually listed in *Town and Country* magazine as one of the top ten stockbrokers in the United States, described the scene this way: "The majority of wealthy Texans were already sort of overextended in real estate and other ventures. When the bottom fell out of the price of oil, it was like you're walking down the street naked and all of a sudden, the cops drive up."

With the entire structure of the Texas banking industry geared to income from energy-based loans, the financial aorta of the state's economy had been severed. The biggest names in Texas finance, in fact, were suddenly in jeopardy. Real estate markets, which had been riding a crest, began to crumble. The building boom of the late 1970s and early 1980s, which had glutted the market with unoccupied office space, turned into a bust. Unemployment in the building trades skyrocketed, and the men who had flocked to Texas from Michigan and other northern states packed their families and belongings and fled. Building cranes, which were jokingly called the official birds of cities like Dallas and Houston, were suddenly idled, then dismantled and relegated to storage yards where they were sold for pennies on the dollar or simply rusted into uselessness.

Banks were particularly affected. Two dominant cathedrals of finance in Dallas, the Republic Bank and InterFirst, were forced to form an emergency merger in an effort to avoid disaster. The new alliance failed and was absorbed by NationsBank after the Federal

Deposit Insurance Corporation stepped in with emergency funds. The massive, Dallas-based M-Bank failed. Texas Commerce merged with Chemical Bank of New York to survive. The Houston-based Allied Bank was absorbed by First Interstate of California. Within a twenty-month span, in some of the most dramatic events in the state's business history, nine of the ten biggest banks in Texas either failed or merged with out-of-state institutions.

The crisis would test the treasury, and the changes Ann had instituted, during the last year, 1986, of her first term. Says a career Texas banking executive, "Under previous administrations in the treasury, these sorts of unprecedented upheavals—the big bank failures—would have created serious complications in the state treasury, if not a crisis. But her operation was automated and flexible."

Two of the greatest changes Ann and her staff had introduced, automation and flexibility, staved off the crisis. Automation kept the system running and made monies available when they were needed. As for flexibility, Paul Williams explained, "By the time the banking industry started coming apart, we had a well-diversified portfolio away from solely being in bank deposits. Just a prudent practice of giving ourselves broader investment horizons to work with. None of this was done in anticipation of the bank collapses."

The banking executive agreed with that assessment, and added, "If [Ann Richards] had made any sweetheart deals with the high-powered Texas bankers of the time, those would have shot to the surface in a highly controversial manner when everything began to crater. The key to Ann Richards's entire tenure as the state treasurer is simply the absence of controversy."

Thanks to that record, Ann received no opposition on the ballot when her first four-year term elapsed in 1986. No Republican chose to run against her. The same could not be said for Democratic governor Mark White, who assumed his office at the same time Ann Richards became treasurer in 1982. With the economy in a shambles, White was defeated handily by the previous Republican governor, Bill Clements, by a vote of 1.8 million to 1.5 million. In fact, Ann, the first woman elected to a state office in Texas in fifty years, was one of the few Democrats on the ballot who retained her office in 1986. "The absence of controversy" was the key: In the minds of the voters, Ann had proved to be everything she had promised.

In the summer of 1988, a political animal known as the yellow-dog Democrat teetered precariously on the endangered species list. The term's apocryphal origins date to the turn of the last century, when Texas was the westernmost state in the old one-party Solid South. The term supposedly caught on when a politician in East Texas told a gathering that he would "vote for a yellow dog" before he voted for a Republican.

The disintegration of yellow-dog solidarity can be traced to the 1952 presidential election, when the Republican Dwight D. Eisenhower carried Texas in his defeat of the liberal Democrat Adlai Stevenson. It had continued when Texas went for Eisenhower a second time in 1956. John F. Kennedy carried the state in 1960, and Johnson prevailed in 1964. Texas swung back to the Republican camp for Richard M. Nixon in 1968 and 1972, but returned to the Democratic fold and Jimmy Carter in 1976. Ronald Reagan of course carried the state in back-to-back elections. Now, in 1988, the Democrats hoped to take Texas back and, in the process of thwarting George W. Bush's bid to assume President Ronald Reagan's mantle, throw the GOP into disarray nationally.

In the midst of these fond hopes, Ron Brown, National Democratic Chairman Paul Kirk's top aide, was dispatched to Houston for his party's state convention in late May. It was his job to rally the forces and leak the news that Texas's Democratic senator Lloyd Bentsen would probably appear on the ticket as Michael Dukakis's running mate.

Bentsen had never been a yellow-dog Democrat. When he unseated Ann and David Richards's political idol Ralph Yarborough in 1970, he did so with the decidedly right-wing tactic of attacking him as a foe of prayer in public schools. After eighteen years in office, however, Bentsen had drifted to the left. Far enough to the left, the party hoped, that the possibility of his being a vice presidential candidate would rekindle the flagging spirits of Texas Democrats and inspire them to raise enough funds to deny Bush.

As it turned out, Lloyd Bentsen was little help to Dukakis, and

George Bush carried Texas handily. But Brown's trip was not totally in vain. For State Treasurer Ann Richards was a featured speaker at the convention, and Brown, after listening to her for some ten minutes, became convinced that she could become a Democratic star on a national scale.

"Ann made a typical Ann Richards speech at the state convention in Houston," says her press secretary, Bill Cryer. "By that I mean it was a real barn burner."

She was at top form. The early lessons taught her by her father, Cecil, and molded by her debate coaches, Mattie Bess Coffield and Prof Capp, had been honed by literally thousands of speeches delivered during the past dozen years. Her carefully measured doses of humor mixed with give-'em-hell-Harry-Truman rhetoric brought the delegates to their feet. Brown was enthralled, and before he left Houston, he decided that he wanted Ann to deliver the keynote address at the Democratic National Convention in Atlanta that August.

"Traditionally, the keynote speaker at the national convention is selected from a reasonably high political echelon," Bill Cryer explained. "That would almost always be a congressman or governor. But a state treasurer? That was unheard of." Ron Brown let it be known that Ann was one of a trio on his keynote "short list." In late June, about seven weeks prior to the national convention, his view carried, and she was selected to become the second woman ever—the first had been Texas congresswoman Barbara Jordan, who was a friend of Ann's—to deliver a national political convention keynote address.

Suddenly, Ann Richards was a national celebrity. The Associated Press dispatch announcing the selection identified her as a "divorced mother of four" adding that she was "a mainstream Democrat and fiery populist from Texas, one of George Bush's adopted states." Upon learning the news, and being asked her reaction to the assignment, Ann answered that she had just that week completed "major addresses" to the Madisonville Cattleman's Association in rural Central Texas and the McAllen Mexican-American Democratic symposium in the Rio Grande Valley. "How do you get to Carnegie Hall?" she asked. "You just practice."

When Ann arrived in Atlanta four days before her heralded

appearance on national television, she was as prepared as ever, considering that she did not have any idea of what she was going to say.

Neal Spelce, an Austin television newsman, accompanied Ann to Atlanta as her speech coach. Four years earlier, Spelce was employed similarly for a spellbinding national convention address delivered by Mario Cuomo. "The national committee had a speech already prepared for Ann," Spelce said. "When I read that speech, I thought it should be included in some book of the greatest speeches ever presented. It rang out like the Gettysburg Address.

"There was only one problem. It was a great speech for anybody but Ann Richards. She had the same reaction. Ann read it and said, 'That's not me.' That was the consensus." Spelce said that her rejection of the script caused "understandable concern" among Democratic party officials, who were understandably keenly interested in discovering exactly what she *would* say.

A committee comprised of Ann, her Austin speechwriter Suzanne Coleman, and another professional supplied by the national party set about creating a new speech. "About every hour on the hour, Lily Tomlin, Ann's old friend and one of her gag writers, would also phone in suggestions," Spelce said. Jane Hickie, an early member of Ann's Good Old Girl network, served as unofficial chairperson of the speech committee.

"Jane supplies a kind clinical approach to things when the circumstances get pressurized. Her presence sort of ensured that everybody remained cool. Which is what happened," Spelce remembers. "Ordinarily, you'd think that writing a national keynote address against a deadline would be a pretty anxiety-provoking experience. But in politics, you know, it's really just something else that goes with the job. The atmosphere with Ann and the others wasn't what I'd call intense. Purposeful is more like it."

Spelce's job did not address the content of the speech but the delivery. "This was a new sort of experience for Ann, but my God. Look at the background and the training, going all the way to the debate days in high school," Spelce continued. "What we did was make her comfortable with the idea that she was approaching two separate audiences. One was the one sitting right there in front of her, thousands of people in funny hats. The convention is just under way, the delegates haven't had time to get burned out and their enthusiasm level is at a peak. They'll respond to anything that Ann says.

"On the other hand, there's that other audience. The millions out there, sitting in their underwear with their feet propped up on a coffee table and sipping a beer. These are the folks that you have to win over."

According to Spelce, the success of a speech in those circumstances is largely determined by techniques and technicalities. "You have to know which television camera is the one that you're on and you play to that camera. When you've delivered a key line, while the audience is cheering and applauding, most speech-makers stop and take a drink of water. With Ann, I thought it would be more effective not to do that, but locate the 'live' camera and continue to look straight into it."

Ann's speech, of course, was considered a raging success by conventioneers and television audience alike. Again and again, the crowd came to its feet and roared its approval. Less than a month shy of her fifty-fifth birthday, Ann was the new "star" of television and the Democratic party. In acknowledgment, Michael Dukakis shook her hand, and told reporters that "she took all my good lines."

The most successful and widely quoted line, "Poor George, he can't help it—he was born with a silver foot in his mouth," was clearly not one Dukakis could have carried off. "In all honesty, I'm not sure who gets credit for that line," Spelce says. "It's been broadly mentioned that it came from Lily Tomlin, but I don't think that's the case."

That single passage proved to be one of the few highlights in an otherwise lackluster presidential campaign. Spelce recalls, "Ann also used this other well-known line about women, about Ginger Rogers having to do everything that Fred Astaire did, but in high heels and backwards. Ann credits Linda Ellerbee with that one, but Linda told me that she heard one woman say that on a bus while having an argument with her husband." Whoever said it first, Ann Richards was the one who brought it to life, and that was what counted.

Ann Richards's memorable keynote address was, in truth, like the house that Jack built, an amalgamation of the creativity and ideas of an ensemble of contributors. Clearly, the address elevated a relatively obscure state official from Texas—George Bush would thenceforth refer to her as "that woman"—into the national spotlight.

Only one individual who saw the speech live would demur. Attorney General Jim Mattox sat in the Texas delegation with his arms folded. Mattox had fought hard for labor, for women, for minorities. He had secured his bona fides as a liberal Democrat, and was already raising funds for his anticipated run for the governorship in 1990, which he fully expected to win. And suddenly, his old friend Ann Richards had become a new, powerful, and dangerous opponent.

"For eight straight years," Ann said, "George Bush hasn't displayed the slightest interest in anything we care about. And now that he's after a job that he can't get appointed to, he's like Columbus discovering America—he's found child care, he's found education."

The audience loved her, loved that Texas drawl that dripped with sarcasm. Loved the smile, and the personality that seemed to speak to each person there.

"Poor George, he can't help it—he was born with a silver foot in his mouth."

The entire convention, electrified, rose to its feet and roared its approval. The Democratic party had fallen head over heels in love with Ann Richards.

"I think," she said, the emotion building as she neared the end, "of all the political fights I've fought and all the compromises I've had to accept as part payment. And I think of all the small victories that have added up to national triumphs. And all the things that never would have happened and all the people who would have been left behind if we had not reasoned and fought and won those battles together."

It hurt, because Mattox had fought those same fights, made his own compromises. He too had made things happen, had fought for the little guy who was always left behind. And he had often had to satisfy himself with small victories.

"And I will tell Lily [her granddaughter] that those triumphs were Democratic party triumphs."

A Democratic party, in Texas, that Ann was bidding for. And Jim Mattox could do nothing but sit, and scowl, and watch the star be born. Elna Christopher, Mattox's press secretary, sat next to Mattox during the speech. Four years later, reflecting back on that night, she wrote, "He was furious."

Nobody ever accused Jim Mattox of being a good sport. After the applause had finally subsided and Ann had relinquished the podium to the next speaker, Mattox told some of his fellow Texas delegates that "two weeks from now, people won't remember who made that speech."

Two years later, he would learn how wrong he was.

CHAPTER 17

THE GOVERNOR'S RACE: THE PRIMARY

Former Travis County sheriff Raymond Frank theorized that Ann Richards was running for governor the day she assumed her post as county commissioner. That is a popular assumption in the zoological garden known as Austin politics. But the notion that Ann's desire to seek the top elective post in Texas was etched in stone comes as news to the candidate herself.

"During Ann's second term as treasurer, she wondered what she might do for a living for the rest of her life," says her confidant and bridge partner, Robert Spellings. "Ann was actually perplexed as to how she was going to support herself. I told her she could land a seat on just about every major corporate board in America and make a fortune. She looked at me in amazement and then laughed and said, 'Hell, let's get some of 'em on the phone.' The thing is that Ann doesn't understand what a star she is."

However, "everyone around [her] pretty much figured that from the time she was elected treasurer that it was a foregone conclusion that she was destined to become governor," Spellings went on. And their dream came to fruition, oddly enough, because of the power of football in Texas politics.

The back-to-back tenures of Texas governors Mark White (1982–86) and Bill Clements (1986–90) were similar in one peculiar regard: both men were driven from office by football scandals. Mark White, elected in 1982, incurred the wrath of the potent Texas High School Coaches Association when he endorsed "no pass, no play" legislation that suspended for six weeks the eligibility of high school athletes who flunked a course. Political analysts pinpointed White's spat with the coaches, parents, and fans as one of the key reasons for his loss to Clements in 1986.

Then it was Clements's turn. Just one month after assuming office in January 1987, Clements casually and unwisely remarked during an interview with *The Dallas Morning News* that he and other members of the Board of Regents of Southern Methodist University in Dallas were fully aware of the fact that several Southern Methodist University football players had received regular payments from wealthy backers of the institution.

The story of Clements's admission caused a firestorm of adverse publicity that culminated with multiple resignations and the National Collegiate Athletic Association's cancellation of the Southern Methodist University football program for two years. And Governor Bill Clements, because of his amazing candor, had committed political hari-kari.

Texas attorney general Jim Mattox, himself a Southern Methodist University School of Law graduate, promptly perceived that the school's misfortune might serve as a political windfall. With Clements now badly crippled, Mattox sensed that a new front-runner was about to surface in the next governor's race, set for 1990, and he was determined to be that somebody.

Meanwhile, the opportunity had not gone unnoticed by Ann and her friends and advisers at the treasurer's office. "I can't say that there was ever a precise moment when a lightbulb went off in Ann Richards's head and that's when she decided to run for governor," Spellings said, "but everyone who was around Ann much pretty much figured that from the time she was elected treasurer that it was a foregone conclusion that she was destined to become governor.

"So when Clements became what amounted to a lame duck, the same sort of opening took place as when Warren Harding got indicted as treasurer," Spellings went on. This was not merely the wisdom of hindsight. Spellings knows his Texas politics. A former University of Texas track athlete, he had been the chief of staff of former Texas lieutenant governor Ben Barnes, who disappeared from politics after the Sharpstown financial scandal of the late 1960s. "Timing," Spellings pointed out, "is everything in politics, and once again, the timing seemed perfect."

Paul Williams, Ann Richards's key aide at the state treasury, remembers the times differently. "Early in 1987, after the Clements business, if Ann had any ideas of running for another state office, that would have been lieutenant governor," he said. Ann's close friend, William Hobby had held the post successfully since 1973, and insiders speculated that the popular Hobby would seek the governorship in 1990.

"If Bill Hobby did that, then it seemed natural that Ann would go after Hobby's job," Williams said. The role of lieutenant governor involved acting as president of the Texas Senate. Ann had proved to be a natural at dealing with the complexities of the state legislature. So moving into the lieutenant governor's post seemed like a reasonable progression.

Williams adds, "But in the spring of 1988, even before Ann made her keynote address in Atlanta, Bill Hobby formally announced that he wouldn't be running for governor or anything else. That sort of took Ann by surprise. Nobody really understood why Hobby finally decided to leave politics. My theory is that he just didn't want Jim Mattox yapping at his heels. In any event, some people who Ann trusted began to convince her that the governor's race was the one she needed to make."

Ann was receptive. In the spring of 1988, Ann commissioned the respected pollster Harrison Hickman to study the chances of a woman's winning a gubernatorial race in Texas. Shortly after the results were in, word that Ann would run started to circulate in Austin. Subsequently, on speaking engagements around the state in the latter months of 1988, Ann pointedly repeated the phrase "I think it's time for a woman in the governor's mansion, somebody who knows how to clean it up."

Mattox regarded Ann Richards as a threat well before she made a formal announcement to run in a ceremony on the south lawn of the capitol building on Saturday afternoon, June 10, 1989. Spellings says that "Jim Mattox called me, oh, it must have been back in the summer in 1988, and told me that I should somehow convince her not to run. Mattox wanted me to support him. I told him, 'Jim, you don't give up old friends for new friends. I'm just not going to do that,'" Spellings said.

"To that, [Mattox] responded by saying that there was no way that Ann could beat him, and I said, 'Jim, you're wrong. If she runs, she's going to win and there's nothing you can do to stop her.' The funny thing about all that was that Jim and Ann had known one another since they were practically kids, back in Dallas when Ann was active with the women Democrats and Jim was running for the legislature. And she and David Richards worked real hard backing him when he got elected to Congress back in 1978."

Spellings realized a battle between Jim Mattox and Ann Richards for the occupancy of the Austin residence at 1010 Colorado Avenue, the governor's mansion, would destroy any prior allegiances. David Richards, who remarried in 1985 and would later father two more children, was apprehensive about the nature of the campaign if his ex-wife entered the ring with his former boss. "Ann had been warned by some people about what she might be up against," David says. "Mattox has an innate knack for utilizing the media to promote whatever cause that he has in mind."

Mattox was artful in his ability to present himself to the public as an underdog. Residents of his congressional district were accustomed to receiving franked form letters from his office in Washington that read: "Dear Friend, Over the past few years, I've made some powerful political enemies because I've tried to represent working people, senior citizens and small business. The big special interests and ultra-right-wing political organizations will STOP AT NOTHING. Their tactics involve gross distortions of the truth." Nobody ever accused Jim Mattox of being the sort of politician who backed off from a good fight.

Ann Richards had enjoyed an acclaimed eight-year stint as state treasurer. The treasury had earned more money for the state than anyone had thought possible. Treasurer and treasury were clean, unsullied by rumors or controversy. Ann was popular on the lecture circuit, turning down many more invitations to speak than she could possibly accept.

Mattox, on the other hand, had stormed from one controversy to the next during his concurrent tenure as Texas's attorney general. The bigger the foe, the better, might have been his motto. In one early case, he "declared war" against Mobil Oil on behalf of a civil lawsuit filed by South Texas oilman Clinton Manges and encouraged Texans to boycott that company's products. Due to a series of complex side issues in the case, he was indicted by Ronnie Earle, the Travis County district attorney who had opened the door to the treasury for Ann with his criminal charges against Warren Harding. Mattox was charged with "commercial bribery" for threatening to drive one of the law firms that had defended Mobil out of the government bond business. The controversy occupied the front pages of Texas newspapers for a year and a half before he was acquitted. Vindicated, he attacked Quaker Oats for what he alleged was false advertising. "The consumers have been duped," he said after pointing out that he could find no evidence indicating that eating oatmeal prevented heart attacks.

His indictment on charges of commercial bribery was merely one of a sequence of episodes that propelled the name Mattox into the seventy-two-point type that introduced many front page news stories. At a victory celebration following his acquittal, he donned boxing gloves for the benefit of the cameras. He was having fun. Stocky and square-jawed, he presented himself as the sort of prizefighter who eschews fancy footwork and relies instead on body punches and elbows thrown in the clinches. Finesse never entered the picture. The basic strategy was to make the opponent appear awkward as well. While this is a time-honored technique in politics, few were as adept at it as he, as his bitterest foes would grudgingly concede.

When Jim Mattox went after an unlicensed Christian home for boys in Fort Worth in 1987, he found himself dragged into a different kind of court. This was "the Court of Divine Justice," so styled by an Indiana minister named Greg Dixon. "He is no friend of religious liberty," Dixon announced, "and I have asked God to remove Jim Mattox from office by whatever method, be it illness or death or whatever He pleases. May his children be childless and his wife a widow."

Mattox appeared to be delighted. "I happen to be a Southern Baptist and I pray myself," he responded. "I pray to God and ask Him to take care of me. So I guess we'll see which one the Lord listens to."

A number of people, usually in private, have accused Jim Mattox of being "possessed," by which they meant that he was willing to do whatever it took to get elected. No one has ever accused him of being a less aggressive attorney general than he had promised he would be, or of neglecting his office. Nonetheless, he had let it be known as far back as early 1987, when he began his second term as attorney general that he intended to run for governor, probably in 1990.

Mattox's "campaign" was low-key at first, but when late in the spring of 1988 rumors surfaced that Ann, too, might be interested in the governorship, Mattox became incensed. As far as he was concerned, he had paid his dues and *deserved* to be governor. Striking preemptively, he attacked before Ann made her final decision to run. In the early summer of 1988, headlines that read "Mattox Says He'd Trounce Richards" appeared. Ann responded with a published statement in which she predicted she would win if she ran. "A lot of people have said that, as a matter of fact, and the cemeteries are full of their bones," Mattox responded in turn. Then he hastily added, "Figuratively speaking, that is."

Mattox initially "declined to comment" on a report that Ann had referred to him, in a conversation with a Democratic party official after her delivery of the keynote address in Atlanta, as "unscrupulous." When told that the Democratic official agreed and added that he was also "crazy," and that Ann had reportedly said "Certifiable," Mattox commented anyway.

He crafted his words carefully. Ann Richards, he said, was "an articulate friend of mine" who might have made negative comments about him "at a time when she was under a lot of pressure, a lot of exhilaration. It kind of reminds me of going to a Baptist revival. You know, you're on the mountaintop and you say and do a lot of things you might not do when you get back to the valley. And [after the keynote speech] she was on that mountaintop. Sooner or later you've got to come back to the valley and when you come back to the valley, you often reflect on what you've done and said. And sometimes you act in a little different way."

However temperate he sounded, Mattox was stung. Retaliating, he attacked Ann's record of efficiency at the treasury and announced that he enjoyed the support of over one hundred county treasurers from around the state. "I'm really pleased to have the treasurers on my team," he said. "We're suited up and ready to run onto the field."

Ann declined to become embroiled in too many skirmishes until her campaign funds were in place. By August 1989, after the formal announcement of her candidacy on June 10, the money-raising effort had shifted into overdrive. At a $125-per-ticket fund-raising staged at the Fairmont Hotel in Dallas, Ann and her old pals Liz Carpenter and comedienne Lily Tomlin put on a three-woman show. Any one of them could have held an audience spellbound; the three together reportedly left the audience gasping for breath and holding their sides with laughter.

One of the routines involved Ann Richards in the role of a fortune-teller. "I have seen the future," she told the audience, "and it looks gubernatorial to me." At that same gathering, Ann cited political gains of females around the country and proclaimed that "it proves once again that the rooster crows, but the hen delivers."

With the filing deadline on December 31, 1989, Jim Mattox officially announced his candidacy that October. He wasted little time establishing the tone of his campaign. Promoting himself as "the people's lawyer," he told a rally, "I just don't know if I can control my Baptist preacher friends any longer from attacking Ann about her drinking." Clearly, Mattox was taking off the gloves and getting personal. "I have many clients and many friends who have been on the wagon and then fallen off. The statistics would show that a relapse occurs in a high percentage of the cases."

In November 1985, Mattox had won a Texas Women's Political Caucus "Good Guy Award," to which he had responded, "I'm glad somebody thinks I'm a good guy." Opinions changed rapidly when he launched an attack on the Alcoholics Anonymous one-day-at-a-time approach that constituted the core of Ann's recovery program. A true political leader, Mattox implied, could not effectively employ such an approach to life and at the same time deal with the complexities of public office, particularly one with as many far-flung responsibilities as the office of governor in a state like Texas. "One day at a time," Mattox said, could "prevent vision" and as such was "harmful."

Lane Denton had savaged Ann and her history of alcoholism during the treasurer's race, and she and her team anticipated no less from Mattox. This time, however, she and her parents and children knew what to expect. At least they thought they did. For with the dawning of the new decade and with the Democratic primary less than three months away, Mattox began sharpening his attacks on Ann. Eventually, those three months would qualify as three of the longest in Ann's life.

There were lighter moments. In December, Mattox produced a private poll that indicated his early 59 percent to 40 percent lead over Ann was growing by the day. Monte Williams, a Richards aide, countered with a "private newspaper poll" showing that 56 percent of Americans believed that Elvis Presley was still alive. "That's our response to Jim Mattox and his poll," Williams said.

———

After the filing date, December 31, 1989, the field for the Democratic race for governor was finally established. As usual, several who had no chance of winning entered to make a point. One who did have a chance was former governor Mark White, who had been unseated by Bill Clements in 1986. No one had expected White to enter the race, and his announcement in December 1989, was unexpected. With the Richards and Mattox forces in opposition primarily to each other, he could hope his two stronger opponents would so harm each other that he could back into a runoff, pick up the losers' votes, and become the Democratic nominee.

During the four years that White had served as governor, he was consistently characterized by the press as "bland." He was not, like Ann, capable of electrifying an audience. Nor was he, like Mattox, given to the partisan polemics that brought opponents' blood to a boil. Now, in 1990, campaigning in "the New Texas," a popular phrase used by candidates of both parties, the nondescript Mark White of 1982–86 reprogrammed himself as a harder character. In the commercials produced by his campaign, he paraded in front of life-sized black-and-white portraits of the eight inmates who were executed at the Texas state penitentiary in Huntsville during his term as governor. He then faced the camera and intoned, "These hardened criminals will never again murder, rape, or do drugs. As governor, I made sure they received the ultimate punishment— *death.*"

Ed Bark, an electronic media critic for *The Dallas Morning News* who specializes in politics, said that the commercial "had all of the subtlety of a tractor pull. But the spot did pass one litmus test at our house. It got our attention."

The commercial also started a macabre contest in which Ann and Mattox felt themselves forced to prove that they, too, were tough on the death penalty. No one was a clear winner, but the spectacle prompted *Saturday Night Live* to lampoon them with a comedian portraying a stereotypical Texas sheriff and an announcer in the background intoning, "Don't stop him before he kills again."

With no presidential race to steal the network media stage, the campaign for governor attracted national attention. Intrigued network news personnel insinuated that the storied Texas myth of "frontier justice" was no myth after all. And Ann and her campaign staff began to fret that her candidacy was being dragged into a morass in which the least common denominator prevailed. The "dignified" campaign they had hoped to run was rapidly becoming a mean-spirited carnival.

The Ann Richards for Governor organizational effort had been structured as a multifaceted operation. Glenn Smith, a former political writer for the *Houston Chronicle* and the *Houston Post* before he worked with then-lieutenant-governor William Hobby, was hired as Ann's campaign manager. A Washington election campaign consultant group run by Robert Squier, who was hugely impressed by the skills of the candidate, had been retained. Mary Beth Rogers, not officially on staff, was available for consultation and advice. Kirk Adams, a union organizer who was married to Ann's daughter Cecile, was in charge of field organization across the state. Two of Ann's children, Dan and Cecile, were assigned to the phone banks and dedicated themselves to a grueling schedule that lasted from early morning to midnight, seven days a week. According to Mary Beth Rogers, Ann's children "worked like field hands. They never seemed to get tired." Jane Hickie, with her immense organizational skills, was once again on board. So was veteran political operative George Shipley, who was known in Austin as "Doctor Dirt." His investigative skills would be called into play later in the campaign.

The first of two live debates, with the candidates answering questions from a panel of journalists, took place in mid-February at a television studio in Houston. It was there that Richards's staff's plans called for her to take charge of the campaign. A former teacher, she would gain a march on Mattox and White by announcing her proposed educational reforms. To that end, she arrived at the station armed with a three-point program that called for incentives for independent public school districts that reduced dropout rates and employed innovative learning techniques; teacher pay raises and state-funded health care for teachers; and increased decision-making authority at the campus level.

As Ann had established with her keynote address in Atlanta, television was her milieu. In a setting that encouraged spontaneous verbal interchange, she and her staff calculated that her natural talents as a debater-communicator would give her the advantage needed to win the night.

Unfortunately, however, the initial debate quickly turned in a direction that was anything but advantageous. An early slip of the tongue, or perhaps only a slurred word, overshadowed Ann's efforts to pursue her chosen topics of education and the environment. Asked about the abortion issue, Ann intended to say that it was not the business of the courts or legislators to determine "whether or why a woman has an abortion." The phrase, however, was widely heard as "whether a white woman has an abortion."

Ann was stunned when she was told about the "slip," and insisted she had said "or why." Others who heard "a white" were equally insistent. According to those who have heard the tape, it did in fact sound as if the "a white" version was more nearly correct. Ann's supportive record on black issues, however, dated back so far, and she was so widely accepted in the black community, that the controversy faded without causing her irreparable damage. Nevertheless, the episode had a sobering effect and heightened her awareness of the pitfalls awaiting a speaker especially in an electronic forum, where a slip of the tongue or a slurred word could be replayed *ad infinitum*.

The controversy could well have been more damaging had not panelist Cinny Kennard asked Ann about reports that Jim Mattox had been circulating during the past month that she allegedly had used illegal drugs. Ann responded with an Alcoholics Anonymous, as opposed to a politically sophisticated, answer. She "hadn't used any mind-altering chemicals for ten years," she said, an answer that only fueled the media's curiosity. She handled the question so ineptly, some thought, that her campaign consultant George Shipley claims that more than one sympathetic lawyer called and offered to coach her on how to lie effectively.

Whether Ann had used drugs was a question that had simmered

from the beginning of the campaign. Kennard's question and Ann's answer opened floodgates of media coverage for the rest of the campaign. White, who had campaigned on the issue from the beginning, stepped up his attacks. Mattox, who has been variously described as a political "pit bulldog" and "the Jimmy Hoffa of Texas politics," intensified his attacks, too, and made drugs very nearly the central issue in his campaign against Ann. He spent approximately two million dollars running a pair of negative television commercials. One made unsubstantiated allegations that Ann had used cocaine. The second "amounted to a combination cocaine abuse and sleaze ad that essentially accused her of being a crook," according to Shipley. Incessantly, as he toured the state during the weeks that followed, he alleged that Ann's visit to St. Mary's in 1980 was for the purpose of overcoming an addiction to alcohol *and* cocaine. Ann denied the charges, which were completely unfounded, but she was clearly on the defensive. Worse, she appeared to be backpedaling.

Lyndon Baines Johnson once said that the one thing a modern political candidate couldn't overcome was to "be caught in bed with a dead woman or a live man." In a conservative, law-and-order state, the charge that a candidate was a divorced grandmother *and* a user of illegal drugs was potentially very nearly as catastrophic.

If the allegations and rumors that flew around the state were not absolutely devastating, they were highly damaging. Early in the campaign, Ann's polls—Mattox's showed different results—showed her with 35 percent of the vote, with Mattox in the mid-twenties and White in the high teens. By late February, her numbers had slipped to 22 percent, barely ahead of Mark White's 18 percent.

"We were in a corner, we were in free fall," says George Shipley, Austin's Dr. Dirt. Suddenly, the game of "who gets in the runoff with Ann" had changed, and there was a real chance that she would be knocked out of the race. In Celia Morris' *Storming the Statehouse,* the author draws a gloomy portrait of the crisis days of February. Ann and her campaign team are depicted as being at one another's throats, and the mood of the candidate is portrayed as being dark, indeed. Tense and irritable, Ann reportedly chided some of her staff for earlier "complacent thinking" when the polls showed her with a clear edge over Mattox and White.

The drug issue was not the campaign's only headache. An article in *Tiempo,* an Hispanic newspaper published in Waco, alleged that during her campaign for the county commissioner in 1976, she had referred to undocumented workers as "wetbacks." Ann pointed to her long record of working for Hispanic candidates and of hiring Hispanics, and charged that Mattox had planted the story.

Ugly rumors of lesbianism surfaced after Mattox supposedly told several reporters to ask Ann about her and Lily Tomlin in a hot tub. (Mattox has insisted the story is untrue.) Lesbianism, Ann's campaign quietly pointed out, was an accusation of last resort by males who were threatened by strong females. Nonetheless, Ann was a proponent of gay rights, and her staff was largely comprised of women, some of whom were openly lesbian. The lesbianism issue became a shadow campaign waged with whispers and a spate of one-liners that made the rounds of bars and parties. However ludicrous the charge, there were those, including women, who chose to believe the rumors, and there is little doubt that votes were lost.

It was alleged that the headquarters of the Texas Council on Family Violence, a state-funded, tax-exempt agency in Austin, had been used for a day to promote a get-out-the-vote phone push for Ann. With the Internal Revenue Service reportedly mounting an investigation, the Council's director, Debby Tucker, wrote a personal check for $123 to the Council for one day's rent on the headquarters. The IRS was satisfied, and the issue dropped out of sight.

Though Ann was preoccupied with putting out these conflagrations, not everyone concurs with the notion that her outlook and demeanor became irremediably grim. "I'm not all that sure how depressed or angry Ann was at that point [late February] of the race," said Robert Spellings. "What might be perceived as a bad mood might have been something else. Ann gets kind of frustrated when people can't keep up with her. But during the whole campaign, we'd talk probably every other day and she seemed pretty much like the same old Ann. She'd call and tell the latest joke she'd heard, or whatever.

"The thing that was truly bothering her was a sense of disappointment in the way that Jim Mattox was running his campaign. What he did, I think, was cruel and unnecessary. Ann likes to believe the best in people. It didn't appear natural to her that this guy who had once been a friend would punch below the belt like that."

Other of Richards's oldest and closest friends remained confident that the Ann they knew and remembered would have the stomach to last out the fight and ultimately prevail. "I wasn't afraid for her," said Kay Coffelt, Ann's backyard neighbor from high school days in Waco. "It was just politics and Ann was a professional." Ann's old Dallas friend Betty McKool added that "Ann has a depth of inner strength that ultimately allows her to see her way through anything."

The second televised debate of the campaign was conducted on the campus of Richland College in Dallas on March 2, 1990. This time, Ann was prepared for questions about whether she had used drugs, and if so what drugs, when, and in what quantities. She was not prepared, however, for the onslaught that ensued.

Ann Richards and drugs had become a media obsession, to Jim Mattox's delight and good fortune. Seizing his chance to inflict even more damage before a state-wide audience, he looked directly at Ann and said, "Ann, you look awfully sober tonight. You look very good and I'll tell you one thing. If you're not off the wagon after what you've been through the last couple of weeks, then you're cured.

"But Ann, both Mark and I have known you too long and we can understand why you don't want to answer the question. The Republicans won't be as gentle, regardless of how much you think it'll hurt you to answer the question."

Ann gave Mattox a look that registered her utter disbelief, and at the same time appeared as if she were literally about to gag. After the formal debate, Richards found herself encircled by crowd of hostile journalists. Their shouts of "Answer! Yes or no! Did you or didn't you use illegal drugs?!" stunned her. Microphones were thrust into her face. In what appeared to be nearly a state of shock, she stiffened and withdrew into a protective shell of silence as the bombardment continued, and finally escaped without further comment. The episode was one of the ugliest in contemporary Texas politics, and the writer Molly Ivins said she never saw Ann enjoy a day of the campaign after it. To this day, her friends shudder when they recall the ferocity of the media feeding frenzy that night, and marvel at her ability to take so much abuse and continue.

"Actually, we'd argued, or least discussed, how to handle this," Robert Spellings said. "I thought Ann ought to say 'yes' or 'no,' but her approach, in the long run, turned out to be the correct one. She said, 'Look, I've taken my stand on the drinking issue. All this business is behind me now and has absolutely nothing to do with the job that I'm running for. So I'm not gonna talk about it.' And, as I say, that turned out to be the correct approach."

Afterward, Ann told her staff, "You'll have to give us this. We're more exciting than the Republicans."

The question remained. Had Ann Richards used drugs? Mattox's allegations that she had were never substantiated. Molly Ivins observed that "anyone in our generation who hadn't smoked dope was such a twerpy goody-two-shoes we wouldn't want them leading the country anyway." Still, no one produced a smoking gun, and Ann's friends to this day will not discuss whether she did or didn't. In any case, the only people who *really* wanted to know seemed to be Ann's opponents and the press. The electorate at large seemed to consider the whole drug issue a nonissue.

The day after the debate, with only nine days to go before the March 13 primary vote, nobody within the Richards camp claimed to have a firm feel for how the election would go. Richard Murray, one of the most respected and highly quoted Texas political analysts, succinctly summed up Ann's situation as the campaign neared its final week. "She just sort of sat on her lead and now she's in a controversy over this drug question that she and her aides find difficult to face."

George Shipley prides himself on being an acute observer of the psychology of candidates and the anatomy of campaigns. It was obvious to him that Ann's campaign was in crisis and about to founder. Actually, he had seen trouble coming from the beginning.

"The reality," he said, "is these races are defined by the players, and Mattox is a thug. Any time you get in the ring with these fuckers, you're going to have to get your switchblade out, because that's the only way you can take them. When you get into a gang fight, that's no time to pull out the Bible."

Shipley had a more jaundiced view of the campaign than Ann and her staff, who had never been in a race as vicious as this one. The consummate professional, he had prepared for the worst. When Ann had announced for governor back on June 10, 1989, he had had her release her back income tax returns. Mattox, he knew, would not do the same, because, among other reasons, they would reveal sizeable campaign gifts from embarrassing sources like Danny Faulkner, a Dallas developer whose land deals were tied to a savings and loan failure. Now, with only nine days to go before the March 13 vote, he pulled the switchblade he had been preparing since the first debate in February.

Mattox had "gone after her with the force of a Soviet armored division," Shipley said. Mattox was also the stronger and less vulnerable of her two main opponents. So with an eye to preserving Ann's spot in the runoffs, they attacked the weaker White. If, they reasoned, White was eliminated, they could then use some of the same issues to drag more skeletons out of Mattox's closet and focus on them in the runoff.

"What we did was, we used White as a battering ram to get Mattox," Shipley said, putting it bluntly. And it was almost too easy. Mark White's salary in his last year as governor, 1986, was $56,000, and he had made $800,000 as a lawyer in 1987. Shipley saw to it that the media "found" a copy of the mortgage on a $1 million house White purchased in Houston that year for no down payment. The lender was a White appointee for the Rice University Board of Regents. In addition to the $1 million house, White had bought a Mercedes-Benz and a BMW for a total of another $100,000. The house and car purchases were documented from public records.

There was more, and it would prove damning. A story was leaked to *The Dallas Morning News* that White's old law firm of Reynolds, Allen and Cook had represented firms that underwrote a disproportionate amount of state bond business during White's tenure as governor. The inference was that if an underwriter's counsel was Reynolds, Allen and Cook, he could usually get a bond deal, and that "White's guys were putting the fix in to take care of Mark White."

The story broke in *The Dallas Morning News* on the morning of May 5th, eight days before the primary. It began, "Officials of bond firms that did millions of dollars in state business with agencies run by Mark White appointees contributed $200,000 to his 1986 [losing] campaign [for reelection]."

On the same morning, Ann held a heavily attended press conference at her campaign headquarters and attacked White and

Mattox. She was standing up against two of the Old Boys, she said, verbalizing the general impression of many women that Mattox and White were using her as an easy target because she was a woman. She was no "shy violet," she reiterated, and was not ready to "roll over and play dead."

White was stunned by Ann's attack and the revelations in the *Morning News* story. Before he had time to issue the standard denials, Ann's campaign blanketed the state with two television commercials. Over a video incorporating pigs feeding at a trough, the commercials said, in part, "Any time anybody gives me a dollar, I feel influenced. Danny Faulkner [the Dallas developer] gave Jim Mattox $200,000. That's a lot of influence, Jim." "Mark White—million-dollar mortgage. Mark White—$4 billion bond deal." And painting both Mattox and White with the same brush, "They line their pockets with taxpayers' money."

"In these kinds of rock-and-roll campaigns," Shipley mused, "the game becomes transformed from a set piece of Kabuki theater into a rugby match." White might well have thought he had walked into a scrum. Reeling from the commercials, he held a press conference in which he "revealed" his tax returns, but only the first page of one 1040 form. With cameras rolling, the reporters pounced. "Governor White, this is only a partial release of your taxes. Why weren't you honest here? How did you get your $1 million home mortgage?" Other questions came hard and fast.

According to Shipley, "White sort of went bug-eyed on camera" and failed to respond. The whole incident was broadcast by WFAA, Dallas Channel 8, and sent via satellite to affiliates around the state. Shipley went on, "[The incident] was seen by six million people. That exploded the race and cost White whatever legitimacy he had as a candidate."

White had been underfunded from the beginning. Now, as the primary neared, he had neither the time nor the money to counterattack. Furious, he could do no more than stand by and watch his chances fade. "If she was a man," the ex-governor said, "I believe we'd be in a fight." And later added, "This is the worst campaign I have ever seen. It stinks."

Mattox professed to be appalled. At a rally in Longview, in East Texas, he told the crowd that Ann's behavior had been so reprehensible that she had disqualified herself in the race.

Dave McNeely is a political columnist for the *Austin American-Statesman*. He later said he wrote a column "saying the ads were bullshit" and that the alleged charges against White were unsubstantiated.

George Christian, President Lyndon Johnson's onetime press secretary, seemed faintly disgusted by the whole affair, but included all three candidates in his indictment. "Scratch them deep enough," he said, "and they're all alike."

A political analyst from Pan American University in the Rio Grande Valley, Jerry Polinard, agreed with Mark White that Richards's late assault had been brutal. "It was vicious and out of character for Ann Richards," Polinard declared. "You've got to go a long way to make Jim Mattox look like a gentle person, but she did it."

Many of Ann's supporters, too, were appalled by the commercials. Everyone had known she was a scrapper, but somehow had not expected her to reach down to Mattox's level of mudslinging. Disillusioned, many asked, "How could she?"

The answer came from Ann herself, when a reporter asked about her participation in negative campaigning. "Do I like it?" Ann responded. "No. Do I want to participate? No. Do I want to govern? Yes. This is what I have to do to pay my dues."

—

Ann's numbers rose and White's plummeted in the final, hectic week of the campaign. Ann was in Houston Friday, March 9, and Fort Worth on Saturday. On Sunday the eleventh, with only two days to go, she returned to Houston to speak at four churches, and finished the day at a rally in La Joya, in the Rio Grande Valley. On Monday, she campaigned through northeastern and eastern Texas, with stops in Sherman, Texarkana, Longview, and Tyler. That night, she went home to Austin for the next day's election.

Watching the returns Tuesday night, March 13, proved to be as nerve-wracking as the campaign had been. From the beginning, it quickly became clear White was no longer in the race. The lead fluctuated between the two front-runners. Mattox led first, then Ann, then Mattox again. Finally, Ann pulled ahead and held her lead. When the votes were fully tallied, her total reached 561,080, or 39.5 percent of the votes. Mattox handily won second place with 521,494 votes, or 36.8 percent of the ballot. Mark White endured a dreary night at his Houston headquarters. The ex-governor's political career was finished after his feeble showing of 274,551 votes. Blaming Ann, he refused to accept her call of condolences.

The runoff was set for April 10. The struggle was extended for twenty-eight more days. "We're not gonna back down. We're not gonna back off," Ann told the exhausted but elated crowd who had joined her to watch the returns. "We're gonna fight to the finish!"

Ann had spent approximately $3.4 million, Mattox approximately $4.4 million during the first stage of the primary. Each would spend another $1.5 million, some $50,000 per day, before the runoff election.

With Mark White outraged and out of the running, the question became, how many of his 274,000 voters could each candidate capture? Mattox needed at least 40,000 more than Ann to make up his 40,000-vote deficit from the primary, and would fight hard for them. Ann tried from the start to smooth the troubled waters of a badly divided Democratic party. "There were people in the primary who supported other candidates and felt they were doing the right thing," she said. "It is time that we reach out to them and tell them that we must be unified."

During the first week, Mary Beth Rogers, Ann's longtime adviser, ally, and friend, formally and officially joined the campaign, replacing Glenn Smith as campaign manager. She and Ann had worked together so often in the past and were so in tune with each other that Ann had complete faith in her judgment and political acumen.

The runoff campaign would prove anticlimactic. The public had tired of the nearly constant mudslinging. Reflecting that apathy, newspapers began to relegate campaign stories to their inner pages, and television slotted shorter stories deeper in the newscasts.

The issues included a state lottery, which both Ann and Mattox wanted. Ann had made insurance reform "her" issue, but Mattox's position on insurance was essentially identical to hers. Ann continued to call for changes in Texas's education system.

However little the electorate seemed to care about Mattox's charges that Ann had used drugs, he would continue to hammer at the issue. At the beginning of the runoff campaign, he called for an end to the mudslinging. Ann was skeptical.

"Given Jim's past, he'll turn it into a mud-wrestling match," she said on March 15, two days after the primary. "He has been trying to rewrite the history of this campaign and come riding out on a white horse. That horse's legs were muddy up to the neck."

When Mattox insisted he was serious, Glenn Smith, who had remained with Ann's campaign as a consultant, met with Kelly Fero, one of Maddox's aides, to work out a truce. Whatever conclusions they reached came to naught when, the next day, March 22, Mattox demanded at a press conference that Ann take a lie detector test and reveal what drugs she took and who supplied them.

By this time, Ann was totally prepared. Her campaign produced a letter from St. Mary's Alcohol Treatment Unit that said she was treated for alcohol abuse *only*. She also released the results of a drug test she had taken two weeks earlier. The results were negative, but the media and the public had become so jaded that the newspapers and television reports virtually ignored both the letter and the drug test results.

Meanwhile, former San Antonio mayor Henry Cisneros began to campaign actively in Ann's behalf. Cisneros was arguably the most popular and influential Hispanic politician in the state, and his endorsement in the Rio Grande Valley, with its predominantly Hispanic population, would prove invaluable.

A compelling speaker, Cisneros told a crowd at a San Antonio rally, "The Ann Richards I know is not the one Jim Mattox describes. When Ann Richards, a modern pioneer, breaks down old prejudices, all Texans win, men, women, white, Afro-American, Hispanic. When she opens doors for some, all of us are admitted to the New Texas."

There were lighter moments. On March 24, an astrologist, Marione Hensley, said that Ann's cycles were better than Mattox's. "They're both Virgos," she said, "but [Ann] hasn't been hit by the eclipses [Mattox] has."

When told of her predictions, Kelly Fero, Maddox's aide, was said to have leaned back in his chair and thrown up his hands in mock despair. "That's it," he said. "We quit!"

Mattox did no such thing, of course. Instead, he continued to hammer away at the drug and alcohol issue. Finally, three days before the runoff at a press conference in El Paso, Ann responded in a voice thick with scorn when queried about the continuing attacks. "It's sickening. It's neo-McCarthyism. It's scurrilous. It's irrelevant, and it's stupid."

The electorate evidently agreed. On the morning of April 10, runoff election day, Jim Mattox personally donned an apron for the news cameras and prepared breakfast tacos for his workers. Ann slept late, and when she rose, she washed her hair, filed her nails, and went to work doing laundry that had stacked up during the campaign.

By the time she reached the Hyatt at 8:00 P.M., the election was essentially over, and the Mattox ordeal was history. The vote ran 639,126 for Richards to 479,388 for Mattox. Ann had prevailed, with nearly 60 percent of the ballot. When Mattox phoned Ann to concede the election, she kissed her granddaughter Lily. Then, looking into the fatigued faces of her embattled crew, she said, "You all have to take a break. You might take a week or two. But don't go too far away."

Because the real campaign to determine if Texas was ready for a woman governor was about to begin.

CHAPTER 18

GENERAL ELECTION

There is only one candidate in this race who is qualified to govern Texas...and you're looking at her.
—ANN RICHARDS addressing the state convention
of the Texas Democratic party, June 9, 1990

Ann Richards's friends and colleagues say her trademark is her ability to identify priorities, focus directly on them, and never be distracted by factors and events that she cannot control. Still, as she fought her way through the difficult campaign for the Democratic nomination for the governorship, she kept a close eye on the Republican side of the ballot, and Clayton Williams.

Williams was a multimillionaire from the Texas old world of cattle and oil. He had founded twenty-six different companies during his business career, including Clayjohn, the largest independently owned natural gas company in Texas. A stereotypical West Texas Good Old Boy, he was "stronger than horseradish," according to one of his millionaire friends. And now, aspiring to political office, he introduced himself to Texas in a series of television commercials during the week following Christmas, 1990.

In one, sporting a white cowboy hat, Williams grinned into living rooms throughout the state. Behind him in the background, young men wearing blue uniforms labored with picks and axes on a rocky hillside. Viewers were informed that this was Clayton Williams's vision of the future, in which youthful drug offenders would quickly become acquainted with "the joys of bustin' rocks."

Elect Clayton Williams governor of Texas, the commercial

suggested, and you will see the beginning of the end of drug problems in the state. The commercials almost immediately made Williams a celebrity. Within a month, his name recognition quotient rose from 4 percent of Texans to 88 percent.

"Sure, we watched those commercials like everybody else in the state," said Glenn Smith. "And it was our opinion that those were the greatest political ads we'd ever seen. They presented a forceful message that defined and framed the candidate in a clear and positive light. Ann characteristically managed to stay focused on winning her own primary, but yes, she was intrigued by Williams and those commercials, which had a production quality that you see in presidential elections and rarely at a state level."

Williams's "bustin' rocks" spots are regarded almost reverently by the professionals of political marketing. Amazingly, the commercials were produced in Williams's West Texas hometown of Midland by a public relations agency that employed only ten people, minuscule by industry standards.

Said Joe Milam, the adman who created the commercials, "The genesis of the commercial actually was in 1985, when we used Clayton Williams on a commercial for his fiber optic phone company. The setting was supposed to be a Pony Express station, and Clayton was dressed in 'period Western attire.' He was a natural. He's got a terrific presence for that kind of TV." So when Williams decided he wanted to become Texas's governor, Milam decided Williams would be his own best spokesman.

The "bustin' rocks" piece was filmed on Williams's ranch near the town of Alpine, the gateway to the Big Bend country in remote southwestern Texas. To play the role of the inmates at Williams's "boot camp" for problem youth, Milam recruited members of the rodeo team from Sul Ross State University in Alpine. "I bought some used security guard uniforms for six dollars apiece and I had a seamstress in Alpine sew stripes on the trousers," Milam recalled. The spot was shot in one weekend. Williams rewarded his "convicts" with fifty dollars a day, all the beer they could drink, and a chuck wagon dinner featuring twenty-two-ounce T-bone steaks.

Of all Williams's ventures and investments, few ever paid off as gratifyingly as that weekend filming session in Alpine. Milam's spots were overwhelmingly popular, and Williams's bid for the Republican nomination against three other more conventional candidates was won before it ever really got under way. According to one political analyst, the man affectionately known as Claytie "got there with those TV spots early and he sawed the rest of the field off at the knees."

Williams's only previous election experience had come when he was voted most popular male graduate in the class of 1949 at Fort Stockton High School. However, he had more than snappy television commercials working in his favor. He marched into the political wars with a campaign fund of $20 million, $8 million of which was his own money.

In two state-wide television debates against the other candidates—Kent Hance, Tom Luce, and Jack Rains—Williams stuck with his hard line on crime and avoided in-depth discussion of the economic problems that had beset Texas for the previous half decade. Claytie was no political scientist, but the polls clearly evidenced that Texans believed he was genuine. In addition, he enjoyed the generous and almost unanimous backing of the Aggies, the alumni of his old school, Texas A&M. Indeed, he stood out as one of the proudest Aggies of them all. He bought the actual A&M emblem that adorned the fifty-yard line at the Aggies' football stadium and installed it alongside a swimming pool shaped like one of the boots worn by Aggie seniors in the backyard of his home in Midland.

Williams's unorthodox cowboy magnetism attracted the attention of not only the national media but journalists from across the Atlantic. Newspapers in the United Kingdom began referring to Clayton Williams as "Blatant Millions." A writer for *The Economist,* England's equivalent of *Fortune* magazine, noted that "Mr. Clayton Williams's television commercials were of a quality that would have met the standards of the most demanding automobile manufacturers. And once he appeared on televised debates with the other candidates, Mr. Williams demonstrated an ignorance of government that would have done Mr. Ronald Reagan proud."

According to campaign manager Glenn Smith, that latter assessment by the British publication was one that was shared by Ann Richards. Smith said, "She never came right out and said so, at least not to me, but I know that Ann felt that if she could get past her own primary, she could handle Clayton Williams one-on-one. She's an astute judge of people, not just public figures, and Ann understood that behind the figure in those commercials was a myth."

Clayton Williams is prominently featured in a private video of a black-tie cattle auction conducted in Midland, Texas, in 1988. Late in the festivities, Williams, in a purple sequined dinner jacket, joins a country and western band and bellows out a tune. Afterward, a friend of Williams's slaps his pal on the back, and says, "Gosh, Claytie, that was great." Williams, now holding a drink in each hand, turns to his wife, Modesta, and yells, "Hear that, honey? These people are so goddamn drunk, they think I'm great!"

In the early months of 1990, a sizeable number of Texas voters appeared similarly infatuated. "People claim I'm going after the Bubba vote," Williams told a small crowd that gathered to hear him speak at the Texas Ranger Museum on the banks of the Brazos River in Waco in early March. "Hell, I *am* Bubba."

Williams would coast through the Republican primary virtually unscathed, although one opponent, Kent Hance, did say that "Claytie would be a good guy to go fishing with, but he'd be a disaster as governor." By early February, 1990, it was obvious that he was the man Ann Richards would ultimately be required to outsmart, outfight, and outcampaign if she were to realize her ambition of becoming governor.

On the night of the primary vote on March 13, while Ann was edging past Jim Mattox only to face the worrisome task of a runoff campaign, Clayton Williams and his Aggie pals were launching into a joyous celebration at his Austin headquarters. Williams faced no runoff. The West Texan had gathered over 520,000 votes, and his nearest opponent, Kent Hance, was sadly out of the running with 132,000. For a political neophyte, Williams had achieved a stunning victory. Even the most die-hard, yellow-dog Democrat probably would not have wagered against his chances in the coming general election on November 6. At his election night party, Williams took the opportunity to needle his Democratic counterparts for the nature of their campaign. Williams grinned into the cameras and proclaimed, "Read my lips! No more mud!"

While Ann and her staff began working through the ordeal of battling Jim Mattox in the runoff, the Williams team met to devise tactics that they hoped would seal the outcome of the general election even before the arrival of summer. The first of these ideas was to invite key reporters from the large Texas newspapers, plus a wire service representative, for a weekend at the Clayton Williams ranch at Alpine.

There, the reporters could watch the Republican candidate for governor work on horseback as the range boss during a real cattle roundup. The plan was to make sure there could be no misunderstanding in the minds of the Texas voters about the legitimacy of the candidate's credentials as an genuine cowboy. Unlike the stars of the old Western movies, Williams needed no stand-in for the riding and roping scenes.

On the first weekend of spring, high winds and a cold, driving rain caused a postponement of the roundup. Some of the news reporters, not thrilled in the first place by the assignment to "rough it" on the ranch with Clayton Williams, attempted to gather some quick quotes from Williams and then return to the comforts of city life.

"Bad weather, it's like rape," Williams sighed to a female political writer from the *Houston Chronicle*. "If it's inevitable, just relax and enjoy it."

Sam Attlesey, of *The Dallas Mornings News* said, "A couple more of us [reporters] partially overheard what Williams said, but we weren't sure. So we conferred with the Houston reporter to be sure those were Williams's actual comments." And then they published them.

Instant indignation resulted, and Williams's candidacy was pummeled by negative press for the first time. Williams apologized to the world at large for what he contended was a "meaningless joke, said in passing." He added he had paid a steep price for his ill-advised comment, having incurred a stern admonishment from his wife and daughter.

One week later, he suffered a similar lapse of judgment. This time, speaking to reporters on the topic of his teenage years, Williams told of trips to Mexican border-town brothels "for service." The candidate explained that excursions of that nature were a standard rite of passage for the genuine Texas ranch hand.

Again, Williams was pelted by a hailstorm of protests from women's groups around America. One of the candidate's media coordinators, Dick Legitt, surveyed the impact of his client's gaffes and believed that the remarks would have little, if any, impact on his standing in the polls. He could not, in other words, lose the support of women and women's groups, since they did not support him in the first place.

Legitt was right when he said Williams's misfires had generated little fluctuation in the polls. When the campaign against the Democrats in the general election began in earnest, Legitt was confident that the gaffe factor would be long forgotten. Nonetheless, other strategists no longer trusted Williams in spontaneous sessions with media and wanted to restrict its access to him.

Legitt opposed the move. A West Texas native himself, he understood the value of the image of his candidate as a throwback to the good old days. Furthermore, his political instincts told him that if Ann Richards defeated Mattox, she should not be taken for granted.

He argued, "How often have you seen a football or basketball team go into halftime with a big lead and their mind-set for the second half is 'Let's forget being aggressive and try not to make any mistakes—fumble the ball or throw an interception—and protect that lead?' How often have you seen that backfire?"

The argument fell on deaf ears. From then on, Williams was kept on a tight rein. But not, in the long run, tight enough.

Said Joe Longley, an Austin lawyer who has represented Ann in civil matters, "At the outset of the primary, Republican leaders thought that Clayton Williams might become the living embodiment of Marshal Matt Dillon on *Gunsmoke*. Instead, Williams was turning out to be Ed Norton on *The Honeymooners*."

The spirit of rejuvenation that might have been anticipated after Ann's victory over Mattox in the primary runoff had not materialized. A post-election-day headline across the front page of the *Dallas Times-Herald*, "Richards Wins in Mudslide," underscored the media perception of her candidacy. Now the highly popular Clayton Williams stood between Ann and the governor's mansion. With no time to celebrate, she and her staff spent the week after the runoff triumph evaluating their position and Ann's chances in the general election. The frank assessment was not promising.

The first task, according to Mary Beth Rogers, who had agreed to continue as Ann's campaign manager for the general election, was to evaluate the whole campaign for the Democratic primary, including the runoff. "We needed to see what went wrong and why, and what worked and why. And then we needed to try and see what we needed to do to rebuild.

"It was obvious," Rogers went on, "that our campaign against Clayton Williams would require a total regrouping. The staff, the campaign workers, were pretty demoralized after the last push, the runoff. The campaign had been so brutal and so hard, the people were just wiped out."

After reading the results of what Rogers describes as a postprimary "benchmark poll" that was compiled to see where Ann Richards stood against Clayton Williams in mid-May, 1990, a prudent call to "abandon ship" might have been in order. "The poll was taken to see how bad the damage Jim Mattox had inflicted on her really was," she says, "and it was pretty bad."

A poll deficit of 15 points in a race involving only two candidates at any point in the campaign is generally deemed terminal to the hopes of the one in the second place. Around June 1, the numbers that Ann's own pollsters regarded as most accurate placed her 27 points behind Clayton Williams. Even more discouraging, according to Glenn Smith, the damage caused by the mudslinging campaign against Mattox lingered in a high "negative" perception by the voters.

Williams had suffered no such damage. He had won his primary easily and relatively inexpensively. The bulk of his $20 million campaign fund was still available for the general election campaign. Ann's campaign could not count on raising enough to match his dollars, which left her at a decided disadvantage from the first day.

Ann carried the Hispanic vote in the Rio Grande Valley when she beat Mattox in the runoff. She could not rely on similar results in the general election, because Williams was fluent in Spanish and his tough antidrug stance was well received by voters along the border.

In early June, common sense might have led another candidate to lose heart. According to friends, however, Ann said common sense told her that she had come too far and endured too much to quit at such an early date. She believed in what she was doing and what she had to offer. Her father, Cecil, now eighty-one, retired, and living with Iona in Austin, agreed, and encouraged her. As far as he was concerned, Cecil said, Williams was "lighter than a June frost," and she could beat him.

Ann and her staff conducted intense planning sessions throughout May and early June. Said Mary Beth Rogers, "We had to realistically look at the damage assessment figures from the primary and figure out how to repair that. We knew that we would have to totally regroup. Behind the scenes, there was a great deal of reorganization, planning, and analysis, and through those kinds of activities, we put a new structure in place in order to run a different kind of campaign."

The restructuring had in reality begun when Glenn Smith was replaced by Mary Beth Rogers as campaign manager. "I was flattered when Ann Richards asked me to help run her campaign when she first announced in June of 1989," said Smith, who was thirty-six at the time. "I admired her for her integrity and how she kept people, the people of Texas, at the center of her agenda. I know that's a cliché, but it's true in her case."

Rogers had proved to be a stabilizing influence on the campaign. "After the primary and all of the tension involved with that, Ann decided that she felt more comfortable with Mary Beth Rogers running the show," said Smith, who continued with the campaign as a consultant. "Mary Beth, more than me, was somebody Ann could confide in. There was no animosity involved in the change. I understood."

He added, "The second big change in the structure of the campaign team for the general election was directly attributable to the increase in donations that flowed into Ann's campaign chest after she won the primary." With that money, they "hired about three times as many people as we had in the primary, and these people were in field offices around the state. The staff that dealt directly with major media was also beefed up substantially."

The revamped Richards team then reevaluated the negative aspects of Williams and his campaign. They did not find much. One of the few weak spots, according to Mary Beth Rogers, was the enormous amount of money he had and would spend. Richards, better than anybody, knew that the public regarded Clayton Williams as "entertaining and different," but she sensed, too, that it was exactly those qualities that made him vulnerable.

Glenn Smith explained, "Ann had Clayton Williams measured all along and was confident that she could beat him, and she sensed that once the voters came to realize that the man in [his] commercials was not the man they thought he was at first, that his image wouldn't hold up. And once that happened, the impact of those commercials would come back as sort of a double negative."

The Richards campaign also realized that they *had* to stop Texas Democrats' internal bleeding from the self-inflicted wounds of the primary. "The party in Texas was a three-way split, and somehow we had to reunify our people with the Mattox and White people," Mary Beth Rogers said, "and that would be no small task." To that end, Ann, Mary Beth, Jane Hickie, and others spent hours on the phones calling Mattox and White supporters in an effort to assuage hurt feelings and heal the wounds left by the primary campaign.

Ann's campaign was in the doldrums as they entered June 1990. Even her good friend Molly Ivins noted in a column that the campaign was flat and listless and seemed to have no direction. Ann had had a falling-out with her media consultant, Bob Squier, who had returned to Washington in a sulk. Minorities were coming to believe that they were being ignored or slighted. Ann was said to be angry much of the time, putting her staff on edge.

Then, as Ann's speech at the state Democratic convention in 1988 had changed the course of her career, the June 1990 state convention changed the course of her campaign. This year, the affair was held in Fort Worth at the Tarrant County Convention Center Arena. The structure was built on the same land that used to house the infamous "Hell's Half Acre," one of the most notorious red-light districts on the old Chisholm Trail of cattle drive fame.

"We really rejuvenated ourselves in that convention," Rogers said. "A black girl, a high school student from Dallas, was chosen to introduce Ann. School kids from Fort Worth were brought onto the convention floor."

Most important, Ann's speech—"Remarks of Texas State Treasurer Ann W. Richards," as the transcript is drably titled— was one of her most inspirational.

The Democrats, of course, were "red, white, and blue," staunch men and women who were "not about to allow Texas to be sold to the highest-bidding Republican."

It was "the season," she said, "when we get to meet these new Republican politicians as they suddenly discover the state.

"They visit down in South Texas and they throw a *pachanga,* put on a sombrero, speak some Spanish, give away free beer...and after the election all you have left is a hangover.

"They visit East Texas and put on their overalls, eat some ribs, get their picture taken next to a tree, go to a church or two on Sunday...and after the election all you have is an empty collection plate.

"And they make a swing out through the Panhandle and West Texas where they put on a cowboy hat and color-coordinated boots, sit around a campfire with reporters, work cattle in front of the cameras for a while...and after the election all you have left is the cow chips."

Then, after the laughter, "Is that enough for you, South Texas?" The convention roared that it wasn't.

"Is that enough for you, East Texas?"

Once again, the raucous answer was no.

"Is that enough for anybody?"

Cheering, shouting, stamping of feet ensued. As Bill Cryer had said of the 1988 Houston convention speech, it was a barn burner.

The convention, and Ann's speech, proved to be the rallying point that launched one of the biggest comebacks in Texas political history. For with the rank and file solidly behind Ann, Mattox and his supporters, and some of White's supporters although not White himself, agreed to back Ann Richards in the campaign.

The Republican convention at the same site in Fort Worth two weeks later took on the superficial aspects of a massive evangelical tent revival, although some tension developed beneath the surface. For instance, in an exhibition hall that connected the Convention Center Arena and a smaller auditorium at the opposite end of the complex, a group of South African Christian missionaries were selling raffle tickets. The prize was an automobile tire inscribed "Mandela Necklace," in reference to the brutal South African practice of hanging tires around the necks of opponents and setting them ablaze. After two days, though few blacks were expected to vote for Williams, a convention organizer suggested to the operators of the booth that they "offer a different grand prize." Williams himself was unaware of the booth or the prize, and, luckily for his campaign, the incident passed unnoticed in the media.

On a more public front, a controversy developed over whether Clayton Williams would appear and speak at a large and emotional Right to Life gathering in the Convention Center Auditorium at the opposite end of the Convention Center from the Arena at the same time as the Republican convention. While Williams and the Republicans opposed Richards's prochoice stance on the issue, he steered clear of the Right to Life rally. Despite the intensely vocal and visible antiabortion forces at the convention, Williams's staff did not wish to alienate the majority of the Texas electorate that held prochoice sympathies.

The highlight of the Texas Republican convention, like that of any convention, came with the address from the candidate at the top of the ticket for the general election. While Clayton Williams spoke, George W. Bush, son of the President of the United States, stood at the side of the stage with a transistor radio pressed to one ear. Bush, a part-owner of the Texas Rangers baseball team, was listening to a game between his club and the Boston Red Sox. At the end of his speech, Williams offered his gratitude to "the great men who have transformed Texas into a Republican stronghold. Governor Bill Clements [massive applause], and Senator Phil Gramm [more applause]!" and then concluded. At that point, George W. Bush approached Clayton Williams and, according to a key Williams aide, "cussed Claytie out royally for not mentioning the President in his speech." Williams hastily returned to the microphone and corrected the omission.

The heat of a typical Texas summer is as relentless as it is intense, and saps the will and endurance of most mortals. But it was in this environment that Ann Richards and Clayton Williams embarked on a torrid state-wide campaign that would ultimately transcend the jejune marketing tactics that characterize modern American politics. In a typical bid for a major office, strategists go to extraordinary lengths to ensure that nothing is unrehearsed. That was not going to be the case in the Richards-Williams confrontation, to the chagrin of the Williams staff.

Republicans, abundantly funded, began peppering the state with pro-Williams television commercials in early July. The candidate adhered to his antidrug, law-and-order theme. Meanwhile, Williams repeated the same story in three or four speaking engagements a day. "I started my business career selling life insurance, and if you can sell life insurance, you can sell anything," he told hundreds of audiences. "Think about it. You've got to talk some old boy into giving you his beer money so that when he dies, his wife will be able to afford a new husband."

That was not the kind of oratory that would send cheering crowds surging to the polls. Neither would it get the candidate in trouble. Williams's handlers were playing it safe. They played it so safe that in early October, during a controversy over a proposed debate, they announced that he would not, under any circumstances, participate in formal television debates with Ann. "Why should he?" Glenn Smith asked. "If you're the front-runner, it wouldn't make sense."

Ann's comments were more colorful. "You can't be John Wayne and run from your opposition," she said, milking all the mileage she could from the refusal.

It was probably a wise choice, given Williams's propensity for, as he put it, "shooting myself in the foot" with occasional gaffes made in off-the-cuff remarks.

"I like to think that we had something to do with that," Mary Beth Rogers said. "Our plan was to put a great deal of pressure on Williams and give him the maximum opportunity to slip up."

George Shipley, who had orchestrated Mark White's downfall during the primary, concurred. "Ann Richards knew she was going to win," he said. "She knew it psychologically long before any of the rest of us did, because she knew that Claytie was Claytie. What we set out to do was cross-examine him electronically and expose him to the kind of intense pressure you put a witness under in the courtroom, and we got lucky and he cracked and his famous gaffes started coming with repetitive frequency."

Clayton Williams attacked Ann Richards on the grounds that she had received the backing of "a Hollywood women's political committee supported by Jane Fonda." For that, a San Antonio editorial writer chided Williams in print for reneging on his "Read my lips; no more mud" pledge.

"That's not mudslinging," Williams protested. "A lot of armed forces veterans look at that business as something offensive. I'm a veteran. Ann Richards is not."

Some observers felt that attacking Ann Richards for not serving in the military was a trifle far-fetched. And most Texans viewed Jane Fonda's activities in Vietnam as yesterday's news. Another Williams remark backfired when he used cowboy jargon to promise voters not only that he was going to defeat Ann Richards in the election but also, "I'm gonna head her, I'm gonna hoof her, and I'm gonna drive her in the dirt."

The time had come to turn Williams's Good Old Boy, West Texas cowboy image back on him, as Ann had hoped to all along. Some weeks after the spat with Bob Squier, the media consultant, had led to him leaving the campaign, Mary Beth Rogers and Jane Hickie had flown to Washington to court him and hire him back. Now, with Squier, the campaign produced, according to Glenn Smith, "a series of TV spots around the theme 'Getting to Know Clayton Williams' that would keep drumming away at his weak spots."

Williams's "head her, hoof her, and drive her in the dirt" quote provided material for the first commercial. In it, an announcer asked, "What do you really know about Clayton Williams?" followed by, among other things, footage of Williams making the gaffe. Underneath the video, "Getting to Know You," the song from *South Pacific,* played softly.

By mid-August, Ann Richards's pollsters, gathering results in standard sample lots of 1,500 inquiries, began to detect upticks in her popularity rating. The morale and confidence of the candidate and her staff were beginning to grow. Earlier, the *Wall Street Journal* had remarked that Ann, during the the primary, "had rarely shown the dash that she demonstrated in the Democratic keynote address in 1988." Now, as she crisscrossed the state on Southwest Airlines commercial flights and in leased and sometimes borrowed planes, Ann demonstrated some of the bounce and vigor that people remembered from that keynote speech.

"By Labor Day, I really think that Ann had made up her mind that she was going to win," says Robert Spellings. "The wit and charm were coming on full force. She inherited a lot of her material [the aphorisms and one-liners] from her father, Cecil, by the way. She learned at the knee of the master."

Ann was fifty-seven, and Cecil, the "master," was still as much an inspiration as he had been when she was a child. "I would lie in bed as a child," she once commented, "and listen to my father and his friends talk well into the night, telling stories of plain people. Basic, gentle, and optimistic stories, forever taking aim at the self-important and dishonest."

Fifty years later, deep in the campaign of her life, she worked him into a positive commercial that aired in late September. In the commercial, Cecil, casting a fishing line, appears on camera while Ann narrates. "Cecil Willis spent his life working hard and saving his money," she said. "He's retired now, and he's worried. Worried about rising insurance rates. I've got a plan. I'm going to appoint a state insurance board that is for the people who *buy* insurance. My plan is important for people like Cecil Willis. I should know because he's my dad."

From September on, to quote one of Cecil Willis's favorite sayings, Ann was "busier than a one-legged man in an ass-kicking contest."

There was no room for mistakes in the last two months of the campaign. One bad error, her staff feared, would have defeated her. They were especially careful to downplay Ann's humor, and for three reasons. One, many men, especially, found her occasionally biting comments threatening, and the male/female issue was problem enough without emphasizing it. Two, Ann needed to appear a *serious* candidate, not a wisecracking, bawdy comedienne. Three, the very nature of Ann's humor, which depends in great part on rhythm, tone of voice, gesture, and eye contact, made it problematic. Often, a sequence that leaves a crowd convulsed with laughter seems flat and uninspired when played out of context on a radio or television newscast, and on occasion can be totally misconstrued once it finds its way to the printed page.

Mary Beth Rogers says that "Ann got some rest in the early part of the summer, and from August on, she was the perfect candidate.

She had recovered from the bitterness and difficulty of the primary and never made a misstep. Her instincts were good, her stamina was good. She did everything that was necessary. You couldn't ask anything more. No matter what kind of organization you have, the campaign still hinges on the candidate and who he or she is and what they are capable of doing. And Ann was capable of pulling out the very best in her."

Strategist George Shipley believes that the summer respite created a revitalized candidate. "This is just my theory," Shipley says, "but it's my opinion that during the early summer before the general election, Ann sort of decompressed, looked over the events of the primary, and finally said to herself, 'Oh Jesus. Is this what I have to do to win?' and then she worked it out in her mind and was at peace with herself.

"The Texas Democratic governor's primary was the most barbaric in the country that year [ironically, the three principal candidates were graduates of the Baptist Baylor University], but the process that she walked through, I think that toughened her enormously," Shipley contends. "On balance, it was a healthy psychological thing. She would deny that. But there was a toughening process that I think very, very clearly gave her a better feel for who she was and what she was doing."

The overall picture was brightening, but the back-breaking job of recovering from a 27-point deficit in the early polls continued to be a daunting project. Funding—"matching Claytie's millions"—continued to be a problem. In mid-September, Ann left the state for a fund-raising tour in the north and east for five days. On September 18, addressing the Women's National Democratic Club in Washington, D.C., she told the assembly not to "get caught up in the rhetoric that we're not going to win. You write us checks and if you get money to us, we're going to win this race. The only thing I have to do is be on television. We can track this and track it very clearly. When I'm on television, my numbers are up, and when I'm not, my numbers are down."

She raised $100,000 on the trip, and bought more airtime. "We felt that if we cut the margin to 10 points by October 1, we might have a chance to win. That's what we had plotted. Anything more than 10, with less than six weeks to go, would have been too much,"

Rogers says. "But from mid-August on, we had a very different campaign structure in place [as compared to the primary].

"We had become a very smooth campaign machine. We were flowing. Everybody was operating pretty much at their highest level. The candidate and staff hammered through all of the problems and we had a game plan and we were capable of sticking to it," she added. "And we did. The media didn't see at the time [in September] when the tide began to turn, but we had established a pattern and a rhythm that might enable us to travel the very long road that would get us to within 10 points, and on October 1 we were *right* there."

Ann's campaign was finally beginning to generate good reviews from the media. A Houston columnist noted that "Clayton Williams is most successful with his television commercials and at staged events. Ann Richards has the ability to rouse crowds. He's playing to the cameras, she's playing to the crowds." By October 1, Ann was relying heavily on her children to help pull off the upset. Again, Dan Richards served as her traveling companion for the final three months on the road.

"You can't underestimate Dan's contribution," Rogers said. "He was a nurturing source of support for his mother."

Son-in-law Kirk Adams continued his organizing activities. By this time, he had volunteer organizations working in nearly all of Texas's 254 counties. Daughter Cecile worked the phone bank in Austin, raising funds. Other phone banks in 150 counties worked daily, soliciting funds and exhorting people to get out to vote. Ellen, Ann's youngest daugher, then twenty-six years old, and the only one of her children who was not drawing a salary, made speeches and organized Richards for Governor committees on college campuses.

Ann and her whole staff appeared revivified. Earlier, because many of Ann's wisecracks were perceived as men-bashing, they had reined back on her proclivity for tossing out one-liners. Now, the humor started to creep back in, especially when she spoke on the stump. A group of women headed by Liz Carpenter, who was fiercely dedicated to seeing Ann win, toured Central and East Texas and were occasionally joined by Ann. They did not reach the numbers of voters any single television commercial would, but they buoyed up the campaign.

"The tricky part came in planning Ann's itinerary," Mary Beth

Rogers noted. "It's real complicated and the travel becomes a grueling venture. You have to figure out where you have to go to influence the votes you need to get and balance that against what else is going on. And once you decide where to go, you have to decide the mechanics. You have two separate teams working on that. You try to plan things at least a week in advance, but some stops are planned six weeks in advance."

One of those stops that Ann Richards's campaign planners booked six weeks ahead of time was a meeting of the Greater Dallas Crime Commission slated on October 11. As matters turned out, this event became the turning point in the entire campaign.

—

By October 1, with Ann Richards's campaign gathering momentum by the day, a series of minor annoyances began to nibble at what had once been considered the unstoppable Clayton Williams. Williams drew criticism for his refusal to debate Ann face-to-face. At one Williams rally in Houston, the candidate was approached by a handful of protesters including a "Claytie Bird" character dressed in a chicken costume and carrying a sign that read Claytie Won't Debate. Williams laughed and tipped his hat to the protesters.

More serious issues quickly materialized. A story appeared on a wire service on October 9 that indicated that Williams's bank in Midland had once had questionable dealings with a loan broker who was later identified as a drug dealer. Williams himself was not directly involved in any of those transactions, but questions were asked and doubt was sown in the minds of the electorate.

While the press that Williams was receiving deteriorated, Ann's continued to improve. She received another boost on October 16 at a fund-raiser at the Austin Opera House. Featured among others were Barbra Streisand, Cybill Shepherd, James Garner, Carol Channing, and Steven Spielberg. It was a lucrative evening. Spielberg, who liked Ann's environmental position, donated $40,000. Don Henley of the rock band the Eagles gave $13,500; television producer Norman Lear, $6,000. Among others writing checks for lesser amounts were Streisand, designer Liz Claiborne, and writer James Michener. Actress Annie Potts, then starring in the sitcom hit *Designing Women,* announced that she would appear on a Richards prochoice commercial, in which she would say, "Ann Richards won't trade your rights away."

The evening generated stories in papers across the state. In reaction, Reggie Bashur, a Williams aide, remarked sourly that "it only serves to remind voters that Hollywood crazies embrace her positions on issues and those are definitely liberal."

Meanwhile, Ann continued to promise sweeping insurance regulation and reform, as she had throughout the primary. She would appoint a board that was consumer-oriented. She would attempt to provide and authorize penalties for insurers that delayed paying claims, prohibit insurers from canceling policies after a policyholder filed one claim, and kill the insurance industry's exemption from antitrust claims.

Williams, on the other hand, endorsed a hands-off policy. On October 15, Ann's campaign began airing more television commercials that exploited his probusiness, anticonsumer position: "Theft, fraud, customer rip-offs. That's today's Texas insurance industry. Does Clayton Williams care?" the spots asked. They were effective. By October 20, polls showed Williams's lead over Richards had shriveled to 5 percentage points. Considering the standard margin for error, the race now belonged to either candidate.

But the whole tenor of the race changed dramatically on October 11, when Ann and Williams both addressed the Greater Dallas Crime Commission. It was one of the rare occasions where the two candidates crossed paths. They made standard policy statements. Afterward, surrounded by the customary armada of news cameras, Ann extended her hand to Williams.

Williams's arm stayed at his side. "I'm here today to call you a liar," he said, astonishing everyone in the room when he refused to shake her hand.

"I'm sorry, Clayton," Ann said, trying to interrupt.

Williams didn't let her finish. "That's what you are. You've lied about me. You lied about Mark White. You lied about Jim Mattox."

Ann could only shrug, drop her hand, and walk away as nonchalantly as possible.

In the minds of the still "undecided" element in the polls, many of whom remained uncertain as to whether they really wanted a woman in charge at the governor's mansion, Clayton Williams had committed the unthinkable. His refusal to shake the hand of the lady was universally viewed as ungentlemanly and decidedly un-Texan. "That one event, that's what won the election," says Bill Cryer, Ann's press secretary. "At campaign headquarters, phones began ringing off the wall."

Ann's old river-rafting companion, Democrat Bill Kugle, saw the handshake "happening" and got on the phone to his state representative in Austin. "I may be insane, but I suddenly feel very optimistic," he said. The words summed up the feelings of thousands of Ann's backers around Texas.

Ann, too, was quick to capitalize on the affair. "The Texas men I know," she said, "simply don't behave in that fashion. [That kind of behavior] is why the rest of the United States thinks of us people as cartoon characters."

"That whole handshake episode, I think, was a product of something that happened earlier in the campaign in mid-September," says consultant Glenn Smith. Prior to the events at the Greater Dallas Crime Commission, the only other occasion in the campaign when Williams and Richards met face-to-face was at an Hispanic forum held in the historic and picturesque South Texas city of Victoria.

Smith recalls, "After the forum was over, Clayton Williams was out mingling in the crowd and Ann confronted him, face-to-face, about some negative radio spots that he'd been running. Ann handed Clayton an audiocassette containing the radio commercial of the spot and said, 'What about the mudslinging? You've got to do something about this, Clayton.' I was standing right there and I thought Williams handled himself all right. He said something like, 'This is a tough campaign, Ann.' But the confrontation startled him and I don't think Williams thought he'd handled it well.

"So the second time they met, up in Dallas," Smith continued, "I think Williams and his people were prepared for another 'stunt' from Ann, which never happened, but they had decided ahead of time not to shake hands, as what they thought would be an effective reaction to whatever Ann might have up her sleeve."

On October 12, the day after the incident, Williams said, "She accused me of laundering drugs. The only thing I ever laundered was my T-shirts and socks when I was in the army. I still believe she stepped over the line." But Williams knew, too, that the image of the cowboy included treating a woman courteously, no matter who she was or what she had said. He had reacted badly, which he as much as admitted when he added, "I may have made a mistake. My own heart doesn't feel good about that."

In Mary Beth Rogers's mind, the unshaken hand was the turning point in the campaign. "But Williams had started laying the seeds of his own destruction in September. The little gaffes, here and there. So when it got to the handshake, it was the weight of other accumulated incidents that made people start to say, 'Wait a minute. Who is this guy, anyway?' There were simply too many little incidents to overlook, all of a sudden."

On October 29, a Gallup poll showed Ann had drawn even with Williams. As the campaign drew toward the finish, Williams's problems continued to snowball. One example was the embarrassing constitutional amendment gaffe. When asked how he had voted on Proposition One, Williams asked which one that was, and was informed it was the only proposition on the ballot, concerning procedures on how the governor would make individual appointments. Williams, who had voted absentee in Midland a few days earlier, admitted he hadn't known that. "I wasn't up to snuff on that one," Williams told astonished reporters. "I asked my wife what to do."

The newspapers described Williams as befuddled, and Ann once again responded quickly. "This is not a toy," she said. "You've got to know your business to make government work. The governor's office is not a good place to get on-the-job experience."

On Friday, November 2, four days before the Tuesday election, Williams continued his self-styled march to the gallows. Earlier, in August, when Ann called for him to release his income tax statements, he had said, "It would take a Mack truck to haul it and I'm not going to do it."

In response, Richards's staff had rented a two-ton Mack truck that they parked in front of Williams's campaign headquarters in Houston. Now, on November 2, while being kidded by some reporters about the truck incident, Williams recalled the havoc caused by the oil bust and casually remarked that he had not paid any federal income tax in 1986.

By Saturday, the revelation was headline news. Williams attempted to explain. "Oh, I've paid taxes. Lots and lots of taxes. But in 1986, when I was fighting for my life, Ann Richards was drawing a fat government paycheck."

In response, Ann immediately reissued her returns for 1986. They showed she paid $47,000 in taxes on $152,000 of income, $68,000 of which was her salary as treasurer, the rest capital gains, interest income, and funds from her divorce settlement. "Shame on you, Clayton Williams," she said, campaigning Saturday afternoon in the small South Texas town of Alice.

"Shame on you for not paying a cent in taxes in 1986 and then writing an $8 million check this year to finance your campaign. Shame on you for telling the people of Texas that you're going to be a governor who works for them, and not be willing to bear the same burden that all Texans bear, and that is to pay our taxes."

That night, Williams's troubles were compounded when it was revealed that he had donated $10,000 to Republican governor Bill Clements's losing campaign in 1986, the year in question. Ann's campaign could not have invented a more damning piece of news. Working late into the night, they wrote and produced radio commercials that took Williams to task. By Sunday morning, volunteers had driven and flown them to every major city in the state and delivered them to dozens of radio stations. The spots played relentlessly all day Sunday the fourth and Monday the fifth.

Clayton Williams had outspent Ann $20 million to $14 million. He had also "shot himself in the foot" once too often. He could not even count on the popular saying, "The opera ain't over until the fat lady sings." For Clayton Williams, the fat lady *had* sung. And if he did not yet realize that, his aide, Dick Legitt, did. Saturday night, late, he was spotted in the back of Dunstons Steak House in Dallas, drinking heavily.

The same night, on a plane taking her from Alice in deep South Texas to Dallas, where she would finish the campaign the next day, Ann told her son Dan, "I haven't started measuring the governor's mansion for drapes yet. But it looks like this thing may work out."

CHAPTER 19

THE HONORABLE ANN RICHARDS

Ann Richards has walked through the fire...and the fire lost.

—ROY SPENCE, public relations executive

Ann Richards's improbable, come-from-behind victory in the governor's race could be attributed to a synthesis of tenacity and zeal that would have earned the commendation of Harry Truman. Her 1990 campaign contained plot twists strikingly similar to Truman's presidential race in 1948. Both races featured dramatic shifts of momentum in the final days. Otherwise, when Ann visited Washington in 1949 as a teenage delegate to Girls Nation, she would have shaken the hand of Thomas Dewey in that Rose Garden reception.

In the days that followed the Texas election, Ann and her staff cheerfully analyzed the ingredients that had fueled a victory that was as close as it was spectacular. With 3,892,746 ballots cast, her margin over Clayton Williams was less than 100,000. A myriad of factors surfaced as prime elements in the victory, one of the paramount being the vote from Dallas County. A surge to the polls in minority-dominated South Dallas, supplemented by heavy support from women voters in the usually archconservative north end of the county, could be pinpointed as the deciding factor in Ann's win and Clayton Williams's loss. For Ann, who had worked in diligent anonymity for liberal causes in Dallas a quarter of a century earlier, the outcome was especially gratifying. As campaign aide Lena Guerrero put it, a Democratic candidate for governor "had won Dallas County for the first time since the earth cooled."

Ann's margin over her Republican adversary in Dallas County—211,000 votes to 192,000—becomes significant in light of what happened just two years earlier, when the Republican presidential candidate, George Bush, carried the same county with a cushion of over 100,000 votes against Democrat hopeful Michael Dukakis. At home in Travis County, where it all started with a race for county commissioner in 1976, Ann pounded Williams by an over two-to-one margin.

While a mood of apprehension darkened the land as the Iraqi invasion of Kuwait pushed the United States and its allies ever closer to the Persian Gulf War, the euphoria of the events of the autumn lingered almost viscerally among Richards's supporters. "She'll be a whirlwind of activity and you'll see her on the news every day," was the assessment of Sarah Weddington, whose campaign for the House Ann had managed back in 1972. Ann, in the meantime, set about the task of assembling a staff to help her sculpt her New Texas. She would be surrounded by the "usual suspects."

Mary Beth Rogers, who had managed her campaign since the first week into the runoff with Mattox, would serve as chief of staff for the new administration. When Ann announced Mary Beth's appointment, she said, "She has been my right hand and my brain. Judge and executor of my bright ideas. Every time I have a job to do, I turn to Mary Beth."

Jane Hickie was quickly named the governor's appointments secretary, an innocuous-sounding title for the person who controlled the gateway to the governor's office and served as the arbiter of who would or would not be given Ann's time and attention. One columnist who appraised the ebb and flow of Austin politics speculated that the "would not" list must surely be headed by the huge law firm of Jenkins and Gilcrist, which had fired Hickie when Ann was far down in the polls. Interestingly, a computer analysis of late contributions to Ann's campaign revealed $190,000 worth of better-safe-than-sorry donations from Clayton Williams supporters. One such contributor, Donald Bonham, head of a huge Houston-based grocery store chain, said, "Basically, I didn't want to be on her 'out' list."

Paul Williams, the accountant whom Ann had placed in charge of restructuring the state treasurer's office when she was elected to that job in 1982, had stayed on for the entire eight years. Williams decided to stay with his boss and accept the job of executive assistant.

Another longtime Richards loyalist, lawyer John Hannah, would become her secretary of state. In Texas, that post is a multifaceted administrative position that oversees the chartering of corporations and nonprofit entities, and all Texas elections. Hannah, a former state senator, had been a member of the famed Dirty Thirty liberal reform bloc in the Texas legislature in the 1960s that pressed for investigations that toppled the speaker of the House and the lieutenant governor. Perhaps Ann had a warm spot in her heart for Hannah, since he, too, had been battered and scarred by Jim Mattox in a losing runoff campaign for attorney general in 1982.

Richard Moya, her old colleague from the commissioners' court in Travis County, was brought on board as deputy chief of staff. Ann directed Moya to assist her in carrying out a campaign promise to streamline the vast and convoluted state bureaucracy. Other deputy chief of staff appointments were forwarded to Joy Anderson, who was Ann's legislative liaison during the years at the treasury, and Carl Richie, a thirty-one-year-old African-American lawyer who had caught Ann's eye as a "get things done" operative working in urban community affairs as an aide to a Houston city councilman. Bill Cryer, a former newspaperman who had served as Ann's press secretary at the state treasury, continued in that capacity.

Also, Ann successfully recruited another distinguished name to her administration's masthead. Barbara Jordan, who had voted to impeach Richard Nixon when she served on the U.S. House of Representatives' Judiciary Committee, agreed to serve as Ann's special adviser on ethics. Some recent events in the Texas legislature, such as East Texas chicken baron Bo Pilgrim's openly handing out ten-thousand-dollar checks on the House floor to any lawmaker who wanted one, gave rise to what lawyers call "the appearance of impropriety." If Texans were to trust their government, Ann felt it imperative that the legislature pass a strong ethics bill.

With the critical posts filled, Ann still faced a final and perplexing personnel decision as inauguration day rapidly approached. Her cats, Tater and Tina, she finally decided, would not move with her into the governor's mansion. That painful decision made, she announced that Cathy Bonner, proud member of the Old Girl network, had been placed in official custody of Tater, and that it was in Tina's best interests to move in with Dan Richards.

When Ann took the stage at the Hyatt Hotel on the unforgettable election night of November 6, 1990, she shouted into the pandemonium that she and her supporters would lock arms on inauguration day and proceed in a triumphant and symbolic procession along Congress Avenue to reclaim the capitol for "all the people of Texas." On January 15, a festive assembly gathered at the Congress Avenue bridge that spans the Colorado River and, with Ann as marshal, marched exuberantly along the twelve block route to the south lawn of the capitol. There, on the same spot where she had announced her candidacy nineteen months earlier, the Honorable Ann Richards was sworn in at high noon as the forty-fifth (or, some conflicting historical data suggests, the forty-sixth) governor of the great state of Texas.

The actual inauguration was followed by a fried chicken picnic on the capitol grounds, at five dollars a ticket, accompanied by music by the Getting Better Every Day band. Lyrics for a special inaugural song, "There's a Little Bit of Texas in Everybody and a Whole Lot of Texas in Me," were written by Governor Ann Richards herself. True to the inaugural tradition, four separate balls spilled over into the early morning hours. Ann traveled from party to party, wearing a royal blue outfit woven from 100 percent Texas fabrics. The dress was the creation of Dallas designer Richard Green, who situated a staff of seamstresses, armed with sewing machines, in an Austin hotel. Green, who served as Ann's fashion adviser throughout her four-year term, says that his client is "bright, straightforward and so easy to work with."

The average ticket for the various galas cost only thirty dollars, meaning that Ann's main inaugural bash became an occasion where a corporate giant and an organizer for Local 134 of the International Federation of Bakery Workers were seen deep in conversation while standing beneath an eight-foot-tall centerpiece fashioned from jalapeño peppers. The menu included Texas wines, mini-*flautas,* sliced ham and biscuits, and a concoction called Rio Grande pasta.

One observer remarked on the "inclusive" nature of the parties. Another, a woman who fancied herself East Texas gentry, surveyed the throng and told a society columnist, "I don't want to be tacky, but it looks like they came in off the street."

Ann's escort for the evening was former sportswriter and author Bud Shrake, whose friendship with Ann and David Richards dated back to Dallas and the early 1960s. Shrake's designation as what one friend termed "the governor's official consort" did not come without a steep price. Ann insisted that Shrake take waltz lessons prior to the inaugural events. "I was tutored," Shrake quipped, "by someone who told me that Texans do the waltz like nobody else in the world. By 'world,' I presume she also included Europe." On the big night, Shrake said, "I'm as ready as I can be" but lamented that his waltzing technique appeared to some as an exaggerated version of the Texas two-step.

Dolly Parton, identifying herself as a "Tennessee volunteer," flew in for the inaugural. As she commented on her roles in the motion pictures *Nine to Five* and *The Best Little Whorehouse in Texas,* Parton told bystanders that "now, thanks to Ann Richards, the women of Texas might get to be known for being something other than secretaries and prostitutes."

Entertainment for the main ball, handpicked by the governor, included the off-the-wall antics of a comedy group, Esther's Follies, that performed a sketch in which an Ann Richards look-alike popped out of a giant box of laundry detergent and was joined on the set by a dancing can of Aqua-Set hair spray. The dancing spray can was intended as a joke about Richards's famed bouffant coiffure. "I take a lot of cracks about my hair," the new governor said. "Mostly from men who don't have any."

The Ballet Folklorico from San Antonio and a gospel choir, Claudia Williams and the Voices of Christ, also performed. Naturally, the famed Three Tenors of the Austin sound—Jerry Jeff Walker, Willie Nelson, and Kris Kristofferson—took the microphone for a set. Later, Kristofferson patted Ann on the back and said, "I'm glad to be part of this celebration. We've had damn few things worth celebrating lately."

On the morning after the inauguration—Day 1 of the Richards administration—Ann's name disappeared from the front page of

Texas newspapers for the first time in months. While the nation gawked at television footage supplied mostly by CNN, the United States had attacked Baghdad from the air. Ann, like many Americans, had been gravely concerned by events in the Mideast and throughout the latter stages of the campaign and her short tenure as governor-elect had worn a yellow ribbon on her lapel to show support for U.S. troops. Still, she privately welcomed the respite from the prying eyes of the media as her term began. She knew that the decisions made in the first four weeks of office would influence the success or failure of her administration over the next four years. However traumatic the war, Desert Storm let her go about her work with a minimum of media distraction, for at least a little while.

—

"Being governor in Texas is a trap," Ann's onetime county commissioners' court colleague, Bob Honts, has said. "You have all the blame and not nearly enough power."

Since the 1880s, the powers available to Texas governors have been limited by intentional restraints written into the Texas constitution. In an effort to offset the influence of federally selected governors during the post–Civil War Reconstruction era, the state's chief executive officer's powers were limited to appointing the heads of certain agencies,, and vetoing bills passed by the legislature. For whatever other policies the governor wishes to implement, he or she must rely on well-thought-out appointments, good old-fashioned political arm-twisting and horse-trading, and the skillful use of President Teddy Roosevelt's "bully pulpit."

With that in mind, Ann closely screened and researched the people she appointed to head key boards and commissions, some of whom were empowered with greater authority than the governor herself. The person with the archaic-sounding position of railroad commissioner of Texas, for instance, is equipped with far-ranging powers involving the regulation of the state's oil and gas industry in addition to railroads and trucking. Ann appointed Old Girl network member Lena Guerrero to fill a commission seat vacated by John Sharp, who had just been elected state comptroller. When an old-line West Texas oilman heard of the appointment, he phoned a friend and asked, "Who is this guy Lane Gerro?' His friend responded, "You better take a seat. This 'guy' is a gal and she's Hispanic."

Still another member of the core group from the Texas Women's Political Caucus days, Claire Korioth, was named to fill the one vacant chair on the three-person Texas Insurance Commission. The man she replaced was former University of Texas football all-American James Saxton, who, as a cowboy-boot-clad teenager, used to run down and catch jackrabbits. Ann, unable to correlate catching jackrabbits and running an insurance commission devoted to giving ratepayers a fair shake, had been bitterly at odds with Saxton throughout the campaign. Guerrero's and Korioth's appointments were typical of Ann's appointments. Of 384 "hires" for the judiciary and for top spots on state boards, commissions, and agencies, half were woman, blacks, or Hispanics.

Bob Honts gave her credit. "Ann Richards has done a better job of appointing the people she's promised to appoint than any other governor," he said, "often to the detriment of herself. She said, 'I'm going to give them a chance,' and she has. The people who she's appointed often don't totally appreciate what she's done for them, and those she hasn't—able people—resent that they've been left out of the process."

Ann's campaign promise that her appointments and administration would reflect the population of the state had not been rhetoric, and as Honts pointed out, "You can't blame a politician for honoring a commitment."

With Tater and Tina safely relocated, Ann set up full-time residence in the Greek Revival governor's mansion at 1010 Colorado Avenue. The old structure that dated back to the post-Alamo days of the Texas republic had been largely restored by Rita Clements, wife of the governor Ann replaced. As the first full-time beneficiary of the restoration, the new occupant called the mansion "one of the most beautiful homes in Texas." She added that she felt awed, and yet somehow comforted, with the knowledge that "Sam Houston, Jim Hogg, Jimmy Allred, and other great governors slept here and wrestled with problems equally difficult as the ones Texas faces now, and they survived the experience."

Legend has it that Lyndon Johnson often won the hearts of congressmen with a tactic that is loosely defined as blackmail. Ann's usual style was more benevolent. Early in her administration, the mansion, almost daily, became the site of breakfast and lunch meetings with Texas legislators in a position to implement the changes she had promised to make during her campaign. Representative Pete Laney, a native of the far northwest Texas Panhandle and soon to be elected Speaker of the House, was a good example. After Ann, according to one report, stuffed him "with doughnuts and bagels at those breakfast meetings," he became instrumental in pushing Texas's new lottery bill through the legislature.

She could, however, take off the gloves when necessary . In one instance, Ann quickly donned the mantle of the activist heading into battle against what one wag called "a government of, for, and by the insurance industry." When the Texas Insurance Commission, whose two Clements appointees outvoted Claire Korioth, tentatively recommended an across-the-board 23 percent rate increase on automobile insurance rates, Ann put pressure on individual legislators and mounted a media attack.

"Outrageous," she said. "There is a strong perception by ratepayers that these astonishing suggested rates run counter to the public good. I want all of you [members of the Insurance Board] to fulfill what I believe is a mandate to monitor insurance rates for the public good. Unfortunately, these rates suggest otherwise and what the public sees is business as usual at the Insurance Committee." She got her way. The final recommendation made by the board was a token 3 percent raise in rates.

After the vital first month, Ann's administration was firmly in place, and most aspects of it appeared to operate smoothly. Outsiders took note. The syndicated political columnists Rowland Evans and Robert Novak visited Austin and wrote that Richards "had stolen the Republican flag...bashing bureaucracy and crusading for trimmed-down government."

Time magazine presented a comprehensive report on the first weeks of the Richards administration. Reporting on "the maverick governor," the magazine noted that she had "seized control of the state's insurance industry, declared a two-year moratorium on the establishment of new toxic waste dumps in Texas and was accomplishing meaningful progress in an effort to make government mean something in people's lives."

CBS's *60 Minutes* dispatched a production crew to Austin and prepared a segment on the governor who, according to one staffer, "had the tongue of an adder."

Texas state comptroller John Sharp, whom Ann counted upon to locate and pinpoint target areas of excessive corpulence in the budget, summarized what he thought to be the underlying message of the Richards regime. "Too many people are being screwed by government."

After Ann's celebrated keynote address to the Democratic National Convention in Atlanta in 1988, press secretary Bill Cryer estimated that her invitations to speak "multiplied by twenty-five times." Since her November rally to overcome Clayton Williams, that figure had doubled again, and her office was inundated with requests for interviews and appearances.

Ann's mother, Iona, sensed that fame had become a distraction. "When Ann was first elected to the treasurer's office," she said, "all the people wanted to know was when she was going to run for governor. Now that she's governor, all the press can ask is when she'll be running for President. The next person I hear ask that, I might hit them in the mouth."

Ann herself, in private, was said to feel very much the same way. She was more gracious, but curt, in public. When asked, she dismissed out of hand all speculation about national ambitions. "Frankly," she said, laying the matter however temporarily at rest, "I am more concerned at this point about what to do about my own administration."

Ann's disavowal of national ambition did not divert the spotlight. At the National Governor's Conference in Washington in April 1991, the "woman with the flashing eyes and snow white bouffant hairdo" stood out as the headliner of the gathering. Pickett Wilson, a top aide for Mississippi governor Roy Mabus, noted that "Ann Richards is the star of this meeting. People are in awe of her."

The governor who had been in office the longest of any at the session admitted to having been taken by Ann Richards's star quality. "She's highly regarded outside her own state," Arkansas's Bill Clinton said.

Lawton Chiles of Florida assured Texans that Ann was the sort of person who makes good on her promises. After she lost a bet with Chiles over the outcome of the University of Miami–University of

Texas 1991 Cotton Bowl football game, Ann promptly delivered Chiles a box of Texas beefsteaks.

The only governor to demure on the potential firepower of Ann Richards's political skyrocket was Republican Carroll Campbell of South Carolina. "Despite all the hype and the big speech [referring to Atlanta in 1988], she's like any other new governor coming in," said Campbell, who resembles Billy Graham in his prime. "She's got to prove herself."

No matter how much Ann wanted to avoid national publicity and get on with the job at hand, she couldn't. Everywhere she turned, she seemed to attract network television cameras. President George Bush, who had written her a cordial letter of congratulations after she the defeated Clayton Williams, came to Austin to address the Texas legislature in the spring of 1990. When Governor Ann Richards greeted him, she wore a silver lapel pin in the shape of a foot. Bush himself had mailed her the pin after the keynote speech. "When a man gives you something, you wear it when he comes calling," Ann explained.

The merry-go-round did not slow down. In November 1991, Ann traveled to New York City to be recognized as one of ten "Women of the Year" by *Glamour* magazine. Other honorees included University of Oklahoma law professor Anita Hill, fresh from her remarkable testimony at the Clarence Thomas confirmation hearings in the United States Senate; broadcast journalist Cokie Roberts; Johnetta Cole, the president of Spelman College in Atlanta; California congresswomen (destined to become U.S. senator) Barbara Boxer; breast cancer video creator Lilly Tartikoff; video producer Callie Khouri; Washington, D.C., mayor Sharon Pratt Dixon; *New York Times* columnist Anna Quindlen, and Jodie Foster, that year's winner of the Oscar for Best Actress for her portrayal of a rape victim.

The cast of ten was selected for what the magazine termed "beacons of integrity who have shown humor, guts and grace in an often graceless and cold-blooded world." One member of the all-female selection board, former Vermont governor Madeleine Kunin, said that Ann Richards "stands out as a role model for women in politics. There are not many members of that club—yet."

The Ann Richards who had attained national celebrity still

attempted to maintain a profile at home in Austin that was as close as possible to the less glamorous years of her service on the Travis County commissioners' court. She was frequently seen dining at some of her favored stops, enjoying the chicken-fried steak at the Broken Spoke Restaurant or Tex-Mex fare at La Zona Rose or El Arroya. She also indulged her love of basketball and regularly attended both men's and women's University of Texas Longhorn home games. Tom Penders, coach of the "Runnin' Horns," was thrilled when Richards gave his team a pregame pep talk. "She really lit the guys up," Penders said.

Ann's frequent escort to the basketball games was Bud Shrake, her "official consort" at the inaugural balls. "Since I got to be governor, I'm a much more desirable date," Ann said. "I get tickets right down on the court."

Shrake nodded enthusiastically and added, "Great parking, too."

Despite the heady trappings of running a populist administration in Texas and consistently enjoying high popularity ratings in the approval polls, Ann had never been so naive as to believe that her administration would be problem-free. Indeed, she both anticipated and predicted some deep ruts in the road ahead. She was not to be disappointed.

What surprised virtually everyone was the nature of the early problems, for they involved some of her key appointments to state posts and commissions, a territory where all assumed she was on solid, stable footing. As one example, her deputy chief of staff, Richard Moya, came under fire at the end of her first year in office. Having been directed to pare down the bureaucracy, Moya's many firings quickly earned him the nickname "the Angel of Death." Not a universally popular man in the labyrinth of state offices in the first place, Moya found himself the subject of an investigation that questioned a contract he had approved without a bid on his previous job with the Department of Housing and Community Affairs. Embarrassed, Ann put Moya on paid leave until he had been cleared in the investigation.

Another example concerned Terese Hershey, a Richards appointee to the influential Parks and Wildlife Commission. Hershey was said to have gained her post because she reminded Ann Richards a little bit of herself, but at the first official meeting of the commission, the outspoken sixty-eight-year old environmental advocate told outdoor enthusiasts that "hunting makes me want to throw up." Immediately, a media war between animal rights advocates and hunting enthusiasts ensued. Ann could only shrug and comment that the number of Texans who owned a hunting license, and that included her, constituted a considerable percentage of the electorate. Hershey remained on the board but issued no further condemnation of hunters or hunting.

The problems stemming from the Hershey and Moya affairs could be viewed as minor annoyances, however, when compared to an embarrassing 1992 scandal that prompted questions about Ann's judgment regarding her appointments. In the 1990 election, John Sharp, a member of the Railroad Commission, was elected state comptroller. Lena Guerrero, Ann's appointee to fill the Railroad Commission chair Sharp left vacant, had claimed she had won a degree with honors from the University of Texas School of Journalism. After running unopposed in the Democratic primary, and some two months before the November 1992 general election, Guerrero's budding political career was destroyed when reporters learned that she had not only not graduated with honors, she had not graduated at all. Her difficulties were magnified when she refused to offer a "full confession." After first being criticized for not checking her appointees more thoroughly, Ann was then, after she refused to defend Guerrero, criticized for abandoning her. "People judge me on what I do," Ann said, somewhat lamely, and left matters at that.

There was no shortage of embarrassment, either, after a special election held in 1993. Ann's reputation was on the line on two issues. One was a Texas constitutional amendment designed to equalize the funding of Texas school districts. Ann ardently backed the share-the-wealth, so-called "Robin Hood" amendment.

The other was the bipartisan election to name a United States Senator to fill the vacated seat of Lloyd Bentsen, who had accepted newly elected President Bill Clinton's appointment as Secretary of the Treasury. Some key Texas Democrats felt, and so advised Ann, that she should run for the senate seat herself. She responded that she would not abandon the governorship in mid-term, and supported

Bob Krueger, whom she had named to fill Bentsen's post until a special election could be held.

The May 1 special election was a disaster for the Democratic party, and for Ann personally. The Robin Hood amendment was soundly rejected by Texas voters. Worse, Krueger had run a weak race and, though he won a runoff spot against the then Texas treasurer, Republican Kay Bailey Hutchinson, was obviously destined to lose, as he did a month later, when Hutchinson trounced him.

Ann would continue to be criticized for her position on the Robin Hood amendment. Some of the pressure concerning her choice of Krueger was removed, however, when, within a week of her election, Hutchinson's treasury offices were raided by Travis County District Attorney Ronnie Earle. The charges Earle was said to be preparing, ironically enough, were similar to those he had filed against Treasurer Warren Harding.

Texas Republicans, seeking vulnerable spots in Ann's armor, located a promising issue in the size of the governor's staff. They produced figures that showed Ann's office listed 337 employees in her second year on the job, a dramatic increase from the 188 staffers on the payroll during Governor Clements's last year in office. Even Amazing Grace, the parrot Ann was given on her sixtieth birthday, got into the act when Karen Hughes, executive director of the Texas Republican party, quipped, "I wonder if they taught it how to say 'Polly wants a bigger staff.'"

Problems aside, Ann's ship of state appeared generally seaworthy as her first-term administration charted a course for its final year. Ann's efforts to promote insurance reform had met with appreciable success. In 1993, when the auto insurers sought a 52 percent rate increase, a state board by now dominated by Ann's appointees approved an increase of 3.7 percent. Additionally, the company's practice of not renewing the policies of drivers involved in accidents not their fault was banned.

The Texas lottery that Ann backed began operating in May of 1992 and promptly became an overwhelming hit, shattering national sales records. Ann's push for ethics reforms achieved moderate results. Laws were passed that forced lobbyists to report spending on public officials and made bribery of public officials a penal offense. Ann was disappointed that the legislature failed to enact promised measures that would have limited campaign contributions and required all officeholders and public officials to disclose tax returns.

On other fronts, environmental groups largely offered high marks for Ann's first term. And, according to the results of a survey published in the *Wall Street Journal* in June 1993, so, too, had the Texas business community, which rated her performance as "surprisingly favorable."

In summarizing Richards's first term in office, Dave McNeely, the respected columnist for the *Austin American-Statesman,* wrote:

> Richards has put a distinctive face and personality on her office. Her sparkling smile and white bouffant hairdo are known nationwide. She has the best sense of humor and speaking ability of any Texas governor since the late John Connally—maybe even better. Perhaps ironically, the woman decried by Republicans as just another tax-and-spend liberal actually has been rather tightfisted. She agreed with Lt. Gov. Bob Bullock and House Speaker Pete Laney to have a no-new-taxes budget in 1993 and she accomplished that. She exudes a sense that she really cares about people—and she does. Her warm personality gets through, even to those who have only seen her on television. Of the Texas Poll respondents, 69 percent said she'd be fun to have over for dinner and 63 percent thought her the kind of person who would be a close and trusted friend. Texans [in 1994] will have a chance to decide who will head their government— and it will be a surprise if they don't hang onto their charming ex-alcoholic divorcee.

Epilogue

Nineteen ninety-four. Election year, again. Ann enters this campaign rested and well financed. She can point with pride to solid accomplishments made during her first term. She has suffered mild embarrassments, but her administration has been scandal-free. Nonetheless, the old days when a Texas governor looked forward to two terms as a matter of course are long gone.

Ironically, her opponent will be George W. Bush, son of ex-President George Bush, who carried Texas in 1988 in spite of Ann's remark about him being born with a silver foot in his mouth. The Republicans have not forgiven that. George Jr., dubbed "the Shrub," will come heavily financed, slickly packaged, and with no record to run against.

This will be the toughest political fight of Ann Richards's life. To win it, she will need the strength of her many friends, and of her upbringing. Which perhaps explains why, on December 13, 1993, she returned to Lakeview, her old hometown, to announce her candidacy for her second term as governor of Texas.

The official announcement took place on the front porch of the house in which she was born. Her parents, Cecil and Iona, accompanied her. So did daughters Cecile and Ellen, sons Dan and Clark, and Ann's grandchildren.

There was nothing grandiose about the setting. Potted chrysanthemums and poinsettia were placed around a simple podium on the porch. Walnut Street, paved now, looks much the same as it did in the early days of the Roosevelt administration and the darkest days of the Great Depression that Ann Richards was born into sixty years earlier. So does the little frame house where Ann was born. Unimaginable in 1933 were the idling TV trucks fitted with satellite dishes that would beam Ann's remarks around the United States.

Approximately four hundred onlookers stood in the sunshine

that brightened the front yard that December morning. A smattering of them remembered Ann from the time when she lived in that house. Boots Douglas, who had carved wooden shoes for the girls, was well into his eighties and still lived across the road. Rusty Hoffman, who grew up with Ann, had driven down from Dallas.

Eventually, the crowd stilled and Cecile introduced her mother. Cecile, a statuesque woman now in her mid-thirties, said the press trucks and cameras reminded her of the night of the 1988 Democratic convention keynote address. "When she finished the speech," Cecile recalled, "[Mother] became an instant national figure. Everybody wanted to see her. The reporters wanted to put her on TV, the delegations wanted her to stop by their meetings. And that night, at about 2 A.M. when we all came back to the hotel room, we watched a tape of the speech. Mom was sitting on the floor in a T-shirt and shorts, and about two-thirds of the way through, Mom turned to us and said, 'Y'all, is that *me?*' And of course it was, but sometimes I know just how that must have felt because when I watch my mother with the President of the United States, or on the television news, and I think, this is the same person who picked me up when I skinned my knees and the same person who took me to Girl Scout meetings and taught me how to ride a bike, and the more I think about it, the more I realize of course it's Mother, because the talent and values that she showed us when she was raising us are exactly those that have made her the effective governor that she is today."

When Cecile finished, it was Ann's turn. As usual, she began with ad-libs, saying her howdys to old friends, and remarking on how she was "surprised on how emotional it was, going back into that house," and then moved to her prepared remarks.

"My momma told the staff," she said, "that they'd know they were in the right place if they could stand on the front porch and see the rock house across the street—like you can't do that anywhere else in Texas. And I think that's the best thing about it. It is like a lot of other haunts in Texas. Lakeview is the kind of place Lyndon Johnson used to talk about, where they knew when you were sick and they cared when you died.

"It is where I learned what is important in my life. It is where I learned my values. Standing here thinking about what it was like to be a kid, playing jacks on this porch and walking on eggshells through that perfectly kept living room, and the first thing that comes to my mind is hard work. My parents didn't know anything different, and they didn't accept anything less. My daddy left early and worked late. I don't think I ever saw Mother idle."

Ann talked about the accomplishments of her first term and spoke of the work that remained to be done. She made her formal announcement and closed with her vision of Texas's future. "I'm telling you, my friends, that this state is literally the crossroads of North America. It is going to be an international economic player. Texas is going to be reckoned with in the competition for the future. And we truly have created a New Texas and we're not turning back. I'm proud to be part of a state where you can start out on a front porch in Lakeview and end up on the front porch of the governor's mansion. The challenge today is to be sure the little girls [of Lakeview] who live here now will have the same opportunity to go wherever their ability and determination will take them. And so, my friends, God willing, that's what we will be doing the remaining year of this term and the next four years we'll be serving as governor. God bless the people of Texas."

While Ann emphasized the inevitability of change during her fifteen-minute address, a chilling north wind blew in and the sunshine in Lakeview was replaced by clouds. Cecil Willis, in ill health, was hustled away from the old house and into a warm car. Her speech over, Ann remained in the front yard, shaking hands with childhood friends and a legion of supporters for perhaps a full hour before making the hundred-mile drive back to Austin.

One week after Christmas, Cecil Willis died in an Austin hospital at age eighty-three from a rapidly spreading cancer complicated by pneumonia. The old friends gathered, this time for Cecil's interment just south of Waco, in Waco Memorial Gardens.

Today, even as she realizes how heartbreaking it can be to say goodbye to the old, Governor Ann Willis Richards remains dedicated to her dream of a new Texas. A Texas in which all Texans— men, women, African Americans, Hispanics, Native Americans, Asian Americans—have a voice. A Texas in which all can share her dream and dare aspire to a place in the Dome.

SOURCES

BOOKS

BENTON, WILBOURN E. *Texas: Its Government and Politics*. Englewood Cliffs, N.J.: Prentice-Hall, 1972.

CARLETON, DON E. *Red Scare! Right-wing Hysteria, Fifties Fanaticism, and Their Legacy in Texas*. Austin: Texas Monthly Press, 1985.

CRAWFORD, ANNE FEARS, and Crystal Sasse Ragsdale. *Women in Texas*. Austin: State House Press, 1992.

————. *Me for Ma*. Austin: State House Press, 1982.

FORD, BETTY, with CHRIS CHASE. *Betty: A Glad Awakening*. Garden City, N.Y.: Doubleday, 1987.

FRIEDAN, BETTY. *The Feminine Mystique*. New York: W.W. Norton, 1974.

GREEN, GEORGE NORRIS. *The Establishment in Texas Politics (The Primitive Years)*. Norman: University of Oklahoma Press, 1984.

KINGSTON, MIKE, SAM ATTLESBY, and MARY G. CRAWFORD. *Political History of Texas*. Austin: Eakin Press, 1992.

LESLIE, WARREN. *Dallas City Limit*. New York: Grossman Publishers, 1964.

McDONALD, ARCHIE P. *Texas: All Hail the Mighty State*. Austin: Eakin Press, 1983.

MORRIS, CELIA. *Storming the Statehouse: Running for Governor With Ann Richards and Dianne Feinstein*. New York: Charles Scribner's Sons, 1992.

O'NEILL, JOHN, and PAT O'NEILL. *Concerned Intervention*. Oakland,

Calif.: New Harbinger Publications, 1993.

RICHARDS, ANN, with PETER KNOBLER. *Straight from the Heart: My Life in Politics and Other Places.* New York: Simon and Schuster, 1989.

SCHUTZE, JIM. *The Accommodation: A History of the Politics of Race in an American City.* New York: Citadel Press, 1986.

VANCE, LINDA. *Eanes: Portrait of a Community.* Dallas: privately published, 1986.

WEDDINGTON, SARAH. *A Question of Choice.* New York: G.P. Putnam's Sons, 1992.

INTERVIEWS

Guy Bizzell (9/93)
Gerald Bolfing (12/93)
Helen Brant (11/93)
Dr. Glenn Capp (7/93)
Suzanne Coleman (2/94)
John Collins (8/93)
Bill Cryer (11/93, 2/94, 3/94, 4/94)
Bill Dosher (12/93)
Shirley Frank Eller (8/93)
Larry Fitzgerald (12/93)
Raymond Frank (8/93)
Frances Goff (2/94)
Del Groese (8/93)
Phil Hardberger (8/93)
Warren G. Harding (2/94)
John Hawes (8/93)
Norman Hay (8/93)
Rusty Hoffman (8/93, 10/93, 1/94)
Bob Honts (9/93)

Karen Hughes (10/93)
James Hyde (8/93)
Ed Kirk (8/93)
Nick Kralj (5/93, 1/94)
Joe Longley (6/93, 1/94)
Dr. Ralph Lynn (7/93)
Eve McArthur (8/93)
David McHam (7/93)
Betty McKool (11/93)
Dave McNeely (3/94)
Pancho Medrano (11/93)
Otto Mullinax (12/93)
Al Ragle (1/94)
Bob Reid (7/93)
David Richards (2/94, 3/94)
Patty Linehan Rochelle (2/93)
Mary Beth Rogers (6/93, 1/94, 2/94, 3/94)
Peggy Romberg (9/93, 4/94)
Fritz Sackett (8/93)
David Samuelson (8/93)

Jim Schutze (2/94)
George Shipley (3/94)
Doris Shropshire (8/93)
Spencer Shropshire III (1/94)
Dr. James Slatton (9/93)
Bessie Smith (8/93)
Glenn Smith (3/94)
Neal Spelce (2/94)
Robert Spellings (10/93, 2/94)
Kay Trautschold (7/93)
Debby Tucker (9/93)
Raymond Vickery (8/93)
Jay Vogelson (1/94)

Mary Vogelson (1/94)
Johnny Voudouris (9/93)
Bob Wade (10/93)
Christina Walsh (2/94)
Bruce Weaver (12/93)
Dan Weiser (7/93)
Richard West (10/93)
Robert Allen White (2/94)
Paul Williams (3/94)
Cecil Willis (12/93)
Iona Willis (1/94, 2/94)
Jimmy and Juanita Willis (9/93, 11/93)

MAGAZINE ARTICLES

"The Crash at Crush." *Frontier Times Magazine,* Oct. 1951.

DuBose, Louis, and Alan Pogue. "Q and A With Ann Richards." *Texas Observer,* Jan. 12, 1990.

"How One Woman Candidate Came Through." *U.S. News,* Aug. 15, 1983.

Ivins, Molly. "A Texas Treasure." *Ms. Magazine,* Oct. 1988.

Jarboe, Jan. "Ann's Plans." *Texas Monthly,* July 1992.

Kennedy, J. Michael. "The Cowboy and the Good Old Girl." *Los Angeles Times Sunday Magazine,* Oct. 21, 1990.

Shropshire, Mike. "Texas Crude." *D Magazine,* Sept. 1990.

Starr, Roberta. "Ann Richards: A Personal Account." *Third Coast,* Feb. 1984.

Stern, Linda. "Sarah Weddington: Advocate With Clout." *Working Woman,* Feb. 1980.

"20 Years of Miracles: St. Mary's Has Helped Thousands Since 1968." *St. Mary's Journal of Recovery,* Dec. 1988.

"The Women of Girls State." *American Legion Auxiliary National News,* July–August 1991.

WOODBURY, RICHARD. "Winds of Change Sweep the Lone Star State." *Time,* April 20, 1991.

WYSE, L. "The Way We Are." *Good Housekeeping,* Feb. 1989.

MISCELLANEOUS

Multiple gleanings from the following publications:

Austin American-Statesman, 1968-current
Austin Citizen
Daily Lariat, (Baylor University daily newspaper), 1951–54
Daisy Chain, (Waco High School yearbook), 1948–50
Dallas Morning News, 1960–94
Dallas Times-Herald, 1960–92
Houston Post
Los Angeles Sunday Times Magazine
Roundup, (Baylor yearbook), 1951–52
Texas Observer
Third Coast
Waco Tribune-Herald, 1940–55.

The quotation on page 16 is from *The Notebooks of Lazarus Long* by Robert Heinlein (New York: G.P. Putnam's Sons, 1973).

ORAL HISTORIES

George Allen, in the Dallas Public Library.
Ann Richards, in the Austin Public Library.

Appendix

**Remarks of
Governor Ann W. Richards
at the
Democratic Issues Conference
sponsored by the
National Legislative Education Foundation
January 30, 1992
Piney Point, Maryland**

Note to the reader: Governor Richards frequently deviates from prepared remarks.

Well, you all, when my friend Jack Brooks invited me to speak today...I accepted in all innocence.

Then I heard the vicious rumor that Bob Squier was putting the word out that I would come up here and give you all THE MESSAGE.

Of course, I reassured myself that anyone smart enough to get elected to Congress would know better than to listen to Squier.

If you all *were* expecting a messiah with a message, all I can say is that when I was born, my parents did not have the foresight to reserve a manger.

I make no pretense of having the keys to the kingdom, much less the keys to the White House.

But I do have one thing going for me...I'm not running for anything this year.

So I can say whatever I please.

Naturally, it pleases me to talk about Texas.

And, if you need a message, here it is.

Read my lips: This nation's ox is in a ditch.

I told you that so you would know what this speech is about.

We Texans like to consider ourselves a breed apart but, truth be told, we are having the same sorry experience as a lot of other states.

It began back in the early eighties with our basic industry being undermined by a competing foreign product.

Not only did the federal government allow the market to be flooded with a sea of cheap oil, but they sent the Navy out to escort the tankers, spending billions of dollars to bring oil out of the Middle East.

The Defense Department may not like to call it a subsidy...but you can put lipstick on a hog and call it Monique...and it is still a pig.

And whatever you call it, the fact of the matter is that if we added the cost of defending the gulf to the cost of oil, Texas would never have had a recession.

Once the price of oil went through the floor, real estate values followed.

Right on their heels were the banks—which, thanks to Ronald Reagan and George Bush, had been deregulated just in time to wade into the boom up to their necks and get stuck in the mud of the bust.

Since it happened in Texas, there was a lot of talk coming out of the White House about how it was all the work of outlaw bankers.

We had our share of bad actors, but mainly we had bankers trying to loan money on real estate—which is what most of us thought banks were supposed to do.

Then, realizing the barn was on fire, the federal regulators slammed the door shut with the cattle still inside...took over our real estate—and sold it at fire-sale prices...and then cut off capital— which, course makes it almost impossible to work our way out.

Meanwhile, anyone with any sense figured out that if you wanted help from the government, the only place to go was the defense budget which was the only economic development program we had.

In communities all across this nation, we've built up massive industries and scientific research projects and told the workers that they were vital to our national security.

Now in my home state, in Tarrant County, Texas, they've sent pink slips to almost 11,000 defense workers in 18 months—with at least 1,200 more to come.

They've been told the war's over, go home.

But no one has told them where to get their next job.

Every one of these federal actions has repeated itself all over the country.

You could hear the story in Michigan, in California—and we know George Bush is hearing it in New Hampshire.

When it happens in our own state, we feel like we're isolated but we're not.

Other states are just beginning to find out that what happened to industries and banks and jobs in Texas will happen to them.

In his 1961 farewell address to the nation, President Eisenhower worried about what would happen to this country as the influence of the military industrial complex grew in government and the economy.

And it is too bad that his own party did not listen to him.

For the last twelve years, Reagan and Bush have acted like the only thing we need a government for is defense.

Now that our need for defense is reduced and the American people want to know where we go from here...they don't have a clue.

And while we sacrificed at home for defense, they sacrificed our economy to a foreign trade policy that surrendered jobs and market share.

That's why it surprises me when anyone suggests that Bush is good at foreign policy.

Diplomacy maybe...but not policy.

Even a seventeen-year-old debutante can bow from the waist.

The bottom line is that since 1981 this country has bought one trillion three hundred billion dollars more than it has sold.

So it is no wonder that we find ourselves in what is generously called a recession.

And here at home?

What good does a tax cut do us if all we can spend it on is a Hitachi?

How do lower interest rates help when you can't get a loan or refinance a house that is worth half what you paid for it?

And while all of this is going on, down at the state level—where the federal mandate rubber hits the road—we are being forced to raise taxes and cut services in the middle of a recession.

I know you all get sick of seeing us in your offices…but by the time the White House and the O.M.B. get through with us, the Congress is our only hope.

I get tired of the Republicans blaming Congress for everything, when Congress is the only thing saving us.

There's no better example than the fight we just had over the ridiculous Medicaid regulations proposed by the White House and the federal bureaucracy.

If you had not reversed those regulations, state budgets would have been short billions of dollars…and our taxpayers would have been on the short end of the stick again.

The last time I checked, the states and the federal government were still sharing the same tax base.

We've got the *same* taxpayers.

It is not like we are living in a foreign country.

Come to think of it, we would probably get more attention if we were.

The way this cockeyed system works, the people who pay the taxes are on the receiving end of everything but the benefits.

The people of this country are coming perilously close to believing that no one who is in charge—in either the public or the private sector—gives a damn about them.

They are told their government is cutting all the fat, but riding past all the new construction of those big government buildings on the way in from the Washington airport, it sure doesn't look that way.

And it is hard to explain how their federal government can spend one trillion, four hundred and ninety-one billion, five hundred and sixty-three million dollars a year…and still can't produce jobs, health care or anything that helps hold families together.

What they see is government in a stretch limousine cruising down the fast lane to nowhere…while they're stranded on the shoulder with their thumbs stuck out.

And as far as government is concerned, that is not their hand signal of choice.

And the private sector?

Most Americans do not care anymore about C.E.O.'s salaries than they care about how much ball clubs pay their players.

But what they can't understand is that these salaries are paid in enterprises that are in trouble and pleading for public support while they lay off their workers.

Wealth has rarely been a divisive issue in this country; most people are for it.

One of the most basic premises of America has always been that everybody has the chance to get rich.

That is what has kept us from falling into class distinctions and warfare seen in so many countries.

After eighteen years of economic decline and frustration, everyone who makes less than $50,000 a year is finally beginning to doubt their potential to move up...and the myth of wealth is coming apart.

In the homes of the poor, it's old news.

But now in the middle class, the Horatio Alger story is becoming a fairy tale.

After generations of believing that the road to success is open to everyone, families just getting on the freeway are looking up to see a sign that reads, "road closed."

That is a dangerous sign in a capitalist democracy.

Every warning light in America is flashing out "dead-end"...and the Bush administration is like everybody's stubborn Uncle Ferd who would wander in the wilderness for forty years before he would stop and ask directions.

Last Tuesday, we heard a state of the union address that offered more of the same meandering...a dribble of this and a dabble of that...sort of a Brylcream agenda—"a little dab'll do ya."

There were proposals in that speech that we can agree with.

Extending business tax credits for research and development is a fine idea.

So is extending unemployment benefits when fifteen and a half million Americans can't find a full-time job or have given up looking.

Reducing withholding is great...but it averages out to about twenty-seven cents a day per American and you still have to pay your full tax bill—after the election.

Letting first-time home buyers withdraw up to $10,000 from their I.R.A. for a down payment and giving them a tax credit is helpful...but how many first-time buyers have $10,000 in an I.R.A.?

There's a health care tax credit for poor people...but too many Americans still cannot afford health insurance and availability is also a problem. What they've proposed is like treating cancer with an aspirin.

The bottom-line is that it is too little too late.

They spent twelve years drilling holes in our economic boat.

Now that we're sinking, they're handing us a thimble and telling us to bail for four more years.

We have reached such desperate times, that every problem, every need, every real concern of the American people is held hostage in a political stand-off.

We are told that the private sector can't afford to provide Americans with good wages, training, health insurance, child care and pensions.

On the other hand, we are told that it is philosophically incorrect for government to step into these areas.

We are told we have a trade imbalance because other countries engage in unfair practices.

On the other hand, we are told it would be philosophically incorrect to interfere with the free market.

We are told that other countries succeed because their governments helped develop their businesses.

On the other hand, we are told that in this country it is philosophically incorrect for government to pick winners and losers.

So, instead, we forfeit the game.

The American people have heard plenty about what we *can't* do.

It is time for us to tell them what we *can* do.

There are no simple solutions and out there in the real world beyond the beltway, Americans know it.

But they are ready to give someone new a chance, if they will only explain themselves in language that can be understood.

Tell it so my Mama in Waco can understand it.

Don't tell us about sequestration or cloture.

Don't even tell us about the relative merits of capital gains and the distribution of income.

We know that Reagan and Bush have led us into a ditch.

What we want to know is how to get out of it.

Tom Harkin is right; what people care about and need are jobs.

If we are going to have a deficit, let it be a deficit that puts people to work and rebuilds our transportation system, not a deficit that picks up everyone else's military tab.

Bob Kerrey is right; health care should be a right in this country.

If we are going to pay its high cost, let our dollars go for quality medicine, not another bureaucratic and regulatory nightmare like Medicaid.

Bill Clinton is right; education is central to all our hopes for the future.

And if we are going to give them the resources we need, let it be for teachers who challenge students and schools that listen to their communities, not for sloganeering and administrators who never see a classroom.

Paul Tsongas is right: our prosperity will be found in the international economy.

And if we are going to help American business compete in that world, let it to produce of the highest quality products and for work that pays a good wage, not for the title of paper shuffler to the world.

Jerry Brown is right; we can only move forward if we restore faith in our political system.

And if we are going to fight for that system, let our fight be for courage and action...not tinkering on the margins of campaign finance.

The truth is that we've got to do it all...every bit of it and nothing less.

Everyone in this room knows that the risk in detailing a list is leaving something out...but the point is that if we are going to work our way out of the mess we're in, the solutions must be comprehensive, not piecemeal.

We don't need another study of the American family to know that the major concerns of the majority of Americans, from our inner cities to the suburbs, are jobs, health care, education, child care, insurance rates, crime, the environment, retirement—a long, familiar litany.

And you don't have to be rocket scientists to figure out that we've got to use *every* tool at our disposal—from the tax code to the budget to trade negotiations—to free up capital for business, to breathe life into our existing industries, to rebuild the infrastructure, to develop cutting edge technologies, to prove by our actions that come hell or high water, we are moving this country forward.

And we can do it.

We proved in defense that when we dedicate our energies and our resources to a goal, we can be the best in the world. That same comprehensive dedication to build our economy must occur.

Years ago, Eleanor Roosevelt was traveling by train across the United States...and she looked out the window and saw a clothes line drooping against the horizon.

She made a note her journal: two children's play suits, a denim work shirt, a pair of faded dungarees, and a plain cotton dress.

"Not much left to waste here."

Others might have seen only clothes on the line, but Eleanor saw the human beings, the family.

It is time for us open our eyes to truly see the people who live with our policies and hear what they are telling us...and understand that despite everything, they still want to believe that we can do better.

We must be worthy of that belief.

Because it is that belief that has seen us through the last two hundred years and, God willing, it will bring us home and move us forward again.

Remarks of
Texas State Treasurer
Ann W. Richards
to the
State Convention of the Texas Democratic Party
June 9, 1990

Note to the reader: Ms. Richards frequently deviates from her prepared remarks.

We Texas Democrats believe in the greatness of this country and this state. We are red, white and blue...and we are not about to allow Texas to be sold to the highest bidding Republican.

When I hear Bill Clements and his cronies say that we can't win this fight for the future of Texas, I have one message for them: They haven't met the Democratic ticket yet.

And when I pick up the paper and read about how the Republicans think they can buy this election with millions of dollars...I've got another message for them: They haven't met *you* yet.

But it is the season when we get to meet these new Republican politicians as they suddenly discover the state.

They visit down in South Texas and they throw a *pachanga,* put on a sombrero, speak some Spanish, give away free beer...and after the election all you have left is a hangover.

They visit East Texas and put on their overalls, eat some ribs, get their picture taken next to a tree, go to a church or two on Sunday...and after the election all you have is an empty collection plate.

And they make a swing out through the Panhandle and West Texas where they put on a cowboy hat and color coordinated boots, sit around a campfire with the reporters, work cattle in front of the cameras for a while...and after the election all you have left is the cow chips.

Is that enough for you South Texas?

Is that enough for you East Texas?

Is that enough for anybody?

Of course, it isn't.

It never was enough.

Posturing and political game playing won't get it any more.

It's time to get serious about Texas.

We are mid-year 1990, just ten years away from the 21st century.

When I was a child, the 21st century brought images of Buck Rogers...space suits and jet packs.

And now those images are a reality.

We have made incredible quantum leaps of technological change...we take photographs of our solar system, we can send rocks back from the moon and yet, they are still arguing that Texans will not vote for a woman governor.

And they are wrong.

The Republican candidate for governor is not comfortable running against a woman. In fact, he's so uncomfortable that he is afraid to appear at the same event.

Here we are in the space age and they are hanging on to old notions, old prejudices, old ignorance.

And they are wrong.

Communism and apartheid are collapsing...the map of the world is changing every 24 hours...and they are still debating whether or not Texans will share power in our government and in our courts with African-Americans, Mexican-Americans and Asian-Americans.

And they are wrong.

We know that we need nuclear physicists to drive the superconducting supercollider...but they are holding out a tin cup for our children's education.

And they are wrong.

But when it comes to something in our past that is worth protecting—our privacy, civil rights, equal legal rights—they won't fight for us.

They even want to tell women whether or why we can have children.

And they are wrong.

It is clear that they are going to have to be dragged kicking and screaming into *this* century...much less the next one.

Meanwhile, it is our children who embrace the year 2000. They are eager and ready.

They understand the importance of education, they understand the danger of drugs.

Our children are angry that we have fouled the air we breathe and the water we drink.

They know we need more police to keep some junkie from breaking into our houses and stealing the T.V.

And our children don't want to leave Texas to go to Boston or Silicon Valley to find a decent job.

It is our children who inspire us to act on this vision of the New Texas. They are not standing in 1990 looking back at 1950. They are not held back by romanticized notions about the world of what has been.

They are ready for the New Texas.

And we are going to build it for them.

We are going to think smarter, work harder and get results.

We're going to be ready for the 21st century with new technology, new spirit and new hope.

Barbara Jordan said:

> Texas is more than a place. It is a frame of mind. A Texan believes that the individual is powerful. I believe that I get from the soil and the spirit of Texas the feeling that I, as an individual, can accomplish whatever I want to and that there are no limits, that you can just keep going, just keep soaring.

That's the New Texas.

And there is no better place to begin to build the new Texas than with our schools.

Right now, our teachers are so burdened with bureaucratic rules, and paper work and red tape that they don't have time to teach.

We constantly tinker with our schools by naming blue ribbon committees...and you know what "blue ribbon" means...it means you and I aren't on the committee...not one teacher...not one principal...not one person who's been in classroom since they went to public school...if they went to public school.

to public school...if they went to public school.

We've tried to make our schools a catch-all and a cure-all. The bureaucrats have written the rules and the system has failed.

When it comes to education, we're going to restore that fundamental relationship between the students and the teachers.

We'll cut the bureaucracy, cut the red tape and let teachers teach.

We'll make school districts accountable for the money they spend.

We'll put discipline back in the schools.

And we'll teach our children the rules that count in life...you have to study to pass...cheating is wrong...if you work hard, you will get ahead.

Our schools will meet high standards if we set high standards.

We can cut our drop-out rate in half...cut our adult literacy rate in half...make sure every child is ready for school...every graduate ready for college or career...and know for a fact that Texas students can compete successfully with any in the world.

We'll do with the education system what we did at the State Treasury. We got rid of the deadwood, we used new technology, and helped people excel at their jobs.

And as a result, we earned two billion dollars for the taxpayers.

Eight years ago it was quill pens and green eye shades. Now the Texas State Treasury is a model for the nation.

And we can create a New Texas criminal justice system that is a model for the nation.

But now, our penitentiaries are full of high school drop-outs...and they are the most sophisticated crime schools in the country...and the tuition is $33,000 a year for the taxpayers.

And when they're released early what do we have? An older, craftier criminal who still can't read and is still addicted to drugs and alcohol.

We need a governor who will concentrate on stopping crime before it happens.

And we need a governor who will insist that criminals serve their sentences. If they do the crime they'll do the time...and not just part of the time...all of the time.

And we won't let them out until they've learned to read and are treated for their addiction to drugs and alcohol.

Texans have every right to expect safe neighborhoods.

And, Texans have every right to expect decent jobs.

But there won't be good jobs unless we have a thriving, diverse economy.

And the only way we're going to get that strong economy is to have a governor who will lead us to buy Texas, build Texas and sell Texas.

Yesterday our business market was the county seat and the city square. Today it is the Pacific Rim and the European Community.

We must turn our business leaders into Texas Ambassadors...who will go out to the world selling our products, touting our people, and creating our markets.

We need a governor who understands the partnership between Texas business and government...who knows that leading Texas is about partnership, not partisanship...about policy, not politics...about being productive, not pessimistic.

We need a governor who understands how business uses ideas from colleges and universities to create new jobs.

My opponent told independent oil producers he was against government research.

Everybody knows Texas A&M research is vital to our farm and ranch economy.

Everybody knows U.T. medical research is vital to our health.

We all know that the superconducting supercollider is important not only to the Texas economy but to the way all people will live in the future.

A year ago, when he was thinking about running, my opponent asked Bill Clements if being governor was a full time job.

Bill Clements who said day before yesterday that it had taken him seven and a half years to figure out that consensus was part of government...seven and a half years of part-time work and part-time leadership.

In mid-1990, ten years away from the 21st century they still think the governor's office is a prize to hang on the wall...to cap the end of a long career.

For them governing Texas is a retirement sideline, with plenty of time for private wheeling and dealing...because they refuse to govern unless ordered to do so by the courts.

In the seven and half years we've spent with the last part-time governor, we turned our prisons over to the courts, our mental health and retardation services over to the courts...our school system is dodging the courts. We are on the verge of losing health and human services to the judges and the courts.

It's about time we had a governor who will do something about problems before they get out of hand.

It's about time we had a governor who will take our government back from the courts and the judges...and have leadership and tough decisions made in the governor's office where they belong.

It's about time we had a governor who knows what the job is...and who plans to get up and go to work for the taxpayers every day.

It's about time we had a governor who has experience making money for the taxpayers...not just for himself.

It's about time we had a governor who will appoint people to the State Board of Insurance who care as much about the people who buy insurance as the people who sell insurance.

It's about time we had a governor who knows that the health of our economy depends on the health of our environment...who will not allow Texas to be the nation's dump for toxic waste.

It's about time we had a governor who will disclose every financial interest. My opponent has refused. I've given the public all of mine.

It's about time we had a governor who has a proven record of cutting the fat and getting five quarters out of every tax dollar.

It's about time we had a governor who is committed to preserving a woman's right to choose and keeping government out of people's private lives.

And I intend to be that governor.

There is only one party that has a ticket capable of governing in this day and time.

I heard a song on the radio this morning: "21st century problems, 18th century mind." That's where the Republicans are.

We Democrats offer an historic ticket...a ticket that reflects the diversity of Texas. We are ready for today. We are ready for the 21st century.

We Democrats are moving forward while they are hanging back.

Between now and November, we'll need to meet a lot of people—and we can tell each and every one the same thing.

There is only one candidate in the governor's race who knows how to do the job.

There is only one candidate in this race who is qualified to govern Texas...and you're looking at her.

The Keynote Address
by Ann Richards

Following is a transcript of the keynote address to the Democratic National Convention by Ann Richards, the State Treasurer of Texas, as recorded by The New York Times:

Thank you. Thank you very much. Good evening, ladies and gentlemen. Buenas noches, mis amigos!

I am delighted to be here with you this evening, because after listening to George Bush all these years, I figured you needed to know what a real Texas accent sounds like. Twelve years ago Barbara Jordan, another Texas woman, Barbara made the keynote address to this convention, and two women in 160 years is about par for the course.

But, if you give us a chance, we can perform. After all, Ginger Rogers did everything that Fred Astaire did. She just did it backwards and in high heels.

I want to announce to this nation that in a little more than 100 days, the Reagan-Meese-Deaver-Nofziger-Poindexter-North-Wein-berger-Watt-Gorsuch-Lavell-Stockman-Haig-Bork-Noriega-George Bush will be over.

You know, tonight I feel a little like I did when I played basketball in the eighth grade. I thought I looked real cute in my uniform, and then I heard a boy yell from the bleachers, "Make that basket, bird legs."

And my greatest fear is that same guy is somewhere out there in the audience tonight, and he's going to cut me down to size.

Because where I grew up there wasn't much tolerance for self-importance—people who put on airs. I was born during the Depression in a little community just outside Waco, and I grew up listening to Franklin Roosevelt on the radio.

Well, it was back then that I came to understand the small truths and the hardships that bind neighbors together. Those were real people with real problems. And they had real dreams about getting out of the Depression.

I can remember summer nights when we'd put down what we called a Baptist pallet, and we listened to the grown-ups talk. I can still hear the sound of the dominoes clicking on the marble slab my daddy had found for a tabletop.

I can still hear the laughter of the men telling jokes you weren't supposed to hear, talking about how big that old buck deer was,—laughing about mama putting Clorox in the well when a frog fell in.

They talked about war and Washington and what this country needed—they talked straight talk, and it came from people who were living their lives as best they could. And that's what we're gonna to tonight—we're going to tell how the cow ate the cabbage.

I got a letter last week from a young mother in Lorena, Tex., and I want to read part of it to you.

She writes, "Our worries go from payday to payday, just like millions of others, and we have two fairly decent incomes. But I worry how I'm going to pay the rising car insurance and food.

"I pray my kids don't have a growth spurt from August to December so I don't have to buy new jeans. We buy clothes at the budget stores and we have them fray, stretch in the first wash.

"We ponder and try to figure out how we're going to pay for college, and braces and tennis shoes. We don't take vacations and we don't go out to eat.

"Please don't think me ungrateful; we have jobs and a nice place to live, and we're healthy.

"We're the people you see every day in the grocery stores. We obey the laws, we pay our taxes, we fly our flags on holidays.

"And we plod along, trying to make it better for ourselves and our children and our parents. We aren't vocal anymore. I think maybe we're too tired.

"I believe that people like us are forgotten in America."

Well, of course you believe you're forgotten, because you have been.

This Republican Administration treats us as if we were pieces of a puzzle that can't fit together. They've tried to put us into compartments and separate us from each other. Their political theory is "divide and conquer."

They've suggested time and time again that what is of interest to one group of Americans is not of interest to anyone else. We've been isolated, we've lumped into that sad phraseology called "special interests."

They've told farmers that they were selfish, that they would drive up food prices if they asked the Government to intervene on behalf of the family farm, and we watched farms go on the auction block while we bought food from foreign countries. Well, that's wrong.

They told working mothers it's all their fault that families are falling apart because they had to go to work to keep their kids in jeans, tennis shoes and college. And they're wrong.

They told American labor they were trying to ruin free enterprise by asking for 60 days' notice of plant closings, and that's wrong.

And they told the auto industry, and the steel industry, and the timber industry, and the oil industry, companies being threatened by foreign products flooding this country, that you're protectionist if you think the Government should enforce our trade laws. And that is wrong.

When they belittle us for demanding clean air and clean water, for trying to save the oceans and the ozone layer, that's wrong.

No wonder we feel isolated, and confused. We want answers, and their answer is that something is wrong with you.

Well, nothing's wrong with you—nothing wrong with you that you can't fix in November.

We've been told—we've been told that the interests of the South and Southwest are not the same interests as the North and the Northeast. They pit one group against the other. They've divided this country. And in our isolation we think government isn't going to help us, and we're alone in our feelings—we feel forgotten.

Well the fact is, we're not an isolated piece of their puzzle. We are one nation, we are the United States of America!

Now we Democrats believe that America is still the country of fair play, that we can come out of a small town or a poor neighborhood and have the same chance as anyone else, and it doesn't matter whether we are black or Hispanic, or disabled or women.

We believe that America is a country where small-business owners must succeed because they are the bedrock, backbone, of our economy.

We believe that our kids deserve good day care and public

schools. We believe our kids deserve public schools where students can learn and teachers can teach.

And we want to believe that our parents will have a good retirement—and that we will too.

We Democrats believe that Social Security is a pact that cannot be broken. We want to believe that we can live out our lives without the terrible fear that an illness is going to bankrupt us and our children.

We Democrats believe that America can overcome any problem, including the dreaded disease called AIDS. We believe that America is still a country where there is more to life than just a constant struggle for money. And we believe that America must have leaders who show us that our struggles amount to something and contribute to something larger, leaders who want us to be all that we can be.

We want leaders like Jesse Jackson.

Jesse Jackson is a leader and a teacher who can open our hearts and open our minds and stir our very souls. He's taught us that we are as good as our capacity for caring—caring about the drug problem, caring about crime, caring about education and caring about each other.

Now, in contrast, the greatest nation of the free world has had a leader for eight straight years that has pretended that he cannot hear our questions over the noise of the helicopter.

We know he doesn't want to answer. But we have a lot of questions. And when we get our questions asked, or there is a leak, or an investigation, the only answer we get is, "I don't know," or "I forgot."

But you wouldn't accept that answer from your children. I wouldn't. Don't tell me "you don't know" or "you forgot."

We're not going to have the America that we want until we elect leaders who are going to tell the truth—not most days, but every day. Leaders who don't forget what they don't want to remember.

And for eight straight years George Bush hasn't displayed the slightest interest in anything we care about. And now that he's after a job he can't get appointed to, he's like Columbus discovering America—he's found child care, he's found education.

Poor George, he can't help it—he was born with a silver foot in his mouth.

Well, no wonder—no wonder we can't figure it out—because the leadership of this nation is telling us one thing on TV and doing something entirely different.

They tell us—they tell us that they're fighting a war against terrorists. And then we find out that the White House is selling arms to the Ayatollah.

They tell us that they're fighting a war on drugs, and then people come on TV and testify that the C.I.A. and the D.E.A. and the F.B.I. knew they were flying drugs into America all along. And they're negotiating with a dictator who is shoveling cocaine into this country like crazy. I guess that's their Central American strategy.

Now they tell us that employment rates are great and that they're for equal opportunity, but we know it takes two paychecks to make ends meet today, when it used to take one, and the opportunity they're so proud of is low-wage, dead-end jobs.

And there is no major city in America where you cannot see homeless men sitting in parking lots holding signs that say, "I will work for food."

Now my friends, we really are at a crucial point in American history. Under this Administration we have devoted our resources into making this country a military colossus, but we've let our economic lines of defense fall into disrepair.

The debt of this nation is greater than it has ever been in our history. We fought a world war on less debt that the Republicans have built up in the last eight years. It's kind of like that brother-in-law who drives a flashy new car but he's always borrowing money from you to make the payments.

But let's take what they are proudest of, that is their stand on defense. We Democrats are committed to a strong America. And, quite frankly, when our leaders say to us we need a new weapon system, our inclination is to say, "Well, they must be right."

But when we pay billions for planes that won't fly, billions for tanks that won't fire and billions for systems that won't work, that old dog won't hunt.

And you don't have to be from Waco to know that when the Pentagon makes crooks rich and doesn't make America strong, that it's a bum deal.

Now I'm going to tell you—I'm really glad that our young

people missed the Depression and missed the great big war. But I do regret that they missed the leaders that I knew, leaders who told us when things were tough and that we'd have to sacrifice, and that these difficulties might last awhile.

They didn't tell us things were hard for us because we were different, or isolated, or special interests. They brought us together and they gave us a sense of national purpose.

They gave us Social Security and they told us they were setting up a system where we could pay our own money in and when the time came for our retirement, we could take the money out.

People in rural areas were told that we deserved to have electric lights, and they were going to harness the energy that was necessary to give us electricity so that my grandmama didn't have to carry that coal oil lamp around.

And they told us that they were going to guarantee that when we put our money in the bank that the money was going to be there and it was going to be insured, they did not lie to us.

And I think that one of the saving graces of Democrats is that we are candid. We are straight talk. We tell people what we think.

And that tradition and those values live today in Michael Dukakis from Massachusetts.

Michael Dukakis knows that this country is on the edge of a great new era, that we're not afraid of change, that we're for thoughtful, truthful, strong leadership, to unify this country and to get on with the future.

His instincts are deeply American, they're tough and they're generous, and personally I have to tell you that I have never met a man who had a more remarkable sense of what is really important in life.

And then there's my friend and my teacher for many years, Senator Lloyd Bentsen. And I couldn't be prouder, both as a Texan and as a Democrat, because Lloyd Bentsen understands America— from the barrios to the boardroom. He knows how to bring us together, by regions, by economics, and by example. And he's already beaten George Bush once.

So when it comes right down to it, this election is a contest between those who are satisfied with what they have and those who know we can do better. That's what this election is really all about.

It's about the American dream—those who want to keep it for the few, and those who know it must be nurtured and passed along.

I'm a grandmother now. And I have one nearly perfect granddaughter named Lily. And when I hold that grandbaby, I feel that continuity of life that unites us, that binds generation to generation, that ties us with each other.

And sometimes I spread that Baptist pallet out on the floor and Lily and I roll a ball back and forth. And I think of all the families like mine, and like the one in Lorena, Tex., like the ones that nurture children all across America.

And as I look at Lily, I know that it is within families that we learn both the need to respect individual human dignity and to work together for our common good. Within our families, within our nation, it is the same.

And as I sit there, I wonder if she'll every grasp the changes I've seen in my life—if she'll ever believe that there was a time when blacks could not drink from public water fountains, when Hispanic children were punished for speaking Spanish in the public schools and women couldn't vote.

I think of all the political fights I've fought and all the compromises I've had to accept as part payment. And I think of all the small victories that have added up to national triumphs. And all the things that never would have happened and all the people who would have been left behind if we had not reasoned and fought and won those battles together.

And I will tell Lily that those triumphs were Democratic Party triumphs.

I want so much to tell Lily how far we've come, you and I. And as the ball rolls back and forth, I want to tell her how very lucky she is. That, for all of our differences, we are still the greatest nation on this good earth.

And our strength lies in the men and women who go to work every day, who struggle to balance their family and their jobs, and who should never, ever be forgotten.

I just hope that, like her grandparents and her great-grandparents before, Lily goes on to raise her kids with the promise that echoes in homes all across America: that we can do better.

And that's what this election is all about. Thank you very much.

Index